Understanding Religious Experience

Understanding Religious Experience

Peter Connolly

SHEFFIELD UK   BRISTOL CT

Published by Equinox Publishing Ltd.

UK: Office 415, The Workstation, 15 Paternoster Row, Sheffield, South Yorkshire S1 2BX

USA: ISD, 70 Enterprise Drive, Bristol, CT 06010

www.equinoxpub.com

First published 2019

© Peter Connolly 2019

All rights reserved. No part of this publication may be reproduced or transmitted in any form or by any means, electronic or mechanical, including photocopying, recording or any information storage or retrieval system, without prior permission in writing from the publishers.

ISBN   978 1 78179 732 7   (hardback)
       978 1 78179 733 4   (paperback)
       978 1 78179 734 1   (ePDF)

British Library Cataloguing-in-Publication Data

A catalogue record for this book is available from the British Library.

Library of Congress Cataloging-in-Publication Data

Names: Connolly, Peter, 1951- author.
Title: Understanding religious experience / Peter Connolly.
Description: Bristol : Equinox Publishing Ltd., 2019. | Includes bibliographical references and index.
Identifiers: LCCN 2018021857 (print) | LCCN 2018035442 (ebook) | ISBN 9781781797341 (ePDF) | ISBN 9781781797327 (hb) | ISBN 9781781797334 (pb)
Subjects: LCSH: Experience (Religion)
Classification: LCC BL53 (ebook) | LCC BL53 .C6533 2019 (print) | DDC 204/.2--dc23
LC record available at https://lccn.loc.gov/2018021857

Typeset by JS Typesetting Ltd, Porthcawl, Mid Glamorgan.
Printed and bound in Great Britain by

Contents

Acknowledgements vi

Introduction 1

Part 1: A critical phenomenology of religious experience

The variety of religious experiences 15
Numinous experiences 19
Mystical experiences 33
Everyday religious experiences 43

Part 2: A reductionist explanation of religious experience

Some cartographic accounts of religious experience 53
Ken Wilber's integral spirituality 62
Roland Fischer's cartography of ecstatic and meditative states 93
My model of ASCs and spirituality 104

Part 3: Loose ends

Neurological research 123
'Authentic' religious experience 131

Notes 153
Bibliography 211
Index 223

Acknowledgements

I would like to express my gratitude to all those people who have contributed to the production of this book. I am particularly indebted to three people who commented on my early drafts: Simon Atkinson, Matthew Clark and Chloe McCarthy. My work would have been much less coherent than it is without their contributions. I would also like to acknowledge my gratitude to all the authors whose works are listed in the bibliography. In February 1676 Isaac Newton wrote a letter to Robert Hooke in which he commented that 'If I have seen further it is by standing on the shoulders of giants'. I may not have seen very far, but what I have seen has only been made possible by standing on the shoulders of those writers. For that privilege I am deeply grateful.

Introduction

Religious experiences provide the foundations for most of the major religious systems. Much (if not most) of what religious people believe and the things they do because of those beliefs ultimately derive from someone's religious experience, such as Moses' encounter with Yahweh in a burning bush, Saul's encounter with the risen Jesus on the road to Damascus, Kṛṣṇa's revelation to Arjuna in the Bhagavad Gītā, Muhammad's revelations from the angel Gabriel (Jibreel) and the Buddha's insights on the night of his enlightenment. Such experiences tend to be treated as self-validating guarantees of the veracity of their contents, even though those contents can be quite varied, and the 'truths' experienced by one religious person are often incompatible with those experienced by another. Hence some religious traditions, e.g. Islām, subscribe to the idea that the ultimate being, God, transcends the universe, others, e.g. Advaita Vedānta, contend that God (brahman/ātman) and the universe are one, and yet others, e.g. Buddhism, claim that there is no God that corresponds to the accounts of either Muslims or Vedāntins.

The diversity of religious experiences and the claims that arise out of them constitute one of the most significant, if not *the* most significant, challenges that the student of religion has to address. Religious descriptions of the world always contain some reference to a realm or dimension of existence that cannot be apprehended by the senses or their extensions, a trans-empirical realm. Various terms have been employed to refer to this realm, some of the most well known being *divine*, *holy*, *sacred*, *spiritual*, *supernatural* and *transcendent*. In this religions share a common element, an element that provides a criterion for distinguishing the religious from the non-religious. This is what anthropologist Anthony Wallace calls *the supernatural premise*.[1] When it comes to descriptions of that realm, however, as noted above, differences begin to emerge.

In some religious traditions, Buddhism for example, that realm is essentially passive. According to Buddhist teaching, *nirvāṇa*, the transcendent, unconditioned realm is not responsible for the creation of the world. It just is. *Nirvāṇa* is not a being, it does not have a personality, one cannot enter into dialogue with it, nor is it responsive to prayer or rituals of any kind; yet in Buddhist teaching the attainment of *nirvāṇa* is the most fulfilling experience to which any being can aspire. It is the highest good and transcends all gods, goddesses, spirits and the like, which, in the Buddhist understanding of things, are all part of the conditioned world and therefore destined to pass away. For this reason no god, goddess or other spiritual being can be an ultimate source of fulfilment. Other religious traditions, Christianity for example, teach very different things about the trans-empirical realm. According to Christian teaching, at the pinnacle of the transcendent realm is God, the supreme being, creator of heaven and earth. The creator, unlike the creation, will not pass away (though some creations such as the human soul may also be granted eternal existence). God also has a personality, intervenes in the world (not least by taking a human body) and is responsive to the supplications of His worshippers. In Christianity God is the only source of ultimate fulfilment.

These two sets of teachings are clearly incompatible with each other if taken at face value, and a study of the history of these traditions certainly suggests that the promulgators of these doctrines intended them to be so taken. Some more recent interpreters have claimed, however, that they should not be taken at face value but rather understood symbolically or understood as provisional accounts that were designed to get people oriented towards the sacred realm but would be replaced by an accurate, though inexpressible, understanding once an experience of the transcendent reality was forthcoming. Nevertheless, if one takes the *prima facie* incompatibility seriously, as most people do, then one is confronted with a real problem. Religions, not just Buddhism and Christianity, make conflicting truth claims. They also make demands on their members which often involve considerable sacrifices and commitment to the pursuit of the tradition's spiritual goals. For most members the teachings about the goals and the means of achieving them are treated as truthful and accurate, yet all such teachings cannot be truthful and accurate for they are incompatible with each other. Are some of these members being deceived or misled then? Various responses to this question have been offered.

One response has been what we might call *ranking*. This is a strategy adopted by many members of particular faiths and also by some scholars. Essentially, it involves identifying the tradition that is deemed to possess the truest beliefs and then ranking all the others in relation to it. Those that are similar are deemed to be more true or to contain more truths than those which are dissimilar. Not surprisingly, people tend to rank the group to which they belong as the highest. Hindus, for example, sometimes treat Jesus as an incarnation of the god Viṣṇu, while Muslims often regard him as an inferior precursor to Muhammad. How is the student who is studying a number of religions and seeking to understand religion as a dimension of human experience which has manifested differently in different times and places to deal with these kinds of claims? Understanding why believers hold such views is not too difficult. Religions provide ultimate goals for people to pursue. They help people to locate themselves in the world and provide a sense of meaning to life. They also situate people within a particular community and contribute significantly to a person's sense of identity. Indeed, it would clearly be ludicrous for a member of one tradition to regard the teachings of another as superior to his or her own. A member who did hold such a view would probably convert before too long, unless, of course, he or she would attract a death sentence for so doing. Determining which, if any, set of believers is correct presents a greater challenge, however. What criteria might one use to make such a decision? How could they be justified? It may well be the case that the teachings of one religion *are* more accurate with regard to the true nature of things than those of all the others, but what method of enquiry could lead an investigator to a reliable judgment about which one it is? Ranking might be a believer's response to religious plurality, but it is not one that can be commended to scholars.

Another strategy that has been adopted in response to the fact of religious plurality, and one that has found much more favour with scholars, is that which seeks to identify a *common core* or *common goal* that all religions share. The idea here is that the various accounts of the sacred realm, the means of gaining access to it and its relationship with the non-sacred or profane world are all, inevitably, conditioned by historical and socio-cultural factors and should not be taken as literal and accurate descriptions. Lying behind the conditioned accounts though is an apprehension of a deeper reality, the spiritual realm, which is in fact the same for all. Such a view is, of course, somewhat disparaging of the beliefs of faith members who do take the teachings of their religion as literal and accurate, and some scholars would argue that approaching the study of religion in this kind of way is inappropriate. For those scholars, our aim should be to understand the lives and outlooks of religious believers, not to make judgments about them. Others would contend that while such empathetic enquiry has an important place within the study of religion it certainly does not constitute the whole. Scholars cannot ignore the plurality issue and have a responsibility to make sense of it and explain it as best they can. The common core/common goal strategy is one way in which some scholars have sought to meet that responsibility.

Common core/common goal thinking is often associated with what Aldous Huxley called *The Perennial Philosophy*, the idea that texts from various religious traditions can be seen to be offering essentially the same teaching about the deepest levels of existence and experience and that those which deviate from this core account are to be understood in terms of either cultural factors or imperfect apprehension.[2] Sometimes the image of different pathways up a mountain is used to convey this notion. All the pathways get the climbers to the top, though the terrain they traverse en route is different. There is also the possibility of false summits. Some climbers might think they have reached the top when they have, in fact, only scaled one of the lower peaks. Perhaps the major problem with such a view is that the descriptions of the deepest levels of existence and experience that are found in some texts patently do not conform to the core pattern identified by Perennial Philosophers, which tends towards understanding the cosmos as some kind of manifestation or emanation of, or perhaps overlay on, a fundamentally formless ground of being which is the source of ultimate fulfilment and of spiritual longing. In other words, the common core/common goal strategy only seems to work if one is prepared to challenge or reject a number of traditions' understanding of their own teachings. It seems to involve putting the theory or pattern before the data. It may be justified in so doing, though many scholars have also found the arguments of the perennialists unconvincing. The common core/common goal approach, unlike the ranking one, does, however, seek to be inclusive, to find value in all religions, though it does so on its own terms and this is a price many scholars and religionists are not prepared to pay.[3]

A third approach to the problem of plurality is what we might call *the human creation strategy*. The idea here is that the problem of plurality exists because religious teachings are not what they appear to be. Teachings about the ultimate nature of existence, human fulfilment and the means to make spiritual progress are presented within traditions as descriptions of objective reality, a reality that exists independently of the experiencer. When we think about the everyday world we think of it as objective. We may, of course, be wrong. A number of philosophers, known as idealists, have argued that what we experience as the world is actually just a projection of our minds. Some of their arguments are ingenious, though they have failed to convince the vast majority of philosophers and psychologists that idealism accurately conveys the true nature of our experience. A kind of half-way house between idealism and naive realism (the view that we simply perceive what is in the world outside our bodies) is the view generally known as constructivism.[4]

Many constructivists argue that there is a world which exists independently of our perceptions of it (the first-order reality). There is also another world, the world of our experience, which is our image or representation of the first world as constructed by our brains. This is the second-order reality. A crucial issue raised by this way of thinking concerns epistemology, the theory of knowledge (that area of enquiry which addresses questions such as 'how do we come to 'know' things?' and 'on what foundations do our claims to knowledge rest?'). This issue can be put in the form of a question: 'if what we experience is just the second-order reality how do we know that there is a first-order reality?' Philosophers, psychologists and others are still debating the matter quite vigorously and we shall not pursue it further here. Suffice it to say that from a constructivist perspective one can argue that religious experiences are second-order experiences which, like many other second-order experiences, are taken to be first-order ones, i.e. are understood in naïve realist terms. Like most experiences they are susceptible to influence from both the surrounding culture and the previous experiences of the experiencer. But they differ from those 'everyday' second order experiences in some important ways.

First of all, religious experiences tend to lack the capacity for sensory verification. Say, for example, I see a horse in a field near my home and, since the field is normally empty, I think it is worth mentioning the fact to my friend. If he is sceptical he can go to the field and check for himself; so can anyone else who is interested. Religious experiences tend not to be like that. It is rarely, if ever, the case that anyone with an interest in the experience, for example, of visions of the virgin Mary that are periodically reported in various parts of Europe, can go along to check it out like they could the horse in the field. There are, of course, reasons put forward by commentators on such cases which seek to explain their lack of sensory verifiability. The point being made here is simply that although the two experiences can both be described as second order they are of different kinds.

Religious experiences also differ from sensorily verifiable second-order experiences in another important way. Visions of the virgin Mary present at least the appearance of sensory verifiability, but many religious experiences do not. Meditators and mystics often pursue religious experience and understanding by methods that are designed to reduce or even eliminate all influence from the external world. They seek knowledge by going within themselves and often report having profound experiences that frequently have the character of being (or seeming) more real than the everyday world of sensory experience.[5] Knowledge acquired in this way may be compelling for the mystic but, as the philosopher and psychologist William James observed at the beginning of the twentieth century, they can have no authority for anyone else unless that person takes it on trust.[6] Because they are internal, these kinds of religious experiences have a number of features in common with other kinds of internally focused experiences such as imaginative reverie, hypnosis and dreaming. Those who take a *human creation* perspective on the issue of religious plurality tend to regard religious experiences as essentially imaginative second-order experiences that are generated entirely in the minds of the experiencers rather than through some kind of interaction between first and second-order realities, though aspects of the first order reality may act as stimuli to their creation.

The *human creation* position is probably further away from that of the believer than the *common core/common goal* one. Writers who adopt the common core/common goal perspective often think of religious experiences in terms of first and second-order reality interaction. The experiencer's second-order reality might interfere with their apprehension of the first-order one but he or she is at least partly, and sometimes completely, breaking through to genuine knowledge about human beings, the human condition and the nature of the universe they inhabit. By contrast, those who adopt a human creation perspective tend to regard such 'knowledge' as a kind of imaginative fiction or a believed-in imagining. Such a view clearly devalues religious experiences (and by implication religious traditions) as sources of knowledge, though it need not devalue them altogether. Pragmatically, imaginative experiences can sometimes be more valuable than sensorily veridical ones (i.e. those that coincide with the way things actually are). The apprehensions of meaning, value and significance that pervade our lives are probably best understood as second order experiences, and they are no less important for that. Similarly, from the human creation perspective, religious traditions, although mistaking second-order realities for first-order ones, have the capacity – perhaps because they do make that epistemological error – to enrich life in many ways. Religious traditions have sought, from this perspective, to improve human life through the provision of an imaginative account of the world which imbues virtually all experiences with meaning and significance. They *are* different from each other and that is to be expected. The crucial issue from this perspective is not whether what religious traditions teach is true but whether what they teach is helpful and enriching. Of course this way of resolving the problem of plurality generates its own system of ranking. Instead of truth being the criterion of value utility or benefit is, and while it might be easier to determine whether some religious traditions enrich the lives of their adherents more than do others (perhaps in terms of mental, emotional and physical well-being) the epistemological problems of grounding the criteria in a knowledge-base that we can have confidence in still remain.

This discussion of strategies for dealing with the problem of religious plurality helps us to understand the significance of another issue that confronts students of religion: the issue of *reductionism*. In scientific enquiry the word 'reductionism' is used to indicate a practice of explaining complex phenomena in terms of simpler, underlying processes. An example of this might be explaining events or processes from one domain, say chemistry, in terms of those from another, say physics. Sometimes this can be tremendously illuminating. The discovery of atoms led to explanations of chemical processes which up until then had been quite mysterious. At other times reductionism can generate distortions, such as when the activity of an animal is explained by reference to the chemical activity taking place in its cells. Animals interact with the environments in which they live and this is a major factor that has to be taken into account when seeking to explain their behaviour. Explanations couched solely in terms of chemical activity fail to acknowledge this and hence provide an inadequate or even misleading account. In the study of religion the issue of reductionism arises when people (usually scholars) offer explanations of religious phenomena that differ from those offered by believers, particularly when the scholarly account omits a significant element from the believer's such as a reference to the existence of a transcendent reality.

Is reductionism a bad thing in the study of religion? Scholars who think it is tend to argue that to ignore believers' accounts of their experiences and their traditions' teachings is to ignore something crucial, for that, essentially, is what we are seeking to understand. By contrast, scholars who support or apply reductionistic strategies to the study of religion tend to argue that what they want to understand is not so much what religion means to believers or what being religious is like for them. Instead, they want to explore the possibility that whatever is happening when people engage in religious activities and take on religious beliefs is something different from what religious people claim is happening. The student of religion need not, however, make an exclusive commitment to either of these approaches. He or she can take both agendas on board. Indeed, I would argue that a methodologically robust approach to the study of religion will always begin with a phenomenological enquiry (one that seeks to understand the believer's perspective) and then follow up with reductionist strategies. Those elements of the believer's perspective that survive reductionist scrutiny could then be deemed to be, in Karl Popper's terminology, 'corroborated'.[7]

In this book I tend to work within a 'human creation' framework that initially approaches religious experience phenomenologically, drawing upon accounts that are provided by the traditions themselves, and then proceeds to apply reductionistic strategies in order to resolve the problems presented by plurality. I will argue that most religious experiences are rooted in common psychological processes. When these are understood, I contend, the variety becomes intelligible, (a) because none of these experiences are of reality as such, and (b) because most of them arise out of trance states that fabricate a quality of verisimilitude (or, even stronger, more real than real) even though they are actually just 'believed-in-imaginings'.[8] The book is thus organised in three sections:

1. a critical phenomenology of religious experience;
2. a reductionist explanation of religious experience; and
3. what I call 'loose ends'.

In the first of these I attempt to map the contours of both virtuoso/adept religious experiences and everyday versions of them. I will aim to work with descriptions that are largely derived from actual spiritual traditions, letting them speak for themselves as it were, while also filtering out interpretations and generalisations that cannot withstand a rigorous phenomenological scrutiny. In the second section, I will outline and evaluate a number of influential scholarly typologies of religious/spiritual experience. None of them, I will argue, is adequate to the task, and some are positively misleading. I will then outline my own contribution to our understanding of this field, a contribution that is significantly influenced by work on the psychology and anthropology of trance experience. In Part 3, I will outline some of the work on the neurology of religious/spiritual experience, seeking to relate the results to my own model, and, finally, explore the question of what, if any, criteria can be employed to determine whether the notions of authentic and inauthentic religious experiences are tenable. Much of the material in this section will be taken from research on psychedelic chemicals and the inferences that scholars have constructed on the basis of that research.

A phenomenological approach seeks to make sense of and convey to the reader 'that which is presented' (i.e. to explain the phenomenon 'in its own terms' as far as possible). This usually involves the attempt to pursue an empathy with the authors or traditions being investigated, *and* the development of typologies that link various aspects together and also go below the surface to identify patterns and connections that are not always obvious from a 'that which is presented' position. In the methodological literature of Religious Studies these two aspects are often labelled, following Edmund Husserl, *epochê* (from the Greek verb *epechô* 'I hold back') and *eidetic vision* (from the Greek noun *to eidos* – that which is seen, form, shape, essence). The *epochê* element is usually understood in terms of what Ninian Smart called 'structural description'.[9] This does not, for Smart, require students to be members of the faith group they are studying or even to be religious at all.

Rather, he conceives it as being akin to some aspects of anthropological study that involve empathic, imaginative participation.[10] This does not, however, commit the scholar to privileging the believer's perspective since, as Smart indicates, 'Belonging to a faith is no guarantee of a *superior* understanding.'[11]

The *eidetic vision* element has been more controversial, with some writers claiming a kind of intuitive apprehension of 'essences' and others, including Smart, whom I tend to follow, arguing that it is more typological in character, an attempt to construct models that reveal patterns, similarities and contrasts underlying religious data. This enterprise is thus cartographic in nature and, as such, subject to the limitations that apply to the construction of all maps. Maps inevitably delete some information, employ generalisations and distort certain features of the terrain. The best maps use these limitations to good effect. Anyone who studies the evolution of the London Underground map will immediately see that much of the information available to the traveller is irrelevant and can even be a hindrance to effective navigation. The uniformity of the symbols representing stations that connect different lines is a generalisation that makes navigation more simple by emphasising only those features that are essential for the traveller, and, finally, the distances between stations are distorted to a massive degree because the traveller only needs information about the stops and an accurate representation of distances would make the map unwieldy.

The history of phenomenological typology in religion is, in many ways, analogous to that of the London Underground map. Scholars have generated their own maps and modified the maps of others. Sometimes these maps have been complementary and can be combined in various ways. At other times they offer quite different and conflicting representations of the territory. In what follows I shall aim to identify maps of both kinds and aim to show how complementary maps can be woven together to offer fuller, more accurate representations of religious experience in all its diversity, and provide reasons for embracing some and rejecting others. Even so, since the product of cartography is merely a map, a representation of the territory, if it conflicts with or fails to match the data it is designed to explain then it is the map that will require modification. In other words, it is important that scholars who construct phenomenological typologies avoid mistaking their maps for the territories they are supposed to represent. There will always be a degree of mismatch and yet some maps will be demonstrably better than others.

To round off this introduction I will offer readers some biographical information that may assist them in identifying elements of bias in my treatment. I was educated in Roman Catholic schools and subjected to the attempts at indoctrination practised by that tradition during the 1950s and 1960s. Perhaps because of this, I have been interested in religious experiences for most of my adult life. As a teenager I experimented with LSD, and had some profound religious experiences plus a few experiences of recognition that however profound they might seem such experiences could be misleading. I'll recount one of those below. I also experimented with various forms of oriental meditation, from the devotional dynamics of the Divine Light Mission, through Radha Soami Satsang (Sant Mat), Tibetan Lam Rim and Transcendental Meditation to the more austere practice of Buddhist Vipassana. Alongside such experiential enquiries I studied comparative religion, with a specialism in Indian traditions, to PhD level and subsequently went on to teach Religious Studies in two British universities as well as lecturing on the history and philosophy of yoga for a number of yoga training organisations. In the course of developing new modules on the psychology of religion and mysticism I took a degree in psychology and trained in hypnosis and neuro-linguistic programming (NLP). My subsequent research on religious experience developed largely as a process of integrating material from all these sources. That work progressed in piecemeal fashion and was published in stages through a number of journal articles and a chapter in my *A Student's Guide to the History and Philosophy of Yoga*.[12] My aim here is to bring this disparate material together into a single volume so that fellow researchers and others with an interest in this aspect of human experience can evaluate it for themselves and, hopefully, draw upon it as they engage in their own enquiries into this fascinating dimension of human psychology.

Now a story of how I discovered that what seemed to be a quite profound religious experience was, in large measure, a construct of my own mind. As I remember it, recognising that memories tend to get modified over time, my friend Paul and I were at one of the Windsor music festivals in the early 1970s. We had ingested some LSD earlier and, as the night deepened, were sitting on our sleeping bags in a wooded area when two young people, a man and a woman, approached us. Readers who have had LSD experiences will know, and those who have not will need to imagine, that at this time we were deeply involved in psychedelic 'cosmic' inner journeying and that these two people speaking to us pulled parts of our awareness back into Windsor Park while other parts of it continued to be absorbed in the cosmic flow of psychedelic experience. The man was white, tall, had longish blonde hair and was slender of build. The woman was black, short, had curly black hair and of stocky build. They told us that they were at the festival to invite people to meet with Jesus. Wow! There we were, connected to the life energy of the cosmos, and here were two angels (they must be angels: angelic smiles and representing the diversity of human forms) inviting us to meet Jesus. Both Paul and I had been raised in the Roman Catholic tradition, so we had plenty of religious stuff in our subconscious minds just waiting to be activated.

In that moment neither of us was inclined to get up and walk off to meet Jesus with these angels, probably because we were unable to – the LSD-generated experience being in full flow. After a while, however, as the effects of the acid began to subside I remember turning to Paul and saying something like 'are you ready to go to meet Jesus?' He was, though both of us needed to piss first; so we walked towards some bushes that promised a little discretion. As we did so, I remember putting my arm around Paul's shoulder and thinking 'Wow! Peter and Paul, off to meet Jesus.' In that moment the upcoming encounter was completely real to me and, I think, to Paul as well. After we had relieved ourselves we made our way over to the tent that the angels had pointed out to us. Once there a number of different 'realities' began to combine and we began to 'come down'. The 'angels' were members of a Bible group and were quoting the Bible to others who, presumably, had been invited over just as we had. Oh, what a disappointment. The 'angels' were just 'Bible bashers' and we had been misled. We wandered back to our spot in the woods, settled down to enjoy the remainder of our trip and, eventually, fell asleep.

What had happened? We had experienced a profound sense of connection with the 'flow of the universe' and thought we were gaining an insight into spiritual realities to which we were normally denied access because of the ways in which 'normal' consciousness operated – at least that's how we tended to think of it at the time. But something about that 'access' wasn't right. We had projected the angelic identity onto the two members of the Bible group because of what we were experiencing under the influence of the LSD, and the possibility of meeting a reincarnated Jesus was only feasible because of the altered state of consciousness created by the drug. So a question arose in my mind that in various forms has remained with me ever since: how reliable are our perceptions generally and, in particular, how much trust can we place in experiences that arise while we are in altered states of consciousness, whether produced by drugs, 'natural' methods for modifying experience – such as meditation, ecstatic dancing and ritual performance – or spontaneously? My current answer to this question is 'it varies according to conditions', though in the case of altered states it is more like 'not much'. I will comment on this more fully in what follows.

PART 1
A CRITICAL PHENOMENOLOGY OF RELIGIOUS EXPERIENCE

The variety of religious experiences

Religious experiences come in what might seem to be a bewildering variety of forms. Some people hear disembodied voices giving them information and/or instructions; others have visions, more commonly visions plus voices, of supernatural beings; yet others are 'possessed' by deities, spirits or other beings, while yet others engage in activities as diverse as meditating on objects, imagined realities or beings or mental processes. Then there are experiences that seem to be precipitated from involvement in ritualised activities, from sacrifices, through pilgrimages to dancing, chanting and listening to the oratory of charismatic preachers and teachers. Some of these experiences arise 'spontaneously' while others are 'cultivated'. In Western culture the word most commonly employed to label both types of experiences and processes is 'spirituality'. When faced with this kind of diversity scholars tend to quickly move into an eidetic vision stage and start to generate typologies that bring together those experiences that are similar and separate those that are different. There are a substantial number of such typologies and they are of variable quality. In this part I will not be seeking any kind of comprehensive coverage of these models but rather indicate some of the ways in which scholars have addressed the task, selecting the more robust elements for combination in a phenomenological synthesis, to be followed, ultimately, by a reductionistic resolution of the superfluous complexity.

A number of authors have argued, persuasively in my view, that there are two broad yet mostly distinct types of religion, i.e. beliefs and behaviours rooted in the postulation of a supernatural realm. Among the most notable articulators of this view are C.K. Yang and Richard Gombrich. Yang calls these two types the 'institutional' and the 'diffused'. The institutional type 'has a system of theology, rituals and organisations of its own, independent of other secular social institutions'.[1] By contrast, the diffused type has its theology, rituals and organisation 'intimately merged with the concepts and structures of secular institutions and other aspects of the social order'.[2] Gombrich calls these types 'soteriologies' and 'communal religions'. The former, 'is the kind of religion which particularly concerns the individual, his highest goals and his fate after death... adherence is defined by assent to its doctrine and entry into membership is formalised by a declaration of faith'.[3] The latter 'solemnizes what happens to people, both singly and corporately, in the course of their lives in society... The problem to which such religion primarily answers is the ordering of society'.[4] To illustrate the difference, Gombrich quotes from a label in the ethnographic section of the Jaipur museum: 'Marriage occupies the most important position among the sixteen sacred rites of India. After the performance of this rite, one gets into the householder stage of life'. He comments that this 'articulates the central concern of communal religion: the orderly perpetuation of society. No soteriology would regard marriage as a more important rite than initiation'.[5] These typologies are the eidetic visions of Yang and Gombrich. They are grounded in phenomenological enquiry, yet they also simplify the diversity that is presented to any investigator as well as revealing significant structural differences that facilitate a deeper understanding of the phenomena.

These two types are rarely found in pristine form. Communal religions often appropriate soteriological elements to enhance their appeal and explanatory range, e.g. communal, diffused brāhmanism appropriated world-renouncing, yogic forms of spirituality in India. Likewise, when successful soteriologies acquire the powers of social regulation they impose their value systems on whole societies, e.g. the Islāmic drive to create Muslim theocracies whenever possible. Such processes also shed light on aspects of sect formation. When soteriologies take on characteristics that are traditionally associated with communal religions some adherents will become concerned that soteriological purity is being compromised and establish sects that resist what they perceive to be the slide into diffusion. Ultimately, the credibility of both forms (diffused/communal and institutionalised/soteriological) rests on religious experiences. Even when authoritative texts are claimed to be eternal or infallible, e.g. Mīmaṃsā Sūtra (1.7ff.), someone had to have an experience that this was so, for it is not self-evident to most people.[6]

The ultimate aim of scholars who study religious experiences is or should be to explain how they relate to each other and to assign an epistemological status to them. The first of these tasks can be accomplished within a phenomenological framework that embraces both *epochê* and *eidetic vision*.[7] The second requires some form of reductionistic analysis. I will begin with an outline and appraisal of attempts to engage with the first task and then offer my own attempt to accomplish the second.

The German theologian Rudolph Otto coined the term 'numinous' (from the Latin 'numen', 'divine presence') to cover a wide range of experiences that, he claimed, lay at the heart of all the major religions.[8] In its fullest form, he claimed, the numinous experience is one of the divine as 'wholly other' than oneself. It is an encounter with that which is a *mysterium tremendum et fascinans*, a tremendous and fascinating mystery. The term 'mystery' indicates that it can never be known in full. It is beyond conception, ineffable, extraordinary and unfamiliar. 'Tremendum' indicates that what is encountered is awe-ful, eerie, uncanny, majestic and powerful. The mysterium tremendum is also fascinating, uniquely attractive, magnetic. It draws one towards it. The encounter with the numinous is thus an experience of a being, a realm or a dimension of existence that is more profound than we can imagine, more overwhelming than we can imagine and more absorbing than we can imagine. Classic examples of numinous experience are Moses' encounter with Yahweh through the burning bush (Exodus 3.1-4.17) and Saul's encounter with the risen Jesus on the Damascus road (Acts of the Apostles 9.3-9).

Philosopher Ninian Smart was not convinced that the category of the numinous was as comprehensive as Otto had claimed. There are, he argued, many descriptions of religious experience where the encounter was not with a reality that was 'wholly other' than oneself but was, in fact, one's deepest self or where the reality was not mysterious, dynamic and frightening but joyful, tranquil and soothing. The Upaniṣadic ātman and the Buddhist nirvāṇa are classic examples. So Smart proposed a complementary category of 'the mystical', an experience of one's innermost nature rather than an encounter with a reality that is 'wholly other'. Typically, numinous experiences come as revelations, often unlooked for, from a source outside of one's self. By contrast, mystical experiences usually arise as a result of a person's practice, usually of some kind of meditation.[9]

Two points of contrast are prominent in the disagreement between Smart and Otto. One concerns the source or ground of the experience; the other has to do with its character. The former raises questions about the relationship between ontology and epistemology while the latter raises questions about the relationship between psychology and epistemology.[10] So, for Otto, the numinous experience is one of the divine as 'wholly other' than oneself, while for Smart the mystical experience is one of encounter with one's deepest self, an experience that is joyful, tranquil and soothing. Otto's account assumes an ontological dualism or pluralism; Smart's does not. With regard to the ontological question we may note that in much religious writing ontology is often mixed in with theology. In terms of ontology, the three most commonly adopted views are monism, dualism and pluralism. Ontological monism is the doctrine that at the most fundamental level of existence all is one being. Dualism is the view that at the most fundamental level there are two separate beings, e.g. God and the universe (here individual souls/spirits would be understood to be parts of God), or souls/spirits and the universe, as in the

Indian systems of Sāṃkhya and Jainism. Pluralism is an extension of dualism, with more than two kinds of ultimate beings (God plus souls plus universe for example). Because there are many individual souls/spirits in Sāṃkhya and Jainism, they could be regarded as subscribing to pluralistic ontologies. The reason why they are usually described as dualistic is that all the souls (called puruṣa in Sāṃkhya and jīva in Jainism) are identical to each other.

In terms of theology, the three most commonly encountered views are polytheism (many gods), monotheism (one god) and atheism (no gods). The point to note about these alternatives, both ontological and theological, is that the options in each are mutually exclusive. One cannot be a polytheistic monotheist or a monotheistic atheist. Likewise, one cannot be a monistic dualist or a monistic pluralist. One can, however, combine any theology with any ontology. I mention this because many writers have tended to assume that certain ontologies go with certain theologies (e.g. dualism or pluralism with monotheism). This is *not* the case. Schematically, we can represent these options in two columns (Table 1). Any cross-column combination is possible; no within-column combinations are possible without falling into logical incoherence. In other words, one can be, for example, a polytheistic monist, or a polytheistic dualist, or a polytheistic pluralist.

Table 1 Ontology and theology.

Ontology	Theology
Monism	Polytheism
Dualism	Monotheism
Pluralism	Atheism

Within religious traditions it is ultimately religious experiences that provide authoritative answers to ontological questions, though theologians often muddy the waters by, for example, leaving the source of ontological information unspecified (as in the Genesis creation accounts that separate God from his creation: to whom did God reveal this information?) or claiming that scripture is to be accorded equal or even superior status with perception, a device employed by the brāhmanical theologian Śaṅkara.

The second contrast between the accounts of Otto and Smart is central to the present enquiry. It revolves around the question of how many distinctive types of religious experience there are. Is there just one religious experience that is interpreted differently by people from different cultures, or are there two fundamental and distinctive types that differ in terms of content (essentially ontological claims) and means of access (revelation versus meditation), or are there more than two?

I shall begin by concentrating on scholarly attempts to map and explain numinous encounters with supernatural beings; then I will consider those religious experiences that seem to be of a quite different character: meditational/mystical experiences, and finally, in Part 2, develop a case for understanding both as variants of the same psychological processes.

Numinous experiences

In this section I will outline Otto's account of the numinous and explore one aspect of it, possession, in greater detail than he did. Otto was a Christian theologian who tended to think that his own tradition represented the pinnacle of religious development, and his investigations into numinous experiences reflect this bias. They do, nevertheless, offer some fine examples of phenomenological mapping.

A first step for Otto was to recognise that the numinous is intrinsically non-rational and non-moral; yet 'there is no religion in which it does not live as the real innermost core'.[11] This is an important claim. The 'real' innermost core of all religions is *non-rational*. The 'real' innermost core of all religions is *non-moral*. Otto explains this through his analysis of the word 'holy' (German, heilige; Hebrew, qadosh; Greek, hagios). He points out that 'holiness' or 'the holy' is an *a priori* category of mind, a category of interpretation and valuation peculiar to the sphere of religion.[12] In other words, 'numinous' is a psychological term. It refers to a psychological process, a 'distinct' way of experiencing. However, 'the holy' is a composite concept that has three significant segments: the moral, the rational and something else. That something else 'has nothing to do with "reason" and "rationality"', for 'it completely eludes apprehension in terms of concepts'. Nor does it include principles of morality, despite the fact that in modern parlance morality or goodness are often deemed to lie at the heart of the idea, as witnessed in the popular and disparaging phrase 'holier than thou'. But even modern notions of holiness contain more than just the moral element. They also embrace what Otto calls 'an overplus of meaning'. Moreover, he claims, this 'overplus' is not some later addition to notions of the holy but actually its core element:

> 'holy', or at least the equivalent words in Latin and Greek, in Semitic and other ancient languages, denoted first and foremost *only* this overplus: if the ethical element was present at all, at any rate it was not original and never constituted the whole meaning of the word.[13]

Otto's term for this 'overplus' element is the *numinous* – from the Latin *numen*, 'divine presence'. Subjectively, an encounter with the numinous evokes a numinous state of mind, a 'mental state [that] is perfectly *sui generis* and irreducible to any other'.[14] It has an 'entirely non- or super-natural quality'.[15] It is worth noting that descriptions of the numinous, for Otto, are not primarily descriptions of that which is experienced but of the experience itself.

Otto is not alone in locating the distinctiveness of religion in its *postulation* of a supernatural realm, though many scholars have attempted, unsuccessfully in my view, to challenge that claim. Conflicts about definitions of religion usually revolve around issues of scope, that is, issues about what can and cannot be legitimately included within the boundaries of the term 'religion'. If the boundaries are drawn too tightly or too narrowly then much that is commonly recognised as falling within its scope will be excluded. For example, the *Cambridge International Dictionary of English* defines religion as 'the belief in and worship of a god or gods and any such system of belief and worship'. This would exclude some of what is often regarded as falling within the scope of the term 'Hinduism', most of Buddhism, Jainism, Taoism and Confucianism, traditions of belief and practice that are generally recognised as having a religious character. If the boundaries are drawn too loosely then it becomes difficult to know exactly what is being referred to when it is employed. Take, for example, the definition offered by Ronald Cavanagh: 'the varied, symbolic expression of, and appropriate response to, that which people deliberately affirm as being of unrestricted value for them'.[16] If we render 'unrestricted value' as 'highest value' or 'most important', which I think we must because of the problems inherent in the very concept of 'unrestricted' value, then all kinds of things that people value highly fall within the category of 'religion', such as association football, making money, travelling around the world, becoming an opera star.

This does not mean that we cannot define what we mean by 'religion' in a reasonably precise manner or that all definitions are equal. In my view, we *can* both delineate the scope of the term with a workable degree of precision *and*, on that basis make some judgements about the value of the various definitions that scholars and others have offered over the years. Thus, students of religion must tackle the lexical issue: 'how a word has been and is now actually used'.[17] Beattie, Bowman and Harvey cite the *Oxford English Dictionary* definition of religion as an example of an authoritative definition that is nevertheless problematic:

> Recognition on the part of man of some higher unseen power as having control of his destiny, and as being entitled to obedience, reverence, and worship;

the general mental and moral attitude resulting from this belief, with reference to its effect upon the individual or the community; personal or general acceptance of this feeling as a standard of spiritual and practical life.

The framers of such definitions tend to work with established historical and contemporary usage and distil this into some concise expression. Yet such expressions are ultimately dependent on the quality of the sources from which they are derived, and in this case, as Beattie et al. indicate, different assumptions on the part of the framers would produce quite different definitions. Moreover, contemporary usage is quite varied, including, as it must, the various definitions offered by scholars.

The lexical challenge for students of religion is thus one that involves finding a formulation that is at least recognisable to native speakers who use the word while at the same time setting the scope of usage as precisely as possible. So, although I find much merit in James Leuba's claim that 'religion' is a term created by scholars for their intellectual purposes and is therefore theirs to define,[18] it cannot be just that. Unlike, say, 'enzyme', a word that was created by scientists to label a particular type of cellular catalyst, 'religion' is a term that has evolved in meaning over time.

Such evolution may and in this case does constrain the uses to which the word can be put, though it does not determine them entirely. Refinement and reformulation can still take place. Consider, for example, the term 'mammal'. Before the discovery of Australasia animals placed in the category of 'mammal' were all thought to give birth to live young that are attached to a placenta and subsequently nourished on milk secreted from glands on the mother's body. Then kangaroos and koalas were discovered. They feed their young on milk but those young are not attached to a placenta. Instead, they are born much earlier than the young of placental mammals and nourished while protected by a pouch on the mother's belly. So the placenta requirement for inclusion in the class was dropped and mammals were subsequently deemed to give birth to live young and feed them on milk. Then the platypus was discovered. Platypuses do not give birth to live young but lay soft-shelled, pea-sized eggs. When the eggs hatch, the young feed on milk from the mother's mammary glands. This required a further broadening of the term's scope. The current agreement on the common features is that mammals (1) are warm-blooded, (2) suckle their young and (3) have four-chambered hearts.[19]

This example shows that even when terms have everyday usages as well as more scientific or scholarly ones it is still possible to deploy evidence to support the adoption of some uses over others. Initially, the least tenable scholarly ones will be discarded and, over time, everyday use will be refined as well. 'Religion', it seems to me, is a term that has a number of features in common with the term 'mammal'. It has a range of rather imprecise, everyday uses and a range of technical uses that are currently in competition with each other, though in principle capable of being sorted into a kind of hierarchy of accuracy, with the too broad at one end, the too narrow at the other and the 'just about right' in the middle. Some definitions even manage to be both too narrow and too broad at the same time.

Like Otto, I would argue that there is a core element that all definitions of religion must have. Different scholars have described it in different ways, though Anthony F.C. Wallace put it succinctly back in 1966. He called it 'the supernatural premise'. His claim is that:

> It is the premise of every religion – and this premise is religion's defining characteristic – that souls, supernatural beings, and supernatural forces exist. Furthermore, there are certain minimal categories of behavior which, in the context of the *supernatural premise,* are always found in association with one another and which are the substance of religion itself.[20]

In his 1969 version of his 'dimensions of religion' scheme, Ninian Smart echoes Wallace when he writes:

> A religious experience involves some kind of 'perception' of the *invisible* world, or involves a perception that some visible person or thing is a manifestation of the invisible world. The ordinary person in Jerusalem who simply saw Jesus walk by was not having a religious experience, but the disciples who saw him transfigured on the mountain *did* have such an experience...[21]

These are not the only writers who make this point, and it tends roughly to concur with everyday usage, though not all scholars accept it. However, without something like the 'supernatural premise, it is well-nigh impossible to distinguish, for example, religious rituals from other kinds of ritual, religious stories from other kinds of stories, religious beliefs from other kinds of beliefs and, most pertinent to these reflections, religious behaviour from other kinds of behaviour. With that premise, on the other hand, all these distinctions can be made. The challenge for those who deny that premise is, therefore, to identify some robust criterion or set of criteria that can make these distinctions as effectively as the supernatural premise can, and also conform to a similar degree with everyday usage. If definitions omitting the supernatural premise cannot make these distinctions effectively then, like the placental and live young criteria for identifying mammals, they must be abandoned. In the present state of our knowledge it looks like Otto's placing of the supernatural at the heart of what religion is all about is both appropriate and insightful.[22]

According to Otto, the numinous displays/is experienced as having three prominent features: it is mysterious (*mysterium*); it is tremendous/awe-ful/dread-ful (*tremendum*) and it is fascinating (*fascinanas*). About the mysterium Otto writes:

> The truly 'mysterious' object is beyond our apprehension and comprehension, not only because our knowledge has certain irremovable limits, but because in it we come upon something inherently 'wholly other', whose kind and character are incommensurable with our own, and before which we therefore recoil in a wonder that strikes us chill and numb.[23]

It is this kind of claim that led Smart to propose his distinction between the numinous and the mystical, a distinction that has prima facie credibility, though one that I shall argue is ultimately untenable. Briefly, the epistemological 'wholly other' does not entail the ontological 'wholly other'. In other words, having an experience of a mysterious, ineffable, unfamiliar, incomprehensible being, realm, dimension or state of consciousness, an experience that transcends all that is familiar, does not automatically validate the inference that what is being experienced is something that is totally different from oneself, something that is an ontologically distinct entity.

'Tremendum' refers to a fear 'that is more than fear proper', 'a feeling of peculiar dread, not to be mistaken for any ordinary dread ...'.[24] It is a response to manifestations of the numinous such as the wrath (orgé) of Yahweh, which is incalculable, arbitrary and, indeed, 'nothing but the tremendum itself ...'.[25] But the tremendum is not simply terrifying, it is also majestic and overpowering.[26] The 'fascinans' element points to something that is quite distinct from, though intimately connected to the mysterium tremendum. Otto's claim is that however awe-ful, majestic and terrifying it is, the numinous is 'something that allures with a potent charm ... something that entrances ... something that captivates and transports'.[27] In classroom situations I sometimes attempt to convey my understanding of the *mysterium tremendum et fascinans* by cultivating, as best as I can, those feelings within myself and express them through my physiology. So, I open my eyes wide, let my mouth sag, let my arms drop and say 'wwooowww!' Then I make my legs and body shake, raising my arms in a gesture of protection while, at the same time shuffling forwards, seemingly against my will. Students seem to get it: when one encounters the numinous as described by Otto those are the kinds of physiological responses that emerge spontaneously.

Another prominent feature of Otto's account is that he identified different levels, stages or depths of numinous experience. For him, even on 'the lowest level of religious development' the essential characteristic of the 'mysterium' abides 'in a peculiar "moment" of consciousness, to wit, the *stupor* before something wholly other, whether such other be named "spirit" or "daemon" or "deva" or be left without a name'.[28] Likewise, the 'tremendum' element of the numinous has 'an antecedent stage', namely *daemonic dread*:

> It first begins to stir in the feeling of 'something uncanny', 'eerie', or 'weird'. It is this feeling which, emerging in the mind of primeval man, forms the starting point for the entire religious development in history.[29]

The culminatory point of that development comes, for Otto, with Christianity: the most complete development of numinous emotion, in which the 'shudder' of the primitive becomes 'mystical awe'.[30] Finally, he suggests that the 'fascinans' element may not have been present in the first stage of religious consciousness, which, 'at first took shape only as 'daemonic dread'.[31] However, such dread 'can never explain how it is that "the numinous" is the object of search and desire and yearning ...'[32] That yearning leads to attempts at magical identification of the self with the numen 'by formula, ordination, adjuration, consecration, exorcism [and] the "shamanistic" ways of procedure, possession, indwelling, self-fulfilment in exaltation and ecstasy'.[33] In particular, possession of and by the numen becomes a good in itself, 'till finally it reaches its consummation in the sublimest and purest states of the "life within the Spirit" and in the noblest mysticism'.[34]

Otto's ideas about the evolution of religious consciousness and levels of religious insight allow him to incorporate most aspects of supernatural experience into his scheme, but they do so on the basis of some questionable assumptions and assertions. In two chapters, entitled 'Its Earliest Manifestations' and 'The Cruder Phases', Otto offers a list of what he calls 'phenomena preliminary to religion proper' or 'pre-religion'. The first item is *magic*, the second *worship of the dead*, the third *ideas of souls and spirits*, the fourth ideas of *power, mana, orienda*, etc. the fifth ideas of the *aliveness* of natural phenomena such as volcanos and clouds, the sixth *fairy stories*, the seventh ideas about *daemons*, and the eighth notions of *purity and pollution*. The last three items on his list, numbers nine, ten and eleven, are not so much about pre-religion as the transition from the pre- stage to religion proper. It begins with a 'transition from mere feeling to its "explication" and to the positing of the numinous object'.[35] This transition, Otto reminds us, is psychological in character:

> Here we have the obscure basis of meaning and idea rising into greater clarity and beginning to make itself explicit as the notion, however vague and fleeting, of a transcendent Something, a real operative entity of a numinous kind,

which later, as the development proceeds, assumes concrete form as a *'numen loci'*, a daemon, an 'El', a Baal, or the like.[36]

This 'transitional stage', this 'naturalistic foundation of religion – whether animism, pantheism, or another – ... these anticipations of a higher religious experience ...'[37] are eventually transcended 'as the numen reveals "itself"' (i.e. becomes manifest to mind and feeling) ever more strongly and fully'.[38] The full revelation emerges gradually, when 'the numinous feeling becomes charged with progressively rational, moral and cultural significance'.[39] Here, again, we may note, Otto slides from writing about the numinous experience into writing about the numen itself, as though the experience somehow validates the inferences about the objective nature of its content.

Anyone who has undertaken even a rudimentary study of religious traditions and/or engaged in religious practices that go beyond the purely habitual will recognise many of the features that explicate Otto's notion of the numinous. Likewise, anyone who has had the good fortune of an education in critical thinking will be aware that there is a fair amount of arbitrariness in his presentation. In the first place, if we adopt an evolutionary perspective as the overarching frame of our enquiry (as we must if it is to have any evidential credibility) then we have to recognise that on the tree of life we are hominid primates. Our nearest relatives, the other great apes, do not seem to display any kind of religiosity, a fact that has led some writers to substitute the designation *homo sapiens* (wise man/human) for *homo religiosus* (religious man/human).[40] Religion, it seems, is a distinctive expression of human mentation, and, in that sense, *homo religiosus* would seem to be an appropriate designator. Even so, the question of whether religious thinking is sufficiently widespread across human populations to be regarded as an evolutionary adaptation is unclear.[41] On the issue of progression, there is a gulf between biologists, who tend to speak in terms of 'systematic change through time',[42] and claim that 'there is nothing inherently progressive about evolution'[43] and more socially inclined writers, who exhibit a tendency to introduce notions of progress into their accounts.[44]

Few students of religion would dispute the fact that religious beliefs and behaviours are varied or that many of the beliefs of one group will be incompatible with those of another group. Ideas about progress can, to some extent, ameliorate those incompatibilities – in a manner similar to that of ranking, i.e. earlier phases are not so much wrong as merely incomplete. Notions of progress in religion face two challenges, however. The first is that such notions are not simply chronological in nature, i.e. it is not the case that recent expressions of religious ideas are claimed to be superior to older ones.

If that were the case then the simplest way to determine which religious system is best would be to identify the most recent: the older the system the less insightful, deep and comprehensive it will be. I know of no scholar who proposes a simple chronological approach to determining progress in religious understanding. Other potential criteria include adherence: the most advanced are those with the most adherents, and the related idea of survival: less advanced systems tend to wither and become extinct; more advanced systems survive and flourish, i.e. attract more adherents. Again, I know of no scholar who employs such criteria when attempting to explain what progress in religion entails, though some writers use them to question the credibility of existing religious traditions. One of my favourite pieces in this genre is H.L. Mencken's humorous 'Memorial Service', which is worth quoting in full:

> Where is the graveyard of dead gods? What lingering mourner waters their mounds? There was a time when Jupiter was the king of the gods, and any man who doubted his puissance was *ipso facto* a barbarian and an ignoramus. But where in all the world is there a man who worships Jupiter today? And what of Huitzilopochtli? In one year – and it is no more than five hundred years ago – 50,000 youths and maidens were slain in sacrifice to him. Today, if he is remembered at all, it is only by some vagrant savage in the depths of the Mexican forest. Huitzilopochtli, like many other gods, had no human father; his mother was a virtuous widow; he was born of an apparently innocent flirtation that she carried on with the sun. When he frowned, his father, the sun, stood still. When he roared with rage, earthquakes engulfed whole cities. When he thirsted he was watered with 10,000 gallons of human blood. But today Huitzilopochtli is as magnificently forgotten as Allen G. Thurman. Once the peer of Allah, Buddha and Wotan, he is now the peer of Richmond P. Hobson, Alton B. Parker, Adelina Patti, General Weyler and Tom Sharkey.
>
> Speaking of Huitzilopochtli recalls his brother Tezcatlipoca. Tezcatlipoca was almost as powerful: he consumed 25,000 virgins a year. Lead me to his tomb: I would weep and hang a *couronne des perles*. But who knows where it is? Or where the grave of Quetzalcoatl is? Or Xiehtecutli? Or Centeotl, that sweet one? Or Tlazolteotl, the goddess of love? Or Mictlan? Or Xipe? Or all the host of Tzitzimitles? Where are their bones? Where is the willow on which they hung their harps? In what forlorn and unheard-of Hell do they await the resurrection morn? Who enjoys their residuary estates? Or that of Dis, whom Caesar found to be the chief god of the Celts? Or that of Tarves, the bull? Or that of Mullo, the celestial jackass? There was a time when the Irish revered all these gods, but today even the drunkest Irishman laughs at them.
>
> But they have company in oblivion: the hell of dead gods is as crowded as the Presbyterian Hell for babies. Damona is there, and Esus, and Drunemeton, and Silvana, and Dervones, and Adsalluta, and Deva, and Belisama, and Uxellimus,

and Borvo, and Grannos, and Mogons. All mighty gods in their day, worshipped by millions, full of demands and impositions, able to bind and loose – all gods of the first class. Men labored for generations to build vast temples to them – temples with stones as large as hay-wagons. The business of interpreting their whims occupied thousands of priests, bishops, archbishops. To doubt them was to die, usually at the stake. Armies took to the field to defend them against infidels: villages were burned, women and children were butchered, cattle were driven off. Yet in the end they all withered and died, and today there is none so poor to do them reverence.

What has become of Sutekh, once the high god of the whole Nile Valley? What has become of:

Resheph	Baal
Anath	Astarte
Ashtoreth	Hadad
Nebo	Dagon
Melek	Yau
Ahijah	Amon-Re
Isis	Osiris
Ptah	Molech?

All these were once gods of the highest eminence. Many of them are mentioned with fear and trembling in the Old Testament. They ranked, five or six thousand years ago, with Yahweh Himself; the worst of them stood far higher than Thor. Yet they have all gone down the chute, and with them the following:

Arianrod	Nuada Argetlam
Morrigu	Tagd
Govannon	Goibniu
Gunfled	Odin
Dagda	Ogma
Ogyrvan	Marzin
Dea Dia	Mars
Iuno lucina	Diana of Ephesus
Saturn	Robigus
Furrina	Pluto
Chronos	Vesta
Engurra	Zer-panitu
Belus	Merodach
Ubilulu	Elum
U-dimmer-an-kia	Marduk
U-sab-sib	Nin
U-Mersi	Persephone

Tammuz	Istar
Venus	Lagas
Beltis	Nirig
Nusku	Nebo
Aa	En-Mersi
Sin	Assur
Apsu	Beltu
Elali	Kuski-banda
Mami	Nin-azu
Zaraqu	Qarradu
Zagaga	Ueras

Ask the rector to lend you any good book on comparative religion: you will find them all listed. They were gods of the highest dignity – gods of civilized peoples – worshipped and believed in by millions. All were omnipotent, omniscient and immortal. And all are dead.[45]

With this 'memorial service' Mencken is clearly not inviting his readers to think that the gods who are worshipped today are in any way superior to those that have 'gone down the chute'. Rather, the implication is that, in time, they too will 'go down the chute'. There is, of course, some hyperbole in his statements, for not all of these deities were omnipotent and omniscient. Nevertheless, and I have not checked the authenticity of every one, all were powerful supernatural beings. But why should we think that any modern deity is greater than the best of them or that any modern understanding of 'the supernatural realm' is superior to those held by the worshippers of Marduk, Odin or Zeus? Chronology, then, would seem to be an untenable criterion for religious superiority. The fact that Sikhism is more modern than Islām does not make it superior to Islām, and the fact that Mormonism is more modern than Sikhism does not make that tradition superior to its predecessor.

Although Otto hints that chronology is a viable criterion for determining progress in religious understanding with his statements about 'pre-religion', 'transitional stages' and 'anticipations of a higher religious experience' that eventually develop into 'the full revelation', his Christian affiliations prevent him from embracing chronology as a primary determinant of progress. Whatever their merits, Islām and Sikhism cannot, for Otto, be regarded as improvements on Christianity. He thus falls back on normative criteria for determining superiority: morality and rationality. The 'full revelation' only emerges when 'the numinous feeling becomes charged with progressively rational, moral and cultural significance'.[46] The peak of these rational, moral and cultural developments comes, for Otto, at the third and highest stage of religious progress, which takes us 'beyond the prophet, to one in whom is found the Spirit in all its plenitude, and who at the same time in His person and in His performance is become most completely the object of divination, in whom Holiness is recognised apparent'.⁴⁷ Who could that be? The Buddha? Kṛṣṇa? Muhammad? No, none of these. For Otto, the Christian, it is Jesus, though a follower of another religion could easily, on the basis of the material in *The Idea of the Holy*, substitute his or her own favourite charismatic figure. That is, while Otto does an admirable job of mapping some of the diversity of religious experiences nothing in his account requires an uncommitted reader to accept his stage/phase model of religious progress, nor to accept what he achieves largely by sleight of pen: that there is an objective numinous reality that corresponds to the subjective numinous experience. Believing in such a reality and regulating one's behaviour in the light of that belief may infuse a person's life with comfort, reassurance and fulfilment, but, in the end, neither the experience nor the belief can guarantee that the whole package is anything more than a positive (or negative) illusion.⁴⁸

As noted above, for Otto, the 'shamanistic' ways of procedure, possession, indwelling, self-fulfilment in exaltation and ecstasy' belong to a preliminary stage in the development of religious consciousness. It seems to me, however, that experiences of 'possession, indwelling, and self-fulfilment in exaltation and ecstasy' are pretty much as numinous as one can get. If some of the most significant and powerful numinous experiences occur when a divinity speaks to a person through an apparition, as he did to Moses through a burning bush and Saul on the Damascus Road, then surely when a divinity enters into a person and 'possesses' them we have something that is even more numinous, significant and powerful, something that warrants more than the brief, passing comment that Otto makes.⁴⁹

In the course of his extensive work on possession, which, for me, is an example of quality phenomenological mapping, T.K. Oesterreich identifies two primary dimensions of possession and five possessing agencies.⁵⁰ The two primary dimensions are somnambulistic–lucid and spontaneous (involuntary)–voluntary (cultivated), as illustrated in Figure 1. The five possessing agencies are a demonic power, a benign power, the spirit of a deceased person, another living person and an animal. Somnambulistic possession refers to a state in which the personality of the possessor completely displaces the personality of the possessed and when, on return to the normality, the possessed is amnesic for the period of possession. By contrast, in lucid possession, the possessed 'does not lose consciousness of his usual personality but retains it ... he remains fully conscious of what is happening; he is the passive spectator of what takes place within him'.⁵¹

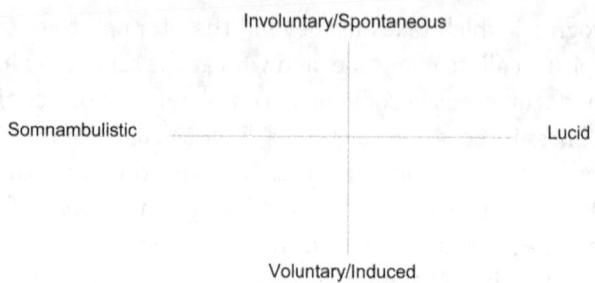

Figure 1 Four types of possession according to Oesterreich.

The other dimension or axis (from involuntary or spontaneous to voluntary or induced) is a little more complex. The individual who is being possessed may interpret the experience as spontaneous or involuntary though it may well have been induced by a third party, an exorcist for example. Involuntary possession is often associated with sickness and is generally treated as unwelcome, at least by the possessed person. But this is not always the case. Many Christians would welcome and count as a blessing possession by the Holy Spirit. Indeed, members of the Church of Jesus, West Virginia, USA, report that they would only consider handling poisonous serpents during church services if the Holy Spirit entered into and 'took hold' of them.[52] Such possession would be welcome and even anticipated – church members often dance ecstatically during services, not least to open themselves to possession by the Holy Spirit – though, ultimately, it is understood as a gift rather than something that the dancers have induced by their own efforts. Then there is the desire for what is sometimes called secondary gain. A number of writers have noted that individuals possessed by demons are often relatively powerless members of their societies, often female, for whom the take-over by a spirit provides an opportunity to express and act out socially unacceptable opinions and behaviours and effect an improvement in their social status at the same time. This latter outcome is largely a consequence of the fact that the successful identification and treatment of demonic possession serves to buttress the belief system and maintain or enhance the influence of the exorcising authority. The possessed can thus be viewed as one of the many vehicles employed for the propagation of a particular ideology. Involuntary possession, even by a demon, may, then, be regarded as beneficial both by the possessed themselves and by the authorities which take on the responsibility for treating such conditions.[53]

Primary indicators

1. A new physiognomy, a change in features.
2. A change in voice, usually involving displacement of the upper registers.

Secondary indicators

1. The new voice speaks for another personality and the host, if commented upon, is usually referred to in the third person.
2. A display of physical abilities beyond those normally available to the 'host', e.g., supernormal strength.

In some cases of voluntary possession it is a specialist who cultivates trance and possession in order to engage in therapeutic or divinatory activity on behalf of the community; a shaman would be a good example here. In other cases many or most members of a group seek possession for their own benefit. The Voodoo religion of Haiti and the related Candomblé religion of Brazil provide good examples of this pattern.[54]

Almost all writers on the subject agree that possession occupies a significant place in the repertoire of many if not most shamans. They disagree, however, on the issue of its centrality. Some, such as Eliade and Arbman relegate it to a peripheral role while others such as Findeisen and Lewis elevate it to the status of a crucial component. Much depends on which shamanic cultures are regarded as prototypical, for this will determine the features that are identified as most significant. In his extensive review of literature on this subject, Hultkrantz criticises a number of authors for over-emphasising one or other features of the shamanic complex. He identifies four central constituents of shamanism: contact with the supernatural world; the social role of mediator with that world; the accomplishment of such mediation through the assistance of spirit helpers; and the shaman's ecstatic or trance experiences. A shaman could thus be said to be a person who, on behalf of a community, enters a trance state and, by means of spirit helpers, obtains a range of benefits for that community.

The role of the spirit helpers is crucial according to Hultkrantz: 'Shamanism is unthinkable without helping spirits',[55] he maintains. The precise nature of the relationship between the shaman and his or her spirits is less clear, however. Certainly he has contact with them during the period of his calling to his vocation, during which he is harassed by spirits and sometimes possessed by them.[56] This suggests, in the case of those who are not members of shamanic families, a spontaneous experience of dissociation and even trance, perhaps prompted by stress and given shape by the motifs that are relevant to this kind of experience in the person's culture. Lewis suggests that the same pattern, albeit in a muted form, is also found in the vocational calling of those who inherit the shamanic role from older members of their families. Here, though, even if the experience is spontaneous it cannot be unexpected, except, perhaps, in terms of timing. At root, however, there may be little by way of significant difference between the two for, as was noted above, even involuntary possession can have its attractions and, at some level, be a desired outcome for the possessed person.

Only some of a shaman's activities appear to involve possession. Hultkrantz identifies four principal shamanic activities: doctor, diviner, psychopomp (soul guide) and hunting magician. Activities undertaken in the context of the first two of these usually require the assistance of and sometimes possession by helping spirits. If the illness is soul loss the shaman employs his own free soul to bring it back, though whether this requires the assistance of spirit helpers is a moot point. If the illness is one of intrusion, where 'an object or a spirit has invaded the patient's body'[57] then spirit helpers are needed. Two techniques of divination are employed. One requires the help of spirits, the other uses natural signs such as patterns of cracks, lines on the hand and so on. The shaman thus performs many of his important tasks with the aid of his spirit helpers. These are of two types: auxiliary, usually animal, spirits; and a main or controlling spirit 'who often takes up his abode inside the shaman ...'[58] Any explanation of the nature and role of possession in shamanism thus requires a clear account of the relationship between the shaman and his or her spirit helpers.

In Candomblé, Macumba, Voodoo and other related traditions possession occurs in a ritual context and is induced by a similar range of trance-promoting techniques: drumming, dancing, rhythmic breathing, etc. The rituals are overseen by a kind of priest (houngan or mambo in Voodoo; Pai de Santo or Mãe de Santo in Candomblé). Unlike the shaman, who is a virtuoso performer, the houngan is more of a facilitator, who provides a location, supplies and expertise.[59] The context he provides is permeated by rhythmic percussion, symbols and stories of the gods (loa in Voodoo, orisha/orixa in Candomblé) to facilitate trance and provide the subjective conditions for possession to occur. The effects of possession in these situations are usually empowering for the participants. As they come to internalise and take on for themselves the personality characteristics of the deities who possess them so they gain access to mental and emotional processes that are not ordinarily available to their conscious selves.

Long-standing members of these groups may well have more than one patron deity who possesses them and, thereby, in psychological terms, have access to a varied repertoire of unconscious processes. As Pierre Verger, a French convert to Candomblé, observes 'this religion ... has the characteristic of exalting people's personalities. People feel strong, people feel protected'.[60] This view is confirmed by Lucia, a Mãe de Santo whose personal Orisha is Iansã. She says:

> Lucia: Iansã ... is the orixa that governs with Xango. She is the goddess of lightning, of fire. She is a very strong orixa. She has a very strong personality and people under her also have very strong personalities ... She is a warrior.
> Interviewer: Like you?
> Lucia: That's it.[61]

The idea here seems to parallel the Hindu notion that people should have a personal deity (iṣṭa-devatā) and the Roman Catholic teaching that each member of the church should chose a patron saint at the confirmation ceremony and cultivate a special relationship with him or her thereafter. The difference is that the followers of Candomblé take their patrons into themselves in the most profound manner possible, through possession.

Mystical experiences

Any survey of books with the word 'mysticism' in their titles quickly reveals that, according to many authors, this phenomenon – if it be unitary – is found in all the major religions of the world. Some even go so far as to claim that mysticism represents a common core of all religions. What then is mysticism?[62]

According to Ninian Smart mysticism refers 'to the contemplative life and experience, as distinguished from prophetism, devotionalism and sacramentalism'.[63] In other words, mysticism, as a concept, embraces both the process of interiorisation or turning attention inwards (contemplation) and the experiences a person has as a result of such interiorisation. The implication here is that mystical experience is, at least in part, dependent on a person engaging in contemplative practices. A further implication would seem to be that mystical experience is sought after by the mystic. These two features of mysticism: an *actively pursued* and *internal* quest, provide the basis for Smart's separation of mystical from numinous experiences. However, it may be that this distinction cannot be pushed too far for, as we shall see, there are some mystical experiences that have a distinctly numinous quality and, after all, even though Yahweh revealed himself to Moses in a burning bush Moses had to climb up the mountain to find him.

Problem

If we follow Smart and give primacy to the processes for obtaining a mystical experience rather than the nature of the experience itself we find that experiences regarded as mystical by some scholars are excluded from the category, perhaps wrongly.

The prime example of such excluded experiences is what William James called 'sporadic' mystical experiences and W.T. Stace 'spontaneous' mystical experiences.[64] Both writers provide a number of examples from spiritual literature to illustrate the distinctive nature of such experiences. Stace, however, goes further than James. He links the spontaneous experiences with what he calls extravertive mysticism and acquired or cultivated ones with what he calls introvertive mysticism. About these two types he writes:

> The essential difference between them is that the extravertive experience looks outward through the senses, while the introvertive looks inward into the mind. Both culminate in the perception of an ultimate unity ... But the extravertive mystic, using his physical senses, perceives the multiplicity of external material objects – the sea, the sky, the houses, the trees – mystically transfigured so that the One, or the Unity shines through them. The introvertive mystic, on the contrary, seeks by deliberately shutting off the senses, by obliterating from consciousness the entire multiplicity of sensations, images and thoughts, to plunge into the depths of his own ego. There, in that darkness and silence, he alleges that he perceives the One – and is united with it – not as a Unity seen through a multiplicity (as in the extravertive experience), but as the wholly naked One devoid of any plurality whatever.[65]

Problem

Stace suggests that spontaneous experiences tend to be extravertive and cultivated ones introvertive, though he does recognise that the connection is not absolute.[66] Indeed, there is plenty of evidence to suggest that introvertive experiences *can* be spontaneous. For example, *The Varieties of Religious Experience* by William James contains a number of accounts of sporadic or spontaneous mystical experiences by John Addington Symonds, 'a renowned Victorian art historian and Renaissance scholar'.[67] Towards the end of one of these accounts Symonds writes, 'At last nothing remained but a pure, absolute, abstract self. The universe became without form and void of content'.[68] This is what Stace would call an introvertive mystical experience but it is clearly a spontaneous one. Likewise, even though the opposite combination: cultivated extravertive experience seems to be rare there are some contenders for this description. The sahaja samādhi state mentioned by Forman and attributed to the Hindu mystic Ramana Maharshi appears to have the characteristics of extravertive mystical experience and it follows on from the practice of introvertive mysticism.[69]

It would seem then, that Smart's process-based definition is inadequate, as it cannot accommodate spontaneous experiences. For Stace, it is not the means employed to gain an experience that makes it mystical but the content of the experience: the experience of unity or universal oneness. This definition certainly allows for the inclusion of spontaneous experiences but it also seems to exclude others that have a decidedly mystical character. The Jain, Sāṃkhya and Yoga systems of India employ contemplative practices very similar to those found in the monistic Advaita Vedānta tradition (which is undoubtedly mystical according to Stace's criteria) yet the aim of such practice is not the realisation of unity, as in Advaita, but the radical separation of spirit from matter – a state called kaivalya (aloneness). Many writers would also claim that Christian Jewish and Muslim mysticism is also non-monistic. It seems to be the case, therefore, that experiences of different and, one might add, mutually exclusive ontological realities can be appropriately described or categorised as mystical.

But if reference to neither method nor ontological content can enable us to distinguish mystical experiences from non-mystical ones, how can we decide what is to count as mystical and what is not? William James offers what might be called a 'characteristics' approach to the issue of definition. In his view, experiences possessing certain general characteristics are to be classed as mystical; experiences lacking these characteristics are not. James lists four characteristics of mystical experience. The first two he regards as primary, the second two as secondary. They are:

1 **Ineffability** – they defy expression; no adequate report of their content can be given in words.

2 **Noetic quality** – they are states of insight into depths of truth unplumbed by the discursive intellect. They are illuminations, revelations, full of significance and importance, all inarticulate though they remain.

3 **Transiency** – they cannot be sustained for long, their quality can be but imperfectly reproduced in memory; but when they recur it is recognised.

4   **Passivity** – when the characteristic sort of consciousness once has set in the mystic feels as if his own will were in abeyance.[70]

Close examination of these characteristics reveals that they too exclude experiences that seem to have a natural home in the category of the mystical. The Buddhist and Yoga traditions describe a number of states variously called jhāna, dhyāna and samādhi. The accounts of these states describe a progression from content-ful, externally oriented experience to content-less, internally oriented experience. This process is common to many contemplative traditions and it clearly falls within the scope of Smart's definition and probably also of Stace's definition of introvertive mysticism, yet it has little or no noetic component. Such experiences provide a foundation for the contemplative's subsequent access to noetic states: truth-bearing insight (ṛtaṃbharā prajñā) and right knowledge (samyak jñāna) in Yoga and Buddhism respectively, but appear to lack the noetic quality themselves. It is clear, however, that they do form an integral part of at least some cultivated mystical experiences.

What seems to be the case then, is that mystical experiences can be spontaneous or cultivated; some have a noetic quality and some do not; some lead to an experience of unity and some do not. James' passivity characteristic also has limited scope. While it might well apply to all spontaneous mystical experience there are some cultivated ones to which it does not seem to apply. James himself recognises that there are 'preliminary voluntary operations' that precede what he regards as mystical experience proper and it has been argued above that such 'voluntary operations' frequently give rise to non-noetic mystical states. But even those mystical experiences that we might call culminatory and which do have a noetic component are not all passive. Perhaps the best example of such an experience is the Buddha's enlightenment. Having attained the fourth jhāna Siddhārtha decided to apply his concentrated mind to the acquisition of three knowledges, the third of which liberated him from the cycle of rebirth and made him a buddha, an awakened one. This can hardly be described as a passive experience. Indeed, the Buddha's primary criterion for deciding whether the 'knowledge' gained through meditation had the capacity to bring release from rebirth was the nature and focus of the attentional activity carried out in that state.

So far, then, we have been unable to formulate a definition of mysticism that will do justice to the range of experiences that seem sufficiently closely related as to form a single category while at the same time distinguish mystical from non-mystical experiences. What we do have, however, is what we can think of as an outline map of the territory that can be extracted from the more robust elements in James's and Stace's accounts (Table 2).

Table 2 Mapping mystical experience – phase one.

Spontaneous	Cultivated
No stages	*Preliminary stages*
Ineffable	Ineffable
Noetic	Transient
Transient	*Culminatory stages*
Passive	Ineffable
	Noetic
	Transient
	Sometimes passive
Introvertive or extravertive	**Introvertive**

This table is, of course, just a provisional representation of the territory and will need to be modified if it is to be comprehensive. It is derived from what can be regarded as the more valid elements of the scholarly accounts to which I have referred. These same accounts, as has already been indicated, also contain elements that are invalid or inaccurate, and it is to these I now turn.

Hierarchical and constructivist interpretations of the mystical literature

Both W.T. Stace and R.C. Zaehner seek to explain some of the differences between mystical experiences by creating some kind of rank order. Stace, for example, argues that:

> the extravertive experience, although we recognize it as a distinct type, is actually on a lower level than the introvertive type; that is to say, it is an incomplete kind of experience which finds its completion and fulfilment in the introvertive kind of experience.[71]

So far as I am aware, there are no grounds for this claim in the mystical literature. If it were accurate, we would expect to find evidence of a progression *from* the extravertive mystical experience *to* the introvertive one. The fact is that there is little or no evidence of such a progression. Moreover, we may recall that the cultivation of introvertive mystical experience usually begins with a restriction and introversion of attention. This progresses or deepens to a point or stage which then acts as a kind of foundation for culminatory experiences possessing a noetic quality that has to do with the nature of existence at a deep level. In other words, extravertive mystical experience seems to have more in common with the culminatory stages of introvertive mystical experience than it does with the preparatory ones. The idea that the extravertive experience 'finds its completion and fulfilment in the introvertive kind of experience' thus appears to be phenomenologically inaccurate.

R.C. Zaehner adopts a similar approach. He distinguishes three general types of mystical experience:

1. the **panenhenic** – an experience of Nature in all things or of all things being one;
2. the **monistic** – the isolation of the soul from all that is other than itself;
3. **theistic** – where the soul is led out of its isolation and is slowly transmuted into the substance of the Deity like a log of wood which is gradually assimilated to the fire.

The first of these is virtually identical with Stace's extravertive type while the monistic and theistic varieties would be subsumed under Stace's introvertive type. Stace, writing some three years later than Zaehner, dismisses the latter's distinction between monistic and theistic mystical experience as reflecting nothing more than two different interpretations of what are essentially identical experiences. He does not, however, explain how this process of interpretation works, though in 1975 Ninian Smart attempted to do just that.

The tool Smart employs for this purpose is the concept of *ramification* or what might be termed 'conceptual embeddedness'. Smart describes ramification as follows: 'where a concept appears as part of a doctrinal scheme it gains its meaning in part from a range of doctrinal statements taken to be true'.[72] In other words, many accounts of mystical experiences are not simply descriptive (e.g. I saw this, I heard this, I felt this – terminology to which all humans can relate), but are doctrinal in nature. That is, concepts which are particular to one or just a small number of religions are used alongside or even instead of more straightforwardly descriptive ones. The extent to which any account of mystical experience is ramified can be determined according to Smart, by employing a simple question: 'How many propositions are presupposed as true by the description?' The more propositions presupposed as true, the higher the degree of ramification. The higher the degree of ramification, 'the less is the description guaranteed by the experience itself'.[73]

Zaehner's typology is based on highly ramified descriptions of mystical experiences and this renders it suspect to say the least. It is also clearly propagandist. Zaehner was a Roman Catholic. It is, therefore, no surprise to find that when he comes to rank his three types against each other the theistic type (which his own tradition endorses) is deemed to be the best. Zaehner's ranking, like Stace's, is not based on any kind of recorded progression through the types but on doctrinal preferences. Smart's concept of ramification is clearly useful when assessing the validity of attempted rankings of mystical experiences. It has less value in the search for the essence of mystical experience. The reason for this is that few accounts of mystical experience are free of ramification. One way to deal with this problem would be to remove the ramified elements from descriptions of mystical experiences. The drawback with this approach is that in most cases de-ramified accounts would contain very little information.

Another approach has been taken by Steven Katz. He takes the concept of ramification seriously, but he does not restrict its application to the post-experience situation. Rather, he argues that ramification occurs at all stages of mystical experience and description. The mystic's background prepares him or her for a certain kind of experience. The experience itself is structured and moulded by that background and, not surprisingly, the accounts of the experience are also permeated by concepts deriving from the mystic's background tradition. For Katz, it is not that mystics reflect on their raw experience and then filter it through doctrinal categories when seeking to describe it. Rather, the categories are constitutive of the experience, they are not separable from it. As he states, 'There are *no* pure (i.e. unmediated) experiences.'[74] If Katz is correct, then mystical experiences are better understood as experiential manifestations of doctrine than as insights into the fundamental nature of existence – despite the conviction of mystics that their experiences are veridical.[75]

Katz's argument has been criticised by a number of writers, and most extensively by the contributors to a volume edited by Robert Forman entitled *The Problem of Pure Consciousness*. In his introductory essay Forman criticises Katz's position with an argument that is reiterated in various ways by other contributors and which offers a different way of understanding mystical experience. Katz is deemed to be misguided because he grounds his account on what his critics call an unwarranted assumption: 'There are *no* pure (i.e. unmediated) experiences ... *all* experience is processed through, organized by, and makes itself available to us in extremely complex epistemological ways.'[76] The import of this claim is made clear in his subsequent comments:

> Properly understood, yoga ... is *not* an *unconditioning* or *deconditioning* of consciousness, but rather it is a *reconditioning* of consciousness, i.e. a substituting of one form of conditioned and/or contextual consciousness for

another, albeit a new, unusual, and perhaps altogether more interesting form of conditioned-contextual consciousness.[77]

This assertion denies the fundamental claim of much mystical soteriology: that mystical experience can provide insight into the truth of things, access to the noumena behind phenomena or experience of a normally unperceived transcendent reality.

It is this assertion that the critics want to challenge most of all. They do it primarily by arguing that not only is Katz's assumption just that, an assumption, it is also unphenomenological because we can find reports in the mystical literature of what the contributors to this volume call a 'pure consciousness event' (PCE for short). A PCE is defined by Forman as 'a wakeful though contentless (nonintentional) consciousness'.[78] An example of such a report can be found at the beginning of Patañjali's *Yoga Sūtra* where the state of yoga is described as 'the cessation of the mind's activities' (citta vṛtti nirodha). Pure Consciousness Events, claim the contributors, *are* unmediated. That is, during such events the mystic is *not* 'employing concepts; differentiating his/her awareness according to religious patterns and symbols; drawing upon memory, apprehension, expectation, language or the accumulation of prior experience; or discriminating and integrating'.[79] In short, PCEs are not conditioned.

Within the context of mysticism, claims Forman, such events occur primarily in the course of what Stace called introvertive mysticism. Here it is to be understood as, to use Forman's words, a rudimentary form of mystical experience, a stage on the introvertive mystical path. The relation between the PCE experience and experience at the culmination of the mystical path can be understood, he suggests, by reference to the distinction between samādhi and sahaja samādhi as described by the Hindu mystic Ramana Maharshi. Samādhi refers to a pure consciousness event akin to the state of yoga mentioned earlier; sahaja samādhi 'is a state in which a silent level within the subject is maintained along with (simultaneously with) the full use of the human faculties ... such a permanent mystical state is typically a more advanced stage in the mystical journey'.[80] So described, samādhi is an introverted mystical experience while sahaja samādhi is an extravertive mystical experience. Seemingly without realising it, Forman has inverted Stace's progression. Stace regarded the extravertive experience as a precursor to the introvertive; Forman regards the introvertive as a precursor to the extravertive. This inversion also challenges Stace's claim that there are no techniques for cultivating extravertive mystical experiences. Forman, however, has the opposite problem to Stace: if samādhi (an introvertive experience) is a precursor to sahaja samādhi (an extravertive experience) how do we account for the fact that many people claim to have had extravertive mystical experiences that have arisen spontaneously?

The solution to this phenomenological muddle is quite simple. If we refer back to the outline map above and the accompanying argument we can see that Stace was wrong in thinking that the extravertive experience was a precursor to the introvertive. In this we can agree with Forman who, however, makes no mention of spontaneous mystical experiences, nor of the culminatory stages of the introvertive path. Once these omissions are corrected we can simply modify Table 2 by adding a column to accommodate sahaja samādhi and an arrow into it from the culminatory stages box in the introvertive column (see Table 3).

Table 3 Mapping mystical experience – phase two.

Spontaneous	Spontaneous or cultivated	Cultivated
No stages	*Preliminary stages*	*Preliminary stages*
Ineffable	Ineffable	Ineffable
Noetic	Transient	Transient
Transient	↓	↓
Passive		
	Culminatory stages	*Culminatory stages*
	Ineffable	Ineffable
	Noetic	Noetic
	Transient	Transient
	Sometimes	Sometimes
	passive	passive
Introvertive or extravertive	**Introvertive**	**Extravertive**

These additions expand our map of the mystical territory but do not complete it, for there is another element in the generation of mystical experiences that all the authors mentioned so far have neglected. This is the fact that some mystical experiences are reported as being directly induced by other people. Two examples, one from Buddhism and one from Hinduism, will illustrate the point.

The texts of the Buddhist Pāli Canon provide us with a number of descriptions of stages in meditational practice and, perhaps more significantly, the stages through which the Buddha passed en route to his enlightenment experience. These stages are called jhāna in the Pāli language and dhyāna in

Sanskrit. Eight and sometimes nine jhānas are mentioned in the Pāli literature but the first four are the most important as it was while he was abiding in the fourth jhāna that the Buddha-to-be obtained the three liberating knowledges: knowledge of his own former births; knowledge of the causes of the births and rebirths of others; and knowledge of the destruction of the defiling impulses (āsava).

In the first jhāna the mind has the characteristics of being 'accompanied by initial thought (vitarka) and discursive thought (vicāra), is born of aloofness and is rapturous and joyful'. The second jhāna is devoid of initial and discursive thought, is born of concentration, and is rapturous and joyful'. The third jhāna is characterised by 'the fading out of rapture, equanimity, attention, joy and clear consciousness. The fourth jhāna 'has neither anguish nor joy and ... is entirely purified by equanimity and mindfulness'.[81] These jhānas are clearly contenders for classification as pure consciousness events. Some of the later ones such as the state of no-thing-ness, the state of neither perception nor non-perception and the state of the cessation of perception and feeling might be stronger contenders, but the significance of the fourth stage within the context of mystical progress in the Buddhist tradition is that it is here that the mind becomes ready for the acquisition of mystical knowledge.

The interesting point from the perspective of the present argument is that a state having the characteristics of the fourth jhāna is also recorded as being attained by people to whom the Buddha gave a progressive talk on dhamma (teachings).[82] Peter Masefield claims to have identified more than eighty accounts of such progressive talks in the Pāli Buddhist scriptures.[83] Similar accounts are found throughout Hindu (and Buddhist) tantric literature. The *Haṭha Pradīpikā* (=*Haṭha Yoga Pradīpikā*), for example, claims that 'It is very difficult to get the condition of samādhi without the favour of a true guru (teacher)' (4.9).[84] The *Gheraṇḍa Saṃhitā* (7.1) tells us that 'The samādhi is a great yoga; it is acquired by great good fortune. It is obtained through the grace and kindness of the guru and by intense devotion to him.'[85] According to Swami Muktananda, a contemporary Hindu tantric, a guru can enter into a disciple through sound, touch or look and awaken the kuṇḍalinī energy, that is, establish a state of samādhi.[86]

Mystical experiences can, then, arise through the practice of some form of mental culture such as meditation or prayer, or spontaneously, or through input from a third party; they can be internally or externally oriented (introvertive or extravertive); they can be content-less or content-ful and, when present, the content can display considerable variety. A map or diagram that accurately and comprehensively mapped the territory of mysticism would thus need to resemble Table 4.

Table 4 Mapping mystical experience – a comprehensive model.

Spontaneous	Spontaneous or cultivated	Cultivated	Initiated
No stages Ineffable Noetic Transient passive	*Preliminary stages* Ineffable Transient ↓ *Culminatory stages* Ineffable Noetic Transient Sometimes passive	*No stages* Ineffable Noetic Passive ↓ *Culminatory stages* Ineffable Noetic Transient Sometimes passive	A number of stages leading to an experience that is: Ineffable Noetic Transient Sometimes passive
Introvertive or extravertive	**Introvertive**	**Extravertive**	**Introvertive or extravertive**

This table places pure consciousness events in the wider context of mystical experience though it does not refute the claim that PCEs are unmediated; nor does it have to, for Katz's claim that mystical experiences are conditioned by the mystic's background prior to, during and after the experience is not as dependent on his 'single epistemological assumption' as his critics might think. Even if PCEs are unconditioned they have no noetic content and are therefore of little doctrinal or soteriological value to religious traditions. Furthermore, as Forman himself admits, such experiences are staging posts on the way to noetic mystical experiences. Even if PCEs are unconditioned this does not establish that mystical insights derive from unconditioned experience and this is what anyone who wants to claim that mystical experiences offer some glimpse or contact with the true nature of things or a transcendent reality has to demonstrate.

Everyday religious experiences

Deep mystical and powerful numinous experiences have had a profound influence on human cultures for thousands of years. Yet no one would describe them as common. Those who have such experiences are often unusual or even socially marginal, liminal characters or groups. Moreover, even when groups of people pursue or open themselves up to these experiences, such as meditating monastics or ecstatic participants at Candomblé rituals or Church of Jesus ceremonies, some people seem to have more success than others. Some monks slip easily into states of deep meditation; some ritual participants find it easy to let the spirits enter into themselves. Such people are the adepts, the spiritual virtuosos. These are the people, those 'most accomplished in the religious life', to whom William James turned when collecting information for his *The Varieties of Religious Experience*. Yet the majority of religious people never have such deep or profound experiences. They may have enough of a glimpse or sniff of them to be persuaded that the hidden depths are there even though a full experiential verification of them is unavailable. Direct recollections of one's previous lives, or perceptions of the 'law of karma', or hearing the voice of a god or spirit, or 'seeing' an angel, or being possessed tend to be rare among most religious people. Much has to be taken on trust. At the same time, researchers have found that many religious people are deeply committed to their faith and seem to derive significant benefits from it. That being the case, no investigation of religious experience can claim to offer any kind of overview if it fails to address its everyday varieties.

Much of the research undertaken by psychologists and sociologists of religion concentrates on the everyday experiences of religious people, and the literature generated by that research is vast. Overviews of this literature can be found in works by Argyle and Beit-Hallami, Hood, Hill and Spilka, Nelson, Paloutzian and Park, and Wulff.[87] Here I want to begin with an exploration of Mircea Eliade's notion of *homo religious,* as I think this gives some insight into important differences between religious and secular outlooks and the ways in which they shape everyday experience. A couple of points to notice about Eliade's usage are, first, his claims that 'Religious man is not *given;* he *makes* himself, by approaching the divine models'[88] and '*sacred* and *profane* are two modes of being in the world, two existential situations assumed by man in the course of his history'.[89] Moreover, according to Eliade, however varied they might be, the lives of those who live within the sacred mode are more similar to each other than they are to the lives of those who live within the profane mode:

> between the nomadic hunters and the sedentary cultivators there is a similarity in behavior that seems to us to be infinitely more important than their differences: *both live in a sacralized cosmos* ... We need only compare their existential situations with that of a man of the modern societies, *living in a desacralized cosmos,* and we shall immediately be aware of all that separates him from them. At the same time we realize the validity of comparisons between religious facts pertaining to different cultures; all these facts arise from a single type of behavior, that of *homo religiosus*.[90]

In sum, some people live within supernatural belief systems and all the customs, behaviours and values that they generate while others, those who live in a desacralised cosmos, live in a world that is devoid of supernatural beliefs, etc.

In these comments Eliade seems to be agreeing that the key defining feature of religion, that which, more than anything else, separates religion from everything else, is what Wallace later called 'the supernatural premise'. Eliade's account, as summarised here, seems to imply a choice of 'existential situations': humans can adopt and live within a supernatural belief system or they can adopt and live within a profane (we might now say 'secular') one. However, for Eliade, the profane mode of life is derivative and essentially incomplete:

> profane existence is never found in the pure state. To whatever degree he may have desacralised the world, the man who has made his choice in favor of a profane life never succeeds in completely doing away with religious behavior.[91]

This is primarily because the secular outlook is, for Eliade, a 'degradation' of 'religious values and forms of behavior'.[92]

It is unclear whether this is a claim that a tendency to believe in a supernatural realm is inherent in human psychology or one that links such belief with other powerful human desires. In support of the latter view we can consider Eliade's comments on chaos and cosmos. The simple occupation of territory is, for human communities, unsatisfactory. The community has a need to understand its place in the world and organise itself accordingly. Supernatural stories are effective in meeting this need. They tell of how the cosmos was created and how the community can continue the divine work, essentially by copying what the divinity/divinities did in the beginning. Ritualistically, this is achieved through rites of consecration that symbolically communicate the fact that 'this land is our land'. He writes:

> An unknown, foreign, and unoccupied territory (which often means, 'unoccupied by our people') still shares the fluid and larval modality of chaos. By occupying it and, above all, by settling in it, man symbolically transforms it into a cosmos through a ritual repetition of the cosmogony.[93]

This kind of view has justified conquest, colonisation and the subjugation of the previous inhabitants of desirable land for much of human history. Its application is inherently violent and oppressive, often involving the demonisation of the earlier inhabitants and, often, sections of 'our' community as well. Moreover:

since 'our world' is a cosmos, any attack from without threatens to turn it into chaos. And as 'our world' was founded by imitating the paradigmatic work of the gods, the cosmogony, so the enemies who attack it are assimilated to the enemies of the gods, the demons ...[94]

Such demonised enemies can be both external and internal to the group, the 'internal' ones being sub-groups that do not share the group's dominant ideology – often because they are disadvantaged or oppressed by it. Hindu scriptures offer examples of both 'external' and 'internal' demonisation.

In the *Rāmāyaṇa* the 'king' of Laṅka, Rāvaṇa, is called a rakṣasa, a demon. He behaves badly, abducting Rāma's wife, Sitā. Eventually, Rāma invades Laṅka, kills Rāvaṇa and rescues Sitā.[95] Every year at the *Dassera* festival this is celebrated by the burning of straw-filled effigies of the rakaṣas: 'the forces of good, embodied in Rāma, have again proved victorious over the forces of evil, symbolized in Rāvaṇa'.[96] As various scholars have indicated, rakṣasa may be 'a metaphor for particular types of human beings'.[97] I would argue that the probabilities point to more than a 'may be'. These rakaṣas are almost certainly outgroups and possibly indigenous people. Somewhat less mythologised references can be found in the *Śatapatha Brāhmaṇa*, which, at 13.8.1.5, refers to the 'demonic people of the east', i.e. east of the *madhyadeśa* (the middle region) or *āryāvarta* (land of the noble ones), who speak a barbarous language (3.2.1.23).[98]

Internal demonisation can be found in a number of influential Hindu scriptures, most notably in The Laws of Manu (*Mānava-Dharma-Śāstra*) and the *Bhagavad Gītā* (especially chapter 16). Here are a couple of examples: '(The name) of a priest should have (a word for) auspiciousness, of a ruler strength, of a commoner property, and (the name) of a servant should breed disgust.'[99] According to the *Gītā* (18.41–48) all humans possess a svabhāva (literally 'own-being' or 'inherent nature', according to Edgerton, or 'the nature of things as they are', according to Zaehner). This nature is determined by the guṇas (the three constituents of nature, prakṛti). Śaṅkara, according to Zaehner, explains that 'Brahmans originate from Goodness [sattva guṇa], princes (and warriors) from Passion [rajas guṇa] mixed with Goodness, peasants and artisans from Passion mixed with Darkness [tamas guṇa], serfs from Darkness with a small admixture of Passion'.[100] A person's nature determines their role in society and the kind of spirituality to which he or she is attracted:

> Calm, (self-) control, austerities, purity,
> Patience and uprightness,
> Theoretical and practical knowledge, and religious faith,
> Are the natural-born actions of brāhmans. (18.42)

Heroism, majesty, firmness, skill,
And not fleeing in battle also,
Generosity, and lordly nature,
Are the natural-born actions of warriors. (18.43)

Agriculture, cattle-tending, and commerce
Are the natural-born actions of artisans;
Action that consists of service
Is likewise natural-born to a serf. (18.44)

Men of Goodness worship the gods,
Men of Passion sprites and ogres,
To ghosts and the hordes of goblins others,
The folk of Darkness, pay worship. (17.4)[101]

Other concepts introduced by Eliade to facilitate an understanding of the mind of a religious person, 'the mental universe of *homo religiosus*',[102] are hierophany, a manifestation of the sacred, and theophany, a manifestation of a god or God.[103] For the religious person the sacred, supernatural realm 'breaks through' into the profane, natural realm with considerable frequency. Stones, trees, streams, rivers, mountains, etc. can all be experienced by the religious person as hierophanies or theophanies that, for the religious mind, can have quite profound effects. 'It is his familiar everyday life that is transfigured in the experience of religious man; he finds a cipher everywhere. Even the most habitual gesture can signify a spiritual act'.[104] For *homo religiosus* all hierophanies are '*experiences* and not simply *ideas*'.[105] Thus, bathing in the river Gaṅgā at the Kumbha Mela festival can, for devout Hindus, cleanse them of past sins/bad karma. In secular, reductionistic parlance, the combined effects of bathing at a 'sacred spot' at a 'sacred time' in a 'sacred frame of mind' can be both psychologically and physiologically profound – in a manner reminiscent of placebo cures.[106] As Eliade insists, the religious person is 'one for whom all these homologies are *experiences* and not simply *ideas*'.[107] Presumably, he means by this that they are taken to be perceptions, perhaps made dynamic through the incorporation of emotional charge. This sounds like a big difference, though for reductionists it carries little force, for 'experiences' are as susceptible to distortion or error as ideas. Psychological research on eyewitness testimony and 'recovered' memories provide numerous examples.

Religious traditions support hierophanic and theophanic experiences in a number of ways, both regular and occasional. Examples of regular support are the liturgical year of Roman Catholic Christianity and the annual cycle of festivals in Brahmanical Hinduism. Occasional support can be seen in what van

Gennep called 'The Rites of Passage',[108] and optional activities such as going on pilgrimage. Details of these forms of support are provided in the notes.[109]

Finally, for this section on Everyday Religious Experiences, I will illustrate some of the differences between the minds of religious people (Eliade's *homo religiosi*) and those of a secular outlook. For Eliade, the secular outlook can only ever be partial:

> profane existence is never found in the pure state. To whatever degree he may have desacralized the world, the man who has made his choice in favor of a profane life never succeeds in completely doing away with religious behaviour.[110]

Many modern atheists would naturally dismiss this as wishful thinking. They might well agree with Eliade that 'it is only in the West that nonreligious man has developed fully' and that belief in the sacred 'is the prime obstacle to his freedom. He will become himself only when he is totally demystified. He will not be truly free until he has killed the last god'.[111] As Denis Diderot is reputed to have said, salvation would only arrive when 'the last King was strangled with the entrails of the last priest'.[112] They would, nevertheless, disagree with his claim that those who have adopted a secular outlook, who have managed to kill the last god and relegated the supernatural to the realm of fiction have, thereby, lost something of great value. Rather, they would argue, freedom from the religious mindset of *homo religiosus* represents true intellectual and emotional progress for human beings.[113]

I will illustrate the contrast between these two minsets with a couple of anecdotes about the religious mindset in action. In August 2006 *The Believer* published an interview with Francis Collins, the former head of the Human Genome Project.[114] In it Collins reveals that he had been an atheist but converted to Christianity following a number of profound personal moments. When he was 27 years old and attending medical school he had a conversation with a patient:

> after telling me about her faith and how it supported her through her terrible heart pain, [she] turned to me and said, 'What about you? What do you believe?' And I stuttered and stammered and felt the color rise in my face, and said, 'Well, I don't think I believe in anything.' But it suddenly seemed like a very thin answer. And that was unsettling. I was a scientist who was supposed to draw conclusions from the evidence and I realized at that moment that I'd never really looked at the evidence for and against the possibility of God.[115]

Then he read *Mere Christianity* by C.S. Lewis and found himself well on the way to becoming a Christian. His final step, according to the interview, was taken a couple of years later while walking in the Cascade mountains of Washington state in the USA:

> I turned the corner and saw in front of me this frozen waterfall, a couple of hundred feet high. Actually, a waterfall that had three parts to it – also the symbolic three in one. At that moment, I felt my resistance leave me. And it was a great sense of relief. The next morning, in the dewy grass in the shadow of the Cascades, I fell on my knees and accepted this truth – that God is God, that Christ is his son and that I am giving my life to that belief.[116]

The most salient element of this account for the present book is Collins's experience of the frozen waterfall. It was an unusual natural phenomenon, both beautiful and, in Otto's terms, awe-inspiring. For Collins it was a hierophany, and it was pivotal: 'At that moment, I felt my resistance leave me. And it was a great sense of relief.' For students of conversion Collins's experience exemplifies a common pattern. Writing in the 1950s, psychologist W.H. Clark proposed a four-stage model:

1. A period of unrest (Collins's response to the woman patient?).

2. Crisis (the years of struggle prior to his 'leap of faith' followed by the waterfall experience?).

3. A sense of peace (the 'sense of relief' that came from accepting that 'God is God, that Christ is his son and that I am giving my life to that belief'?).

4. A concrete expression of conversion (sharing his faith perspective with journalists, through his writings and working as Bill Clinton's speechwriter when the president announced that 'Today, we are learning the language in which God created life'?).[117]

Other researchers, notably Lewis Rambo, have refined Clark's model, largely by broadening its scope, both in terms of the number of disciplines employed to investigate the dimensions of conversion and also in terms of the stages involved. In the 1980s Rambo formulated a five-stage model the first stage of which begins before Clark's first stage. Rambo calls this the context: 'the total social, cultural, religious and personal environment'.[118] Consideration of this stage helps us to understand why Collins's initial enquiries about religion led him to a Methodist minister rather than a Brāhman priest, a Buddhist monk or a Muslim imām and also why he was directed towards *Mere Christianity* rather than Sarvepalli Radhakrishnan's *The Hindu View of Life* or Anagarika

Brahmacari Govinda's *Why I am a Buddhist*. It also helps us to understand why, when encountering the triple waterfall, he interpreted its symbolism in terms of the Christian 'three in one' rather than as symbolic of the three bodies of the Buddha or Śiva's trident. Buddhists, Christians and Hindus might all experience/impose different symbolism on the frozen waterfall, though as Eliade notes, they also do something very similar that separates their experience from that of a non-religious person: they experience it as a hierophany.

My second example of the religious mindset in action comes from Bill Maher's documentary film *Religulous*.[119] One of the people he interviewed was Steve Bug, a member of the 'Ex-Jews for Jesus' movement. In response to Maher's questions about how he came to his conversion Bug responded by saying that it was the many miracles performed by god that persuaded him. The sceptical Maher asked for some examples and Bug offered the following: on one occasion he was at a party and asked where he could get a drink of water. He was handed a glass and advised to stick it out of the window and pray for rain. He did so. The heavens opened. Torrents of rain poured down and Bug's glass was filled. Miracle or coincidence? Bug had no doubt that it was the former; Maher was equally convinced it was the latter. Here then is a fine example of the contrast identified by Eliade. Bug experienced a hierophany; Maher a natural phenomenon.

PART 2

A REDUCTIONIST EXPLANATION OF RELIGIOUS EXPERIENCE

As indicated in Part 1, religious experiences take many forms and can be created in many ways. Scholars have adopted a variety of approaches in order to make sense of the diversity. A number of these were mentioned in Part 1, such as ranking and universalising (seeking a common core). Another favoured strategy has been cartographic: the mapping or arranging of different experiences and the methods of producing them in relation to each other. Such efforts have contributed significantly to our understanding of the variety of religious/spiritual experiences and the ways in which they are obtained. At the same time, it seems to me that all, or at least all that I have examined, fall short in one way or another. My procedure in this section will, therefore, be to outline a number of such cartographic approaches, identify some of the limitations with each and then present my own account, which, while featuring a number of cartographic elements also offers an explanation of what is occurring in religious experiences from a primarily psychological perspective. Some of these cartographies are mainly descriptive and phenomenological (i.e. working with the categories provided by the traditions themselves). These, I will argue, tend to be complementary and amenable to combination in different ways. Others, two of which I discuss in detail, combine information from a variety of sources and seek to provide explanations of religious experiences that place them within a kind of value framework.

Some cartographic accounts of religious experience

First of all, I will present a number of largely phenomenological typologies that purport to map the main varieties of spiritual practice, and then use the information gleaned from this to show that certain practices go with certain beliefs/theories and not others; that theories, practices and experiences are interlinked, and, therefore, that, contra Werner,[1] it is misguided to think that any practice can be pursued to any significant degree without reference to theory (= teachings or beliefs). Theory answers the crucial questions about why a practice should be undertaken. If one doesn't know why one is practising one is hardly likely to be motivated to persist if the going gets tough. Moreover, the internal experiences generated by spiritual practice are many and varied. Without theory most meditators would quickly become lost in their experiences and come to many false conclusions, as the gurus of all mystical traditions are quick to point out. Theory tells the practitioner whether practices are helpful or not, whether they are indicative of progress or not and whether they are veridical or delusional. In other words, if a person is a spiritual practitioner and wants to understand the experiences that their practices generate then they should let theory/theology be their guide. A humorous example of the wisdom of this advice can be found in Lewis Carroll's *Alice in Wonderland*:

> Having wandered away from the Duchess's kitchen, where she had just seen a cat grinning at her ('because it's a Cheshire cat' the Duchess had said, which was no explanation at all) she was a little startled by seeing the Cheshire-Cat sitting on a bough of a tree a few yards off. The Cat only grinned when it saw Alice. It looked good-natured, she thought: still it had *very* long claws and a great many teeth, so she felt that it ought to be treated with respect. 'Cheshire-Puss', she began rather timidly, as she did not at all know whether it would like the name: however, it only grinned a little wider. 'Come, it's pleased so far', thought Alice, and she went on. 'Would you tell me please, which way I ought to go from here?' 'That depends a good deal on where you want to get to,' said the Cat. 'I don't much care where –' said Alice. 'Then it doesn't matter which way you go,'" said the Cat.[2]

Consider Patañjali's *Yoga Sūtra*. When we seek to make sense of this text we inevitably try to work out how the different parts fit together or, in Smart's terminology, how they are ramified. Patañjali distinguishes between seer and seen and argues, though some might challenge this, that the two exist independently of each other. He also distinguishes between the seer abiding in its own, unconditioned nature (svarūpa) and being conditioned by the activities of the mind (vṛitti). The experience of dhyāna is the (temporary) experience of svarūpa. It is made permanent by the process of pratiprassava – where the guṇas (the constituents of the seen, i.e. prakṛti) return to their unmanifest state. This abbreviated description of Patañjali's yogic path reveals that it is deeply metaphysical. It is not simply a set of instructions: do this; then do that; then do something else. It is an explanation of the context in which the doing takes place and functions as a kind of guide or map to help keep the yogin on track. It is profoundly theoretical.

Now some typologies.

Typologies map out a conceptual landscape by grouping phenomena together and identifying relationships between them. They are, therefore, often controversial and sometimes misleading if they are inaccurate. The controversies and inaccuracies arise out of the fact that typologies are created by people to make sense of a complex world. They do not exist in the world itself. Without them, however, we would live in a world of particulars that we would be unable to understand. Indeed, much of what we call understanding is rooted in our ability to create categories that group particulars together (e.g. the category of 'fruit') and typologies that explain the relationships between categories or sub-categories.

The first three typologies I will consider here (Goleman's, Naranjo's and Rawlinson's) are largely phenomenological in character, i.e. are generally faithful to the traditional sources from which they obtained their information. I tend to think of them as progressive, i.e. each improves on the previous one. The next two (Wilber's and Fischer's) move beyond phenomenology and seek to explain phenomenological accounts in terms of concepts and data taken from research in a variety of disciplines.

One simple typology was offered by psychologist Daniel Goleman in *The Varieties of Meditative Experience*.[3] He distinguishes between what he calls the path of concentration and the path of mindfulness, a distinction taken primarily from Buddhist sources. Concentration refers to the focussing of attention on a single point, which, if continued, eventually produces a state where the mind is described as 'concentrated, purified, cleansed, spotless, with the defilements gone, supple, dexterous, firm, and impassable'.[4] Common Sanskrit terms for concentrative meditational experiences are dhāraṇā, dhyāna and samādhi. 'Mindfulness' is common translation of the Buddhist term 'sati/smṛti' (Pāli/Sanskrit), the primary meaning of which is memory or recollection. Traditional foci for mindfulness meditations are the body, feelings, thoughts and phenomena.[5] As this distinction is taken from the Buddhist scriptures, it is quite phenomenological, i.e. not imposed by outsiders. Interestingly, there is some evidence from electroencephalographic studies which suggests that different things are happening in the brain during these two kinds of meditation. In simplified terms:

Many electroencephalographic (EEG) and related studies have been undertaken on meditators. Among the more interesting early ones are Kasamatsu and Hirai's study of zazen meditators (zazen is a form of mindfulness practice often referred to in English as 'just sitting'), and B.K. Anand and his colleagues' work on yoga meditators. The former found that:

- Advanced meditation masters could produce rhythmical theta trains during meditation.

- Most zazen practitioners generated alpha waves with eyes open, and with increasing time spent on meditation the amplitude of the alpha waves increased and their frequency decreased.

- Experienced zazen meditators tend not to habituate during meditation.

Anand and his colleagues studied yoga meditators who were practising a form of concentrative (samādhi) meditation. They found that:

- Yogis demonstrated alpha wave activity of increasing amplitude during meditation.
- Yogis were not responsive to external stimuli during meditation.
- Yogis tended to manifest alpha wave activity in the normal state, though it could be 'blocked' by sensory stimuli, and such blocking was not susceptible to habituation. In other words, the after-effects of yoga meditation seem to be that the yogi is in a state that is quite similar to that of the practising zazen meditator.[6]

Crudely, habituation responses to a regular click stimulus (e.g. a clock) can be represented diagrammatically (Figure 2).

These patterns will come as no surprise to modern researchers on the neurology of attention. Our brains are not only asymmetrical in shape, they are also asymmetrical in function. The left hemisphere controls focal attention

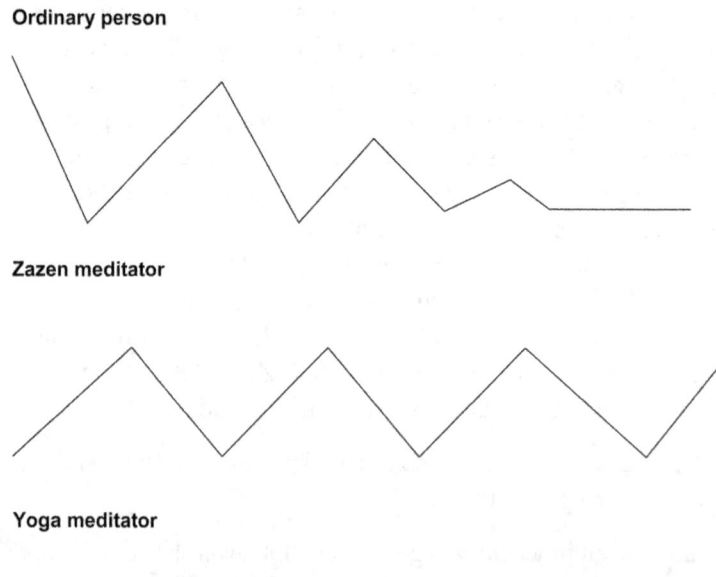

Figure 2 Three types of habituation response to a regular click stimulus.

and the right controls global attention.⁷ Each hemisphere also tends to inhibit the activity of the other, so as one increases in activity the other decreases. What seems to be happening in these two types of meditation is that the zazen meditators are activating their right hemisphere's global attentional processes and inhibiting those of the left, while the yoga meditators are doing the opposite. Both types of meditation can be seen to produce an altered state of consciousness because, as Iain McGilchrist comments, 'Both hemispheres are involved in almost all mental processes, and certainly in all mental states: information is constantly conveyed between the hemispheres, and may be transmitted in either direction several times a second.'⁸ This is the situation that is appropriately called a normal or ordinary state of consciousness. The sustained inhibition of the attentional processes of one hemisphere modifies this state, and produces thereby an 'altered' state. Goleman's simple typology of meditation can be represented diagrammatically thus:

Concentration   Mindfulness

Goleman tends to group all forms of meditation under one of the two headings, though he also maintains, in perennialist fashion, that their outcomes are actually identical: the 'transcendental experience' that is 'veiled by the different names given it by various religions'.⁹ The same two categories have been employed by Claudio Naranjo, who calls them concentrative meditation and the negative way.¹⁰ He also adds a third category that he calls 'the way of surrender and self-expression'. This, he states, is typically the domain of 'visionary experience, automatic movements, the release of dormant physical energies, inspired utterances, automatic writing, spirit possession'.¹¹

These three categories can be arranged along a continuum:

Way of concentration   Negative way   Way of surrender and
                                     (mindfulness)   self-expression

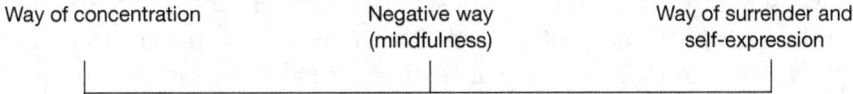

The two poles offer a sharp contrast to each other. *The way of concentration* is highly controlled and systematic; *the way of surrender and self-expression* requires the relinquishing of all control. *The negative way* can be seen as a kind of bridge between the two as it has features in common with both. *It shares with the way of concentration* a disciplined approach to meditation and a detached, dispassionate attitude that can only be cultivated through sustained practice.¹² *The negative way also shares characteristics with the way of surrender and self-expression.*

Both cultivate an 'openness to experience' through the non-manipulation of the contents of consciousness. According to Naranjo, the negative way cannot help being permissive and complete surrender demands detachment.

Naranjo's category scheme seems to offer a pretty comprehensive coverage of cultivated (as opposed to spontaneous) religious experiences. However, a little reflection on its relationship with other categories that were introduced in Part 1 show that it has considerable limitations.

If we arrange the categories of numinous/mystical and self-power/other-power[13] into a single scheme (Figure 3), we can see the major limitation of Naranjo's approach. His first two categories occupy the bottom right-hand corner while the way of surrender and self-expression takes up the other three. In short, the way of surrender and self-expression is a bit of a catch-all that requires further analysis.

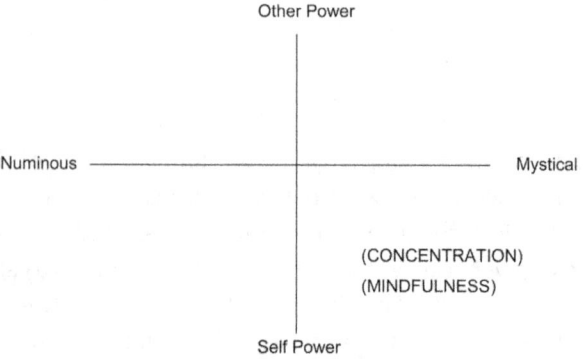

Figure 3 Types of spiritual practice.

This is where Andrew Rawlinson's scheme represents a considerable step forward. In *The Book of Enlightened Masters: Western Teachers in Eastern Traditions* Rawlinson introduces a typology of spiritual traditions that he constructed on the basis of the accounts provided by various texts on spirituality and interviews with modern spiritual teachers. It has two axes: hot-cool and structured-unstructured, which he describes thus:

> *Hot* is that which is other than oneself; that which has its own life. It is not something that one has access to as of right. It is powerful and breath-taking, and is associated with revelations and grace. It is very similar to Otto's numinous.
>
> *Cool* is the very essence of oneself; one need not go to another to find it. Hence, one does have access to it as of right. It is quiet and still, and is associated with self-realisation.

The meaning of *Structured* is that there is an inherent order in the cosmos and therefore in the human condition. There is something to be discovered out there and there is a way of discovering it. A map is required to find the destination.

By contrast, *Unstructured* teachings say that there is no gap between the starting point and the finishing post. Method and goal are identical. We are not separate from reality/truth/God and so no map is required. Everything is available now and always has been.[14]

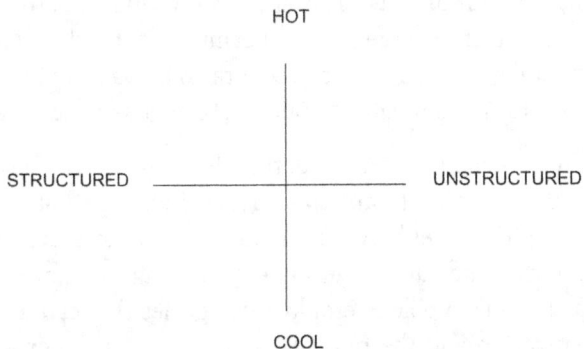

Figure 4 Rawlinson's 4-fold typology of spiritual practice.

Schematically these axes can be represented as in Figure 4. This arrangement gives us four quadrants: hot-structured; cool-structured; hot-unstructured, and cool-unstructured. The primary characteristics of each, according to Rawlinson, are:

- **Hot–structured:** These traditions stress the importance of initiatory knowledge, hierarchy, the exercise of will, and the manipulation of the laws of the cosmos in the service of self-transformation. Images used by such traditions include the magician and the gambler and the idea of a jump rather than a journey. Examples would include Hindu Tantra, Buddhist Vajrayana, the Siddha tradition, Vedic ritualism, Kabbalah, Hermeticism, Alchemy and Shamanism.

- **Hot–unstructured:** These traditions stress the characteristics of bliss, discipline, love obedience, submission and wisdom. Images include the lover and the martyr. Examples include Ecstatic Hindu devotionalism, e.g. Caitanya, Pure Land Buddhism, Sufism, Christian mysticism, e.g. St Teresa.

- **Cool–structured:** These traditions stress the characteristics of dispassionate awareness, order, progress, effort and concentration. Images include those of the craftsman and the yogin and the idea of work rather than grace. Examples include Patanjali's Yoga Sutra, Theravada Buddhism, Zen, early Vedanta, i.e. the Upanisads, Samkhya, Aurobindo, Plotinus.

- **Cool–unstructured:** These traditions stress the fact of Being, the possibility of knowing the truth at any moment (you do not even have to jump) and the absence of any kind of 'path'. Images include those of the sage and the hermit, and the idea of 'letting go'. Examples include Advaita Vedanta, Madhyamaka Buddhism, Mahamudra, Taoism, Tibetan Buddhist Dzogchen and Zen.

It is clear from the examples provided, that different kinds of spirituality are located in different quadrants, and this, in turn, indicates that there are some quite significant differences between the various traditions of spirituality and that the notion that they are all ultimately teaching the same thing is false. Moreover, Rawlinson's typology employs categories that can distinguish the way of concentration and the negative way from each other – though like Goleman and Naranjo he fails to acknowledge the unstructured/detachment dimension of Patañjali's system. His scheme also divides the way of surrender and self-expression into sub-categories. Finally, and perhaps most importantly, it shows that each category involves an interconnected network of theories and practices. In Indian traditions this point is emphasised in a number of ways. For example, it is important to have a guru who is a representative of an established lineage (paramparā), hence texts often begin with a statement about the line of transmission for the teachings they contain, e.g. Upaniṣads such as the Bṛhadāraṇyaka and the Muṇḍaka, and the Sāṁkhya Kārikā. Also, many teachers such as Śaṅkara emphasise the importance of studying the right doctrine over that of using the right technique.

Rawlinson' scheme shows us that, for example, in hot-structured traditions ritual is an important practice. In cool unstructured paths it is irrelevant. Detachment is important in most cool paths but anathema in hot ones. In short, practice is always informed by theory. What is more, Rawlinson's analysis demonstrates quite pointedly that all spiritual practices do not lead to the same goal, even when they fall within the same quadrant. This conclusion becomes obvious when, for example, we consider yogic ontology. As outlined in Part 1, spiritual traditions tend to subscribe to one of three basic doctrines of existence (ontologies): monism, dualism and pluralism. For monists, at the most fundamental level reality is one, for pluralists at the most fundamental level reality is two and for pluralists at the most fundamental level reality is more than two. These ontologies are, then, mutually exclusive. If one is a true and accurate description of reality at the most fundamental level then the other two are false. On the basis of yogic practice some yogins describe reality monistically, some describe it dualistically and some describe it pluralistically. Clearly, yogins do not all teach the same thing, they teach incompatible things. So all systems of yoga cannot lead to the same goal. More generally, religious traditions that subscribe to monist ontologies tend not to seek the same spiritual goals as those which subscribe to pluralistic ones. As the fifteenth-century Hindu devotionalist Ramprasada put it: 'I don't want to be God, I want to taste God.'

To sum up so far: there do seem to be real differences between the various kinds of spiritual practices. They differ in their theoretical/metaphysical underpinnings; they differ in the behaviours they encourage, and they differ in the kinds of brain activities that they produce. So the next question is, do they have anything in common?

I think that they do, but it is not, as many writers claim, that they lead to the experience of a 'superconscious' state in which knowledge about fundamental realities is made available. This idea is common in Indian yogic writing. For example, the Buddha claimed that when he attained the fourth level of jhāna/dhyāna he was able to acquire knowledge of his previous births, an understanding of the law of karma and the ability to eradicate the processes that had kept him trapped in a round of rebirths: kāma (sexual desire), bhava (desire for continued existence) and avidyā (ignorance of the true nature of things).[15] Patañjali claims that in the state of nirvicāra samādhi insight (prajñā) is truth-bearing (ṛtaṃbharā).[16] In more recent times writers such as Swami Vivekananda have reiterated the same point,[17] and a quick internet search threw up this definition from the Ānanda organisation: 'Meditation may be defined as any practice of which the goal is superconsciousness.'[18] I want to claim that these notions about meditation and spirituality more generally are misguided and that we will understand it (in all its varieties) much better if we think of spiritual practices as techniques of trance induction and spiritual/religious experiences as varieties of trance experience. Before embarking on that enterprise, however, I will present and critique two other influential cartographies, not just to identify ways in which they are flawed but also to indicate some of the creative thinking, both insightful and misguided, that they have brought to our understanding of this vast and complex field. Indeed, the fact that they have been so influential is, in itself, a primary reason why no writer on religious/spiritual experience can avoid positioning him or herself in relation to them. The creators of those cartographies are

Ken Wilber and Roland Fischer. Both, I argue, are deeply misguided and their models should be abandoned or avoided by anyone who seeks an accurate understanding of religious/spiritual experience.

Ken Wilber's integral spirituality

Ken Wilber's model of *integral spirituality*, aka the *integral map*, the *integral operating system* (IOS) and *all quadrants, all levels, all states and all types* (AQAL), is an ambitious attempt to fit religion and spirituality into a framework that embraces modern scientific discoveries, postmodernist and related work in the humanities, and a variety of other cartographic approaches to the organisation and representation of human knowledge, speculation and imagination. Like the ranking and perennialist strategies for dealing with differences in claims about the nature of religious experiences and the status of inferences based upon them that were outlined in Part 1, its achievements in terms of comprehensive sweep are purchased at a high price in terms of overall accuracy and plausibility. Here I will content myself with offering an outline of this map along with comments that explain why I deem it unsatisfactory and inadequate as an explanation of religious experience.

Wilber's model has evolved over a considerable period of time, and his first book, *The Spectrum of Consciousness* (1977) explicitly connects his spectrum project with the approach of the perennialists:

> if we adopt the thesis proposed by Schuon, Guenon, and Coomaraswamy – namely the 'transcendental unity of religions' – and then translate this thesis into the terms of the spectrum of consciousness, we can introduce a considerable parsimony to an otherwise complex filed [sic].[19]

His 'translation' yields results that are virtually identical to those generated by perennialist analyses:

> Schroendinger [sic], Christ, and Shankara – who all experienced Mind – would speak of it in different terms, reflecting not a difference in Mind but a difference in symbolic elaborations of Mind. Schroedinger used the terms of physical theory; Christ, those of Hebrew theology; and Shankara, those of Hindu Autology – yet this Reality remains one and the same ...[20]

This is subject to the same criticisms that writers such as Katz and Smart directed towards them. Moreover, the unphenomenological character of such analyses does not seem to make him uncomfortable, for he sincerely believes not only that many religious people do not understand their own experiences, but also that even the virtuosos, the adepts, do not understand them. Fortunately, his model is able to determine the reasons behind that lack of understanding and put people on the right course.

He tells his readers that 'Many fundamentalist Christians gag in horror when any mention is made of the *fact* that all religions are identical in esoteric essence.'[21] Devout though they may be, they do live in ignorance of the true nature of their own religion. They are not, however, discarded altogether. Rather, fundamentalists, and others who reject a perennialist-style model, are simply located on a lower level in Wilber's scheme: 'existence is graded into several levels ... each level has its own peculiar mode of knowing, modes that grade, shade, and range from pure non-dual awareness (Mind) to pure symbolic representation (Ego)'.[22] At that early point in his thinking he claimed that there was a 'primary dualism' between the exoteric and the esoteric. The exoteric is the 'existential level':

> the level of many different selves symbolically knowing many different Gods, with the content of that knowledge supplied by many different Biosocial Bands; while the Level of Mind is the esoteric level, the level of the Universal Godhead, the non-dual awareness wherein many selves and many Gods unite in the timeless omniscience of Reality.[23]

So, you fundamentalists; you monotheists who subscribe to a dualistic or pluralistic ontology; you polytheists, whatever ontology you hold, and you atheists who deny the existence of gods, God or Godhead: don't fret too much. You can take comfort in the fact that you are merely functioning at a lower level than those with non-dual awareness who function at the Level of Mind rather than being simply in error. You too can get there. For guidance on how, just read Wilber's books! Indeed, according to *integral spirituality*, with such guidance the modern seeker can go beyond the Buddha, Jesus or Muhammad, for they were merely 'enlightened in terms of the states and stages that had evolved by the times that they lived.[24] This is not quite the 'more recent is best' approach mentioned in Part 1, though it comes pretty close. It is clearly a claim that modern 'enlightened' beings are more 'enlightened' than their 'enlightened' predecessors: 'A person's enlightenment today is not Freer than Buddha's (Emptiness is Emptiness), but it is Fuller than Buddha's (and will be even Fuller down the road) ...'[25]

To understand or critique this and other claims made by Wilber some acquaintance with the integral map is necessary. It has five core elements: quadrants, lines, levels, states and types.[26]

Quadrants

Wilber's quadrants are perspectives derived from pronouns, though in a rather peculiar way (see Figure 5). He acknowledges that all pronoun-derived perspectives have singular and plural forms (I, me, mine, we, us, ours, you, yours, he, him, she, her, it, that, they, those and them), though he does not explain why 'theirs' is omitted from his list, nor why his 'simplification' of the list boils down to 'I', 'we' and 'it'.[27] That simplification *does* enable him to set up his quadrant framework by, first of all, claiming that:

> every event in the manifest world has all three of those dimensions. You can look at any event from the point of view of the 'I' (or how I personally see and

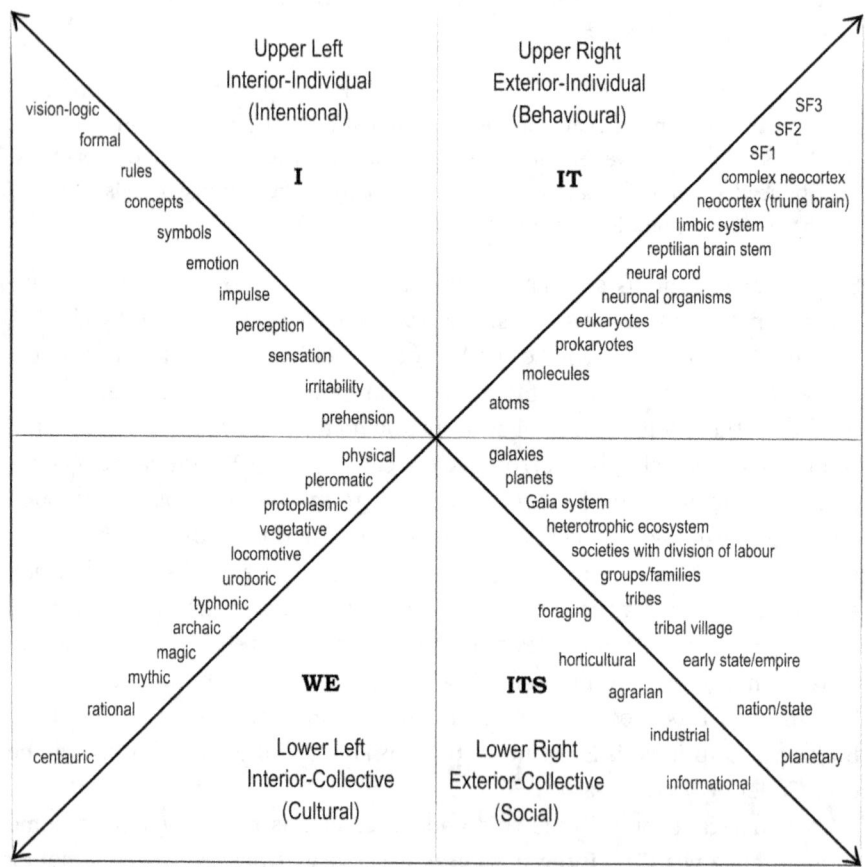

Figure 5 One version of Ken Wilber's integral map
(= integral operating system or integral model).[30]

feel about the event); from the point of view of the 'we' (how not just I but others see the event); and as an 'it' (or the objective facts of the event).[28]

Solution-focused and NLP therapists often guide clients in the use of similar perspective shifts to facilitate a greater understanding of their situations and relationship dynamics, though the 'it' tends to be replaced by a 'detached observer' perspective.[29] Many of the things to which we apply the 'it' pronoun, e.g. rocks, rivers and automobiles, have no 'perspective' whatsoever.

His second quadrant-creating move is to subdivide 'it' into singular 'it' and plural 'its'.[31] Many readers will, naturally, have reservations about both of these moves. In terms of perspectives, the I–we division is insufficiently comprehensive. *I* might have a view or opinion; *you* might agree or disagree with it; *they* might agree or disagree with either or both of us. Moreover, the us–them dynamic (intricately investigated by social identity theorists[32]) is virtually absent from Wilber's account, though it has considerable explanatory value when applied to many real world 'events'. The 'it' and 'its' quadrants are also problematic. In the first place, he claims that 'it' represents what is '*outside* of the *individual*' and 'Its' represents what is '*outside* of the *collective*', but, clearly, the outside of the individual is much more than an I–it dynamic. It also encompasses I–you, I–them, I–that and I–those dynamics. Likewise for the 'its' quadrant: not only is the outside of the collective 'we' (+ us and ours) often they/them/theirs as well as 'its', 'its' is not even the plural of 'it'.

When these ambiguities (misrepresentations?) are added to claims like 'the "I," "we," and "it" dimensions of experience really refer to *art, morals* and *science*. Or *self, culture* and *nature*. Or the *Beautiful*, the *Good* and the *True*',[33] some readers, myself included, cannot help but be sceptical about the viability of the quadrant strategy for arranging 'every event in the manifest world' in relation to all the others. In short, Wilber's quadrant approach, while valuable for its emphasis on the benefits of adopting multiple perspectives when seeking to understand events/phenomena, does seem to be the product of questionable assumptions, claims and moves. His subsequent use of that framework indicates that he thinks his readers will have accepted its validity, though anyone who demands a greater degree of rigour in the creation of such schemes will, necessarily, approach those subsequent moves with considerable suspicion.

One example will serve to illustrate the value of that suspicion. In a section on 'integral medicine' Wilber shows how seductive models can lead to misguided over-generalisation. The image he paints is that factors from all quadrants are causative to some degree in all physical illness, and he claims that:

> psychoneuroimmunology – has made it quite clear that the person's *interior states* (their emotions, psychological attitude, imagery, and intentions) play a crucial role in both the *cause* and the *cure* of even physical illness ... most illnesses have causes and cures that include *emotional*, *mental* and *spiritual* components.[34]

Two words in this quotation require comment: crucial and most. To claim that something is 'crucial' is to claim that it is decisive, essential or very important; to claim that 'most' illnesses have causes and cures that include *emotional*, *mental* and *spiritual* components is to allow that less than half have not. There is a degree of obvious tension between these claims, for the first maintains that all the mentioned components are essential elements in both the cause and the cure of illnesses while the second maintains that this is not the case in some instances. Let us assume that by 'most' Wilber means 'almost all' and by 'crucial' he means 'very important'. This would go a long way to resolving the tension, though the impression created by these comments is that in the vast majority of cases failure to take account of elements from all quadrants would result in deficiencies of both understanding and treatment.

By contrast, I would contend that the all-quadrant dynamic is virtually irrelevant for the understanding and treatment of many illnesses. As it happens, before engaging with Wilber's integral spirituality I had just read Steven Johnson's *The Ghost Map*.[35] This is a book about the discovery of how cholera was spread and how to treat it. The cholera bacterium can kill its victims in less than 24 hours. It thrives in human excrement. 'It cannot be transmitted through the air or even through the exchange of most bodily fluids.'[36] However, if it is present in a medium that is ingested, such as water, it will flourish. Johnson explains how it was discovered that infected water was the source of the cholera epidemics that plagued London during the nineteenth century. He also explains that both the treatment and neutralisation of cholera are pretty straightforward. To treat cholera, 'rehydrate'![37]

> [Cholera] has a shockingly sensible and low-tech cure: water. Cholera victims who are given water and electrolytes via intravenous and oral therapies reliably survive the illness, to the point where numerous studies have deliberately infected volunteers with the disease to study its effects, knowing that the rehydration program will transform the disease into merely an uncomfortable bout of diarrhea.[38]

Emotions, psychological attitude, imagery, intentions and spirituality make little or no contribution to this cure, except, perhaps, in a horse and canary pie kind of way.[39] To neutralise cholera just ensure that the water people drink is uncontaminated.

Is cholera unique? By no means. Many communicable diseases can be treated with vaccines, physical injuries with surgery and inflammatory illnesses with pharmaceuticals.[40] In most of these cases neither emotions nor spirituality, etc. contribute much to the cure. Laser treatment for astigmatism tends to improve the sight of people who are calm or anxious, prayerful or agnostic, high-IQ or low-IQ, etc. Such factors may influence the speed of recovery from the surgery, but in a minor way. The all-quadrant approach to medicine fails to discriminate between the quantitative contributions of different factors. Some factors are horses and others are canaries. All of them may be ingredients in the pie but they do not all contribute equally to its flavour.

Lines

The lines or 'developmental lines' in Wilber's integral map (the diagonals in Figure 5) are what many of us would call intellectual or theoretical constructs, attempts to identify significant divisions in the natural world, which can be structural, e.g. the periodic table of chemical elements, or developmental, e.g. the stages in the development of embryos.[41] Wilber claims that there are over a dozen of these, though he also refers to over 100.[42] Each of them can be divided into (he says 'possess') a number of *levels* that 'unfold in *stages* or *waves*'.[43] Although he claims that they are not lines 'in any strict sense' the fact that the levels/stages are progressive and never go backward does imply that representing the these developmental trajectories by lines is not inappropriate.[44] His 'integral psychograph' represents them diagrammatically as vertical lines rising from a horizontal axis (the *x*-axis) through, in this case, 10 levels', (on the *y*-axis).[45] These developmental lines' are 'relatively independent' of each other ('paths up a mountain' is his preferred metaphor), though he does claim that two of them are necessary and that their development constrains the development of the others. The two are the cognitive developmental line and the consciousness developmental line.

His comments on these constraints are interesting. For example, he claims that a person may be highly developed on the cognitive line but poorly developed on the moral one. However, the reverse (low IQ, highly moral) cannot occur.[46] The same applies to his other 'developmental lines', such as the values line, the interpersonal line the emotional line and the spiritual line. Similarly, the consciousness level (whatever that is) of a person will constrain their development of the others. He is not particularly clear about the ways, if any, in which developments in the cognitive and consciousness lines constrain each other, though the impression created is that they somehow function in tandem. In other words, one cannot progress along (up) the cognition line without also progressing up (along) the consciousness one and vice versa, though these two can develop in tandem without requiring parallel developments along the other lines.

The lines he lists in *integral spirituality* are:

- The cognitive – which addresses the question 'what am I aware of?'
- The self-identity – which addresses the question 'who am I?'
- The values – which addresses the question 'what is significant to me?'
- The moral – which addresses the question 'what should I do?'
- The interpersonal – which addresses the question 'how should we interact?'
- The spiritual – which addresses the question 'what is of ultimate concern?'
- The needs – which addresses the question 'what do I need?'
- The kinaesthetic – which addresses the question 'how should I physically do this?'
- The emotional – which addresses the question 'how do I feel about this?'
- The aesthetic – which addresses the question 'what is attractive to me?'[47]

'Consciousness' is not included in the list of lines because it 'is not itself a line among other lines, but the space in which lines arise',[48] though he does include a graphic representation of its 'levels' (indicated by the colours of the rainbow, where infrared is low and 'clear light', beyond ultraviolet, is high).[49] If this all seems a bit too neat to you then you are not alone. It seems too neat to me too. Moreover, when I look at the levels/stages through which the cognitive line progresses I find myself immersed in what I can only describe as metaphysical and imaginative constructs. The first five levels of sensorimotor, preoperational (symbolic), preoperational (conceptual), concrete operational and formal operational are grounded in mainstream, though not uncontested, psychological research.[50] The next seven will not be found in any psychology textbook:

- pluralistic mind (meta-systemic/planetary mind);
- low vision-logic (paradigmatic);
- high vision-logic (cross-paradigmatic/higher mind/global mind);
- illumined mind, para-mind, trans-global (previously psychic);
- intuitive mind/meta mind (previously subtle);
- overmind (previously causal); and
- supermind.

Such levels/stages, indeed, all of the levels/stages of every line 'are just conceptual snapshots ... real in the sense that there is something actually existing that occurs in the real world and that we call development or growth'.[51] Well, it is one thing to acknowledge that living things develop and grow, but quite another to claim that any of them develop and grow in these specific ways through these specific stages. Some of the developmental trajectories that are represented by his lines are pretty well attested by some reasonably robust, though not uncontested, research, e.g. on cognitive development. Others are more fanciful and idiosyncratic, e.g. which aesthetics does address the question of 'what is attractive to me?' that is far from being its only, or even central, concern. Christopher Janaway, for example, claims that 'The big, obvious question about aesthetic value is whether it is ever 'really in' the objects it is attributed to.'[52] Disagreements between aesthetic objectivists, who maintain that 'aesthetic qualities are properties inhering in objects, and that aesthetic experience gives us knowledge of these properties' and aesthetic subjectivists, who maintain that 'what it is for an object to be beautiful is for it to yield a certain response in the subject'[53] have not, so far, been resolved; so the subjectivism inherent in Wilber's representation of aesthetics ('what is attractive to me?'), and the idea that there are progressive stages of development in aesthetic judgement (which seems to have an objective component), is at least contentious and possibly misguided.

The view that complex organisms such as human beings have developmental trajectories for a variety of their abilities is, in itself, relatively non-contentious, and a substantial number of modern researchers have investigated them in considerable detail. Researchers such as Jean Piaget and Lev Vygotsky (both born in 1886) 'set the agenda' for developmental psychology, though some of their ideas have been shown to be misguided by subsequent researchers. They are, therefore better treated as starting points for investigations in this area than as completely reliable guides. Other research on which Wilber relies is far more speculative than that undertaken by Piaget, Vygotsky, Carol Gilligan or Howard Gardner, e.g. the 'Spiral Dynamics' developed by Clare W. Graves and developed by Don E. Beck and Christopher C. Cowan,[54] and the 'stages of faith' outlined by James Fowler. He does point out some of what he perceives the limitations of both schemes to be, but he also uses them as bases for his own projections. So, for example, he states, in commenting on Fowler's work, that 'there are somewhere around 3 or 4 *stages of faith* beyond his stage 6 (which is roughly a turquoise-level faith) …'[55] This kind of move is pretty typical of the ways in which Wilber proceeds when developing his model. It is, for me, far less critical of the limitations of his source materials than is warranted by any reasonable standard of academic rigour, and it tends to treat any developmental scheme that is broadly compatible with his own assumptions and presuppositions as valid, though incomplete.[56]

Fowler's stage scheme is worth a more detailed examination as Wilber uses it as a kind of foundation from which he extrapolates when filling out his model of 'integral spirituality'. It is an approach to religiosity/spirituality that is mainly theological in character with elements of psychology mixed in, though it is 'religious psychology' (psychology in the service of religion) rather than psychology of religion (a psychological investigation of religion). Wilber tends to treat it as an accomplishment, a framework that is accepted by all serious researchers in the field and a foundation for further research. Such an attitude is, however, demonstrably misguided. For example, Marion Smith, who

> has probably done more than anyone else to bring Fowler to the attention of the British public … maintains that his account is still tentative and provisional, and not, as some may suppose, the end-product of an investigation in which the details have been confirmed after informed and thorough scrutiny.[57]

Other critics, none of whom are mentioned by Wilber, have highlighted some of the more specific limitations of Fowler's model. I will mention just a few, though they should be sufficient to persuade all but Fowler's most blinkered fans that the status accorded to it by Wilber is unwarranted. Sharon D. Parks has identified five 'primary foci' of resistance to and concern about that model:

1   the definition of faith;

2   the description of stage 6 – Fowler's vision of 'mature faith';

3   the adequacy of the theory in relation to particular religious beliefs;

4   the adequacy of the account of affect, process-motion, the unconscious, and the imagination;

5   the adequacy of the theory vis-à-vis a critical socio-political analysis, especially a gender analysis.

The first two of these, she states, 'have dominated the discussion to date'.[58] Let's have a look at both of them.

The concept of faith

Parks mentions a number of critics in her overview of this literature, and interested readers can access their work via her references. Here I simply offer my own evaluation of the way in which Fowler introduces his key concept. Chapter 1 of *Stages of Faith* is called 'Human Faith'; so a reasonable expectation on the part of readers is that they will emerge from it with a pretty clear idea about what faith is and what it is not, that is, with some understanding of the scope of the term: what can and cannot be appropriately included within it. That expectation remains unrealised by the end of the chapter. En route to that end readers encounter a number of definition-like statements that, unfortunately, fail to equip them to provide a reasonably clear and succinct answer to the question 'what are we to understand by the term 'faith'?

Examples of these definition-like statements are: 'Faith is a person's or group's way of *moving into the force field of life*'; 'Faith is a person's way of seeing him- or herself in relation to others against a background of shared meaning and purpose'; and 'Faith as a state of being ultimately concerned may or may not find its expression in institutional or cultic religious forms'.[59] It is, following Niebuhr, 'the search for an overarching, integrating and grounding trust in *a center of value and power sufficiently worthy to give our lives unity and meaning*'.[60] To me, the phrase '*a center of value and power sufficiently worthy to give our lives unity and meaning*' sounds like theologian-speak for god, though Fowler also implies that non-believers (presumably people who do not believe in the existence of a supernatural realm), agnostics and atheists also share in this human faith. Not surprisingly, stage 4 seems to be as far as they can get without converting to some form of theism.[61]

My best shot at making sense of these statements is something like 'Faith refers to the human *search* for meaning in life'. In other words, this 'faith' that Fowler is exploring is a process that has different end points for different people: some find their end point (the point at which they arrive at a position of 'integrating and grounding trust') in a particular supernaturalist world-view such as Christianity or Islām; others find their end point in non-supernaturalist world-views such as Humanism or Stoicism. The problem with my interpretation, reasonable though it seems to me on the basis of the statements in Fowler's chapter 1, is negated by other statements about faith in chapter 2. Here Fowler introduces the ideas of Wilfred Cantwell-Smith. Nowhere in that chapter does Fowler explicitly state that he deems Smith's analysis to be definitive, though by the end readers are left in no doubt that Fowler does endorse it. Smith contends that that faith and religion are different and that neither has much to do with belief! Fowler writes: 'Smith gives a persuasive demonstration that the language dealing with faith in the classical writings of the major religious traditions never speaks of it in ways that can be translated by the modern meanings of belief or believing'.[62] In short, religions do not make truth claims. Well, people find many things persuasive, and the fact that one individual finds the claims of another persuasive hardly constitutes a sound basis for everyone else to accept them. The idea that religion has nothing to do with belief was recently resurrected by Stephen J. Gould in *Rocks of Ages*,[63] and it is still rubbish. I will support this judgement below.

With regard to the relationship between faith and religion, Fowler, following Smith, asserts that 'Faith, at once deeper and more personal than religion, is a person's or group's way of *responding* to transcendent value and power as perceived and grasped through the form of the cumulative tradition.'[64] If we unpack this theologian-speak we get something like – religions are cumulative traditions, i.e. they have a history and a number of dimensions. Faith is people's way of 'responding' to such traditions. Much rests on the meaning(s) of the verb 'responding'. It has an ambiguity about it that theologians find attractive. One can 'respond' to a religion in many ways. One common response to (or one common effect of) participation in a religious ritual is emotional arousal: rituals evoke feelings in people. A common response to religious boundary-markers (the things that distinguish our group from others) such as values and their associated behaviours, e.g. we eat pigs, they don't; we regard women as inferior to men, they don't; we fast on Tuesdays, they don't, is identification: committing oneself to group norms, promoting group interests and incorporating group characteristics into one's sense of who one is. A common response to religious exhortations such as pray at set times or go on pilgrimage or kill animals in a particular way or prohibit women from touching sacramental objects is to act upon them, to do or enforce what is required. A common response to religious statements, such as 'god is great' or 'the Buddha saw the world as it really is' or 'Jesus is the son of god' is to claim that they are true. If a person thinks that a statement or proposition is true then that person believes it to be true. Beliefs are propositional in character.

All of these 'responses' (and others) are constituents of Smith's and Fowler's conception of 'faith', at least there is nothing in what they write that would exclude them. Clearly, not all of them involve belief-formation. Nevertheless, I would argue that all are underpinned by beliefs. The emotions people experience in response to religious rituals are, in part, determined by what the participants think is happening, by their beliefs. People who think that they are ingesting the body (and blood) of Christ when receiving a communion wafer will feel differently from people who think that they are merely ingesting a wafer of refined flour. The differences in feelings derive from differences in belief. The same applies to responses to group boundary-markers generated by cumulative traditions and behavioural exhortations generated by cumulative traditions: people embrace them because they think that the distinctive features of a particular group and the behaviours it demands of its members arise out of an accurate rather than an inaccurate understanding of the way the world/universe is. Indeed, we would think it most peculiar if a person said something like 'I spend my time doing these things, avoiding other things, and promoting yet others because they are required by the cumulative tradition with which I identify, a tradition that misunderstands the true nature of the universe.'

When Smith and Fowler emphasise the 'trust' and 'loyalty' elements of faith: 'the relation of trust in and loyalty to the transcendent ...',[65] they seem, to my mind, to be saying that faith is, essentially, a trust in the whole package (all the dimensions) that cumulative traditions (religions) have put together. On the surface at least, that seems like a lot to ask of anyone. Much depends on what 'trust' means in this context. Trust in a package as large and complex as a cumulative tradition inevitably has many elements. There is obviously a feeling/emotional element in that trust, and, as I argued above, an inevitable belief element, a confidence in the truth of its statements, its truth claims. Then there is the behavioural element – people do things because they have beliefs and associated feelings. So, I find Smith and Fowler's arguments that faith can be separated from religion and belief untenable. Faith has a belief dimension and, if I am correct, this informs and shapes all the other dimensions.

The cumulative traditions to which Smith and Fowler refer are all founded on the assumption that 'the transcendent' exists and that they have some kind of privileged access to it. In other words, as I argued in Part 1, the word 'religion' is most coherently deployed to refer to supernaturalist belief systems and their behavioural manifestations. That is what these 'cumulative traditions' are; that is what people trust in when they have faith, and that is what develops in, perhaps, a stage-like manner as people gain a more detailed and cognitively sophisticated understanding of the tradition with which they identify. Progress through such stage-like phases is not necessarily progress towards greater understanding of reality, a deepening of one's knowledge; nor is it necessarily a progression towards becoming a better human being (moral progress). Rather, it is merely progress in one's understanding of a particular tradition's world-view and its values, both of which may be inferior to other world-views and value systems. Kohlberg's stage theory of moral development, the template for Fowler's model, is, as Moran observes, not actually a theory of *moral* development, i.e. a development that results in one becoming an increasingly moral person at each stage, but rather 'it is a theory of the development of *moral reasoning* or a theory about reasoning about moral dilemmas'.[66] This, perhaps, explains why Wilber, who builds on Kohlberg's work, can claim that 'you cannot be low-IQ and moral'.[67] He seems to have misunderstood the nature of Kohlberg's theory and thought that each stage was somehow indicative of moral improvement rather than of a mere improvement in a person's *understanding* of moral issues.

Fowler's vision of mature faith

Each of the stages that Fowler thinks he has identified in the development of a person's faith is given a chapter in *Stages of Faith*. At the end of each of those for stages 1–5 he summarises the main characteristics of the stage he has just introduced. A notable feature of these summaries is that they all focus on changes that are internal to the person. If there are any behavioural changes that result from stage progression Fowler does not mention them. The chapter on stage 6, Universalising Faith, is different. There is no summary at the end and behavioural-sounding changes are introduced. On the one hand, there is a statement:

> Stage 6 becomes a disciplined, activist *incarnation* – making real and tangible – of the imperatives of absolute love and justice of which Stage 5 has partial apprehensions. The self at Stage 6 engages in spending and being spent for the transformation of present reality in the direction of a transcendent actuality.[68]

So, no room for non-believers, agnostics and atheists here.

On the other hand, he identifies a number of people who exemplify this stage. They are: Mohandas Gandhi, Martin Luther King Jr., Dag Hammarskjöld, Dietrich Bonhoeffer, Abraham Heschel, Thomas Merton and Mother Teresa of Calcutta. Christopher Hitchens's *The Missionary Position: Mother Teresa in theory and practice* had not been published in 1981 nor in 1991, when Fowler summarised his work for the collection of essays he edited with Nipkow and Schweitzer. So he can be forgiven for falling, like so many others, for the propaganda that hid her actual, rather unpleasant, agenda behind a saintly mist.[69]

Fowler conceptualises stage 6 in terms of what Niebuhr called 'radical monotheism', though he also claims that this 'does not negate the possibility of its universal truth and usefulness'.[70] Typical theologian-speak. In order to justify his claims about 'radical monotheism' to his critics Fowler sets out to deal with 'three critically important kinds of claims':

1. what he calls 'the absoluteness of the particular';
2. 'the claim that the Kingdom of God is an *eschalogical reality*'; and
3. 'I want to test with you how seriously we are prepared to take the category of *revelation* – revelation when it is connected with the truth claims [ah, an acknowledgement that beliefs do a place in faith] of our own religious traditions and revelation when it is claimed for truths of others' traditions'.[71]

At that point I became quite curious, since points 1 and 3 are two of the hottest issues around in relation to religion.

He sets out the challenge of point 1, which is given a subsection of its own under the heading of 'The Absoluteness of the Particular', with remarkable frankness:

> Concern about particularity arises out of the collision of communities of faith, each of which – directly or indirectly – makes claims of universal truth and validity for their faith. With these implicit or explicit claims of universality there are usually clear assertions that the alleged universal truth is an exclusive possession of the community that has been formed around it. Religious wars, inquisitions, heresy trials, persecutions, pogroms, holocausts and histories of prejudice and suspicion have been the results.[72]

His response to this challenge did not fail to disappoint. Secularist solutions to 'the clash of religious truths [= truth claims] neither overcome the divisions in the human family that prove so destructive, nor do they address the pervasive hunger for truth that characterizes our age'.[73] One might wonder what he had in mind when referring to 'secularist solutions'. Could it have been 'Abandon religions and with them all the divisions that they create?' That solution has never been tried, though John Lennon did invite us to imagine what it might be like. The question of addressing 'the pervasive hunger for truth' cannot, likewise, be easily dismissed with an assertion. Non-believers, agnostics and atheists are usually quite clear and explicit about how they look for truth, namely through the disciplines of science. Having dismissed 'secularist solutions' to the 'absoluteness of the particular' to his own satisfaction, Fowler proceeds to offer his own. It is couched in what, to me, is typical theological language:

> Absoluteness is that quality of a tradition of religious faith [the 'human' aspect of faith has been well and truly dropped by now] given to it by the instances in which the Unconditioned has come to expression in it ... absoluteness, as a quality of the transcendent that comes to expression, *is not exclusivistic*. Presumably, the absoluteness of the divine character can come to expression in different forms and in different contexts, with each of these instances bearing the full weight of ultimacy.[74]

Let's take a moment to reflect on what is being claimed here. On the one hand, communities of faith make claims of universal truth and validity for their faith, and, usually, clear assertions that the alleged universal truth is an exclusive possession of the community that has been formed around it. On the other, all these claims of universal truth and validity carry 'the full weight of ultimacy'. What does this final phrase mean? The prima facie interpretation, the one we should adopt unless good reasons are provided for abandoning it, is that each of these sets of claims (= world-views) is ultimately true, true at the highest and most fundamental level of truth or reality or whatever occupies an equivalent place in people's vocabularies. If that interpretation is even close to what Fowler had in mind when he wrote it then the theological veil has been lifted. It is all smoke and mirrors.

As I mentioned in Part 1, polytheism, monotheism and atheism cannot all carry 'the full weight of ultimacy'. If there are, irreducibly, many gods and that claim is true, then, at the ultimate level, there is not just one god. If there are, at the ultimate level, no gods, then there cannot be one god or many gods. The simultaneous assertion of polytheism, monotheism and atheism at the ultimate level is nonsensical. It is rubbish. Similarly, in terms of ontology, the three most commonly adopted views are monism, dualism and pluralism. These positions are mutually exclusive. One cannot be a monistic dualist or a monistic pluralist or a dualistic pluralist or any other combination of them. So, how can claims from a tradition such as Advaita Vedānta, which maintains ontological monism at the ultimate level, be as true as those of Jainism, which maintains ontological dualism at the ultimate level? They cannot. Some of these claims must be wrong. All of them may be wrong, but all of them cannot be right, and Fowler's solution to the challenge of 'the absoluteness of the particular' turns out to be no solution at all. Despite the logical problems many theologians do, nevertheless, assert the viability of a variety of blends. Rāmānuja's qualified non-dualistic theology (viśiṣṭādvaita) is a fine example.

The subsection on point 2, entitled 'The Eschatological Character of the Kingdom of God', was simply too theological and obscure for me to make much sense out of it, and, interestingly, point 3 somehow failed to make it onto the page. There was no subsection on point 3 and it is not addressed elsewhere in the book. I wonder why. It is difficult to avoid the conclusion that, for Fowler, stage 6 is deeply tradition-bound, essentially arriving at a nuanced, rather abstract commitment to the cumulative tradition known as Christianity. The 'universal' dimension is opaque, to say the least. Other writers have homed in on different though related weaknesses of the model. So, 'it seems "antipluralistic and condescending"', it 'does not appear as an evolution of the psychosocial structures described by stages 1 through 5', and 'the distinctions between form and content become blurred without adequate explication'.[75] If Wilber wants his readers to take his notion of lines of development seriously then surely he needs to find better, more rigorous examples than he offers at present.

Levels

Wilber uses the phrases 'levels of development' and 'stages of development' interchangeably.[76] The term 'level', he states, is used 'to indicate that there are important *emergent* qualities that tend to come into being in a discrete or quantum-like fashion ...'[77] and 'by "stages" [= levels] we mean progressive and permanent milestones along the evolutionary path of your own unfolding'.[78] I am, as readers might surmise, unclear about what 'the evolutionary path of your own unfolding' refers to, not least because Wilber does not himself restrict his notion of levels/stages to individuals. Indeed, he explicitly includes 'culture' in his list of phenomena that emerge in levels/stages. In addition, some of the other examples of stages/levels that he offers have, to say the least, a controversial status. He cites Jean Gebser's account of five levels of consciousness (archaic, magic, mythic, rational and integral) as one example; the yogic cakra system (there's only one?) as another; the Vedāntic distinction between gross (sthūla), subtle (sūkṣma) and causal (kāraṇa) bodies as another; and those schemes developed by Loevinger and Cook-Greuter, Beck and Cowan, Kagan and numerous other researchers as yet others. Can all these stage/level models be accurate? Wilber himself asks the question 'Which is right?' and answers it: 'All of them; it just depends on what you want to keep track of in growth and development.'[79]

This certainly appears to involve a rather uncritical acceptance of every developmental scheme that has ever been created, which inevitably seems misguided, since not all such schemes are compatible with each other and the evidence supporting some of them is far more flimsy than that supporting others. There is certainly a lot of fudging going on here. To illuminate some of it I will focus on the claims he makes, both explicit and implicit, about material with which I have some familiarity: Indian yogic spirituality. For example, he equates the Vedāntic kāraṇa śarīra (causal body) with the Buddhist dharmakāya, the Vedāntic sūkṣma śarīra (subtle body) with the Buddhist sambhogakāya and the Vedāntic sthūla śarīra (gross/coarse body) with the Buddhist nirmāṇakāya. There is a rough correspondence here, but it falls far short of synonymy, and I cannot imagine either Buddhists or Vedāntins accepting such equivalence.

His treatment of Vedāntic material itself is also suspect. For example, in Vedānta (particularly non-dual or Advaita Vedānta),

> The food sheath [anna-maya-kośa: the sheath (kośa) made (maya) of food (anna)], the grossest of all, is the jīva's [= soul's] physical body (sthūla śarīra) to which birth and death relate. The three kośas of prāṇamaya, manomaya and vijñānamaya constitute the subtle body (sūkṣma śarīra). The subtlest sheath of ānandamaya is the causal body (kāraṇa śarīra) which comes into existence due to the Self's limitation by māyā [illusion].[80]

The ātman (self), as non-dual consciousness, i.e. the turīya (the fourth state – beyond waking dreaming and deep sleep) lies behind 'the conglomerate of these five kośas'.[81] Compare the following account, based on actual Vedāntic texts, with Wilber's. He describes the kośas as five levels of spirit, to which he claims, Vedānta adds a sixth: turīya (literally, the fourth) and a seventh: turīyatīta (literally, beyond the fourth). In Vedānta, this turīyatīta state is only introduced in late Upaniṣads, i.e. post-Śaṅkara (who probably lived during the eighth century). So what was, and still is for many Vedāntins, a four-fold scheme, is converted by Wilber into a seven-fold one: an unphenomenological reworking that hardly inspires confidence in his use of source materials.

Another of his claims about levels/stages concerns Indian yogic ideas about cakras. He writes:

> The 7 chakras, which are simply a more complex version of the 3 simple levels or stages [body/egocentric/preconventional; mind/ethnocentric/conventional; spirit/worldcentric/postconventional[82]], represent 7 levels of consciousness and energy available to all human beings. (The first three chakras – food, sex, and power – are roughly stage 1; chakras 4 and 5 – relational heart and communication – are basically stage 2; and chakras 6 and 7 – psychic and spiritual – are the epitome of stage 3.)[83]

What are we to make of this? In the first place, I suspect that this characterisation is based more on the account that Baba Ram Dass/Richard Alpert published in 1973 than a study of Indian material on the cakras.[84] In the second place, we can note that there is a lack of consensus in Indian spiritual texts about the nature, number and character of the cakras. Many Western writers on the subject of cakras rely primarily on the translation of the Ṣaṭ Cakra Nirūpana included in John Woodroffe's *The Serpent Power*.[85] This text describes six 'major' cakras, the sahasrāra (thousand-petalled lotus), two 'minor' cakras between the ajñā cakra and the sahasrāra (the manas and soma cakras) plus a 12-petalled lotus (the dvādaśarna) situated in the pericarp of the sahasrāra. According to Eliade, the sahasrāra designates 'the plane of transcendence', and hence is not technically a cakra.[86] Jean Varenne makes the same point when he writes that the sahasrāra is not located at the top of the head but 'above the top of the head' – in order to differentiate it from the other six. The best graphic representations, indeed, show it in the form of an inverted lotus (stem upward, corolla opening downward) emitting a radiance that bathes the subtle body in its entirety.[87]

Woodroffe writes: 'Above the ajñā is the causal region and the lotus of a thousand petals, with all the letters, wherein is the abode of the supreme bindu, Paraśiva.'

Despite being mentioned in a number of texts (most tantric texts have not been translated and the teachings they contain are 'still extremely obscure'[88])

Table 5 The six major cakras according to the Ṣaṭ Cakra Nirūpana.

Cakra	Situation	Number of Petals	Letters on petals	Dominant tattva/element	Colour of tattva
Ajñā	Between eyebrows	2	ha, kṣa.	Manas	?
Viśuddha	Throat	16	a, ā, i, ī, u, ū, ṛ, ṝ, ḷ, ḹ, e, ai, o, au, aṃ, aḥ.	Akāśa (space)	White
Anāhata	Heart	12	ka, kha, ga, gha, ca, ccha, ja, jha, jña, ṭa, ṭha.	Vāyu (wind)	Smoky
Maṇipūra	Navel	10	ḍa, ḍha, ṇa, ta, tha, da, dha, na, pa, pha.	Tejas (fire)	Red
Svādhiṣṭhāna	Genitals	6	ba, bha, ya, ra, la.	Āpa (water)	White
Mūlādhāra	Anus	4	va, śa, ṣa, sa.	Pṛthivī (earth)	Yellow

this scheme of six cakras – seven if the sahasrāra is counted as a cakra[89] – is by no means universal. Dasgupta points out that tantric Buddhist texts tend to treat only the maṇipūra, anāhata, viśuddha and ājñā cakras as major and that different texts describe even these in different ways.[90] Moreover, other Hindu texts such as the Maṇḍalabrahmaṇa Upaniṣad refer to nine cakras: the six of the Ṣaṭ Cakra Nirūpana plus the tālu, ākāśa and bhrū cakras. We may also note that the positions of the three major nāḍīs (subtle channels) are also variously described. There are at least three versions of their relationship:

1. According to the Yāmala Tantra, iḍā and piṅgalā 'go straight up, alternating from left to right and right to left, and, having thus gone round all the lotuses, these auspicious ones proceed to the nostrils'.[91]

2. Another view is that they are shaped like bows on either side of the suṣumnā nāḍī.[92]

3. A third view is offered by Lama Anagarika Govinda who, following Swami Vivekananda, states that 'there is no spiral movement of these nāḍīs around the suṣumnā'.[93] His view is that they run parallel to the suṣumnā, forming a figure of eight with the fine suṣumnā passing up through the middle at the point where the other two meet.

Another mismatch is found in descriptions and depictions of the cakras in relation to the suṣumnā nāḍī. The Ṣaṭ Cakra Nirūpana claims that they are located within the suṣumnā. Most artistic representations show them either as attached to the suṣumnā on some kind of stem or located on its outside. C.W. Leadbeater claims that the cakras are located on the surface of the body, whereas Indian texts almost always locate them at the back of the body.[94] He also omits the genital cakra from his account, substituting a spleen cakra for it. Texts also vary in their descriptions of the number of petals displayed in each cakra, and of the source of the nāḍīs. Table 6 shows some of the variants.

Table 6 Petals on the cakras.

Ṣaṭ Cakra Nirūpana	Heruka Tantra	Sekoddeśa Ṭīkā
Ajñā – 2	32	32
Viśuddha – 16	16	16
Anāhata – 12	8	32
Maṇipūra – 10	64	64

Source of the nadis

Ṣaṭ Cakra Nirūpana – Mūlādhāra;[95]
Haṭha Yoga Pradīpikā – between the penis and the navel;[96]
Triśikhi Brāhmaṇa – navel area;[97]
Heruka Tantra – just below navel;
Most early Upaniṣads – heart.

Finally, it is also worth noting that the very existence of these subtle structures is a matter of considerable disagreement. One the one hand, many tantric practices were sanitised, often by substituting symbols for the materials employed in the rituals, by redefining tantric terms, and by what James Mallinson calls 'corporealisation', that is, the reworking of the rituals into practices that take place within the human body.[98] This is the process that lies at the heart of haṭhayoga. David Snellgrove makes a similar point when writing about 'tantric feasts'. Although much of the material on such feasts has been sanitised or deleted from tantric source materials there is enough remaining to support the thesis that these rituals frequently involved participants in taboo practices, especially sexual ones, and that various sites existed around India where tantric yogis could go to find yoginīs (female tantric practitioners, who were often from low caste backgrounds) as partners for the rituals. Moreover, 'all these places are identified with "veins" [nāḍī] related to the various "lotus-centers" [cakra] up and down the spinal cord'.[99] In other words, the descriptions of the cakras and nāḍīs in the subtle body may well have been nothing more than a coded map of the tantric sites that were located across the length and breadth of India.

These differences between textual descriptions of the cakras and nāḍīs and of their ontological status inevitably raise questions about their use as indicators of 'progressive and permanent milestones along the evolutionary path of your own unfolding', and, indeed, about treating any of these levels/stages schemes as accurate models of human development and progress.

States

According to Wilber, the relationship between states and stages/levels 'turns out to hold *the single most important key to understanding the nature of spiritual experiences* ...'[100] It thus warrants a most careful and critical investigation. 'States', for Wilber, refers to the experiences that individual people have (his upper left quadrant). Some of these, he says, are 'natural' or 'ordinary'. His basic list of these contains five: 'As the traditions themselves often do, I will refer to 3, or 4 or 5 major states of consciousness – but all 5 are implied.'[101] In its three-fold form the list of natural/ordinary states of consciousness comprises waking, dreaming and deep sleep. The four-fold version adds the turīya (fourth) state and the five-fold one the turīyatīta (beyond the fourth) state. The reason why these states are labelled as 'normal/ordinary' is that they 'are available, to some degree, to all humans at virtually any stage of growth [Wow!], including infants, simply because even infants wake, dream and sleep [Mmm, not so wow!]'.[102] In Vedānta the turīya and turīyatīta states are extraordinary and indicative of pronounced spiritual progress; so the claim that they are normal/ordinary and available to all is startling, hence my 'Wow!' However, the justification offered is a damp squib. The fact that everyone wakes, dreams and sleeps contributes *nothing* to the claim that the turīya and turīyatīta states are ordinary.

Other 'states' are not 'ordinary'. Wilber calls them 'nonordinary' or 'altered'. Some are drug-induced; others are trained by means of spiritual practices such as meditation. These latter states 'tend to unfold in a sequential fashion'.[103] Such sequential development does not, however, ensure progress along the developmental lines mentioned above. The two are essentially independent of each other. Wilber calls them 'state-stages' and the developmental lines 'structure-stages'. 'Training' (spiritual exercises) might map the route for progress in states, but how does one progress through structure-stages? Some progress seems to be at least partly automatic, e.g. cognitive development. But the way to progress through Wilber's other structure-stage schemes is far from clear. Indeed, he claims that 'As for *transformation* itself: how and why individuals grow, develop, and transform is one of the greatest mysteries of human psychology. The truth is, nobody knows.'[104]

Components of Wilber's contribution to answering this question are his definition of 'enlightenment', and his account of state and stage progressions. Enlightenment, he assumes, is a good thing, something worth striving for, though he never provides reasons for his judgement.[105] His definition of 'enlightenment' is not taken from, though it is clearly influenced by, Indian traditions of liberation, but is rather idiosyncratic, designed to fit his map: 'the realisation of oneness with *all states* and *all stages* that have evolved so far and that are in existence at any given time'.[106] That's a clever move, but it does not enable him to evade some awkward questions. In the first place, what about all the people who became liberated after receiving orally delivered proclamations of the dhamma by the Buddha and had never practised meditation nor lived exemplary moral lives?[107] They provide obvious counter examples to the idea that 'enlightenment' requires 'progress' through all states and all lines. Secondly, what, for example, does it mean to experience 'oneness with all states and stages? If stages are progressive and do not go backwards, then if one has arrived at stage 3, stage 2 has been left behind. One is in a different cognitive, moral or aesthetic space. Reflect for a moment on a stage theory that is valued and employed by Wilber: Piaget's 4-stage theory of cognitive development. When a child moves from the sensorimotor to the pre-operational stage (s)he no longer thinks in a sensorimotor way, or, as these shifts are not all-or-nothing affairs, finds it increasingly difficult to do so. A person cannot think in sensorimotor, pre-operational, concrete operational and formal operational ways at the same time, cannot be 'one' with all four stages.[108]

Pretty much the same problem arises with regard to state progression. For some opaque reason Wilber uses Vedāntic notions of state progression and Evelyn Underhill's 'stages of spiritual progression' as normative for this field. The Vedāntic five-fold version and Wilber's seven-fold modification of it I have outlined, along with its problems, above. Underhill's stages are:

1   awakening/initiation;
2   purification/pacification;
3   illumination;
4   dark night;
5   unification.

If we take the Vedāntic concept of a turīyatīta state (beyond the fourth or turīya state) then, as with Piaget's shifts from sensorimotor to pre-operational, concrete operational and onto formal operational thinking, which is 'beyond' the concrete operational, the meditator has gone 'beyond' the previous state. The main difference here is that the Vedāntic literature implies that the meditator may re-enter the turīya state after accessing the turīyatīta one. Unlike structure-stages, state-stages may be traversed repeatedly. This, however, is quite different from being 'at one' with all of them.

When we compare Wilber's favoured state-stage models with others found in the spiritual literature we find:

(a) the idea that experiencing non-duality or 'the clear light of the Supermind' as a kind of pinnacle of spiritual development is misguided, or at least unphenomenological, i.e. it misrepresents what the traditions communicate about such experiences; and

(b) that Underhill's stage scheme is *not* an 'almost perfect' representative of a phenomenological approach to spiritual state development.

With regard to (a), the *Yoga Sūtra* of Patañjali provides a clear counter example to Wilber's claimed status for the primacy of non-dual experience. This text, mistakenly described by Wilber as the 'pillar of Hinduism,'[109] has, nevertheless, been influential in many modern yoga traditions, both Indian and Western. Indeed, in recent years it has been promoted by many teachers and writers as the normative and quintessential text on yoga. Here's a selection of their comments. Tirumalai Krishnamacharya, founder of a modern yoga movement of international standing, is quoted as claiming that 'If it is not in the *Yoga Sūtra* it's not yoga.'[110] For Godfrey Devereux, author of *Dynamic Yoga*, it is 'the bible of yoga'.[111] Swami Vivekananda describes it as 'the highest authority and text book on Rāja Yoga'.[112] J. Carrera describes it as 'a timeless spiritual classic whose appeal is founded on a profound and unerring understanding of the human condition'.[113] For Wendy Doniger it is 'essential to anyone's understanding ... of the practice of yoga'.[114] This, then, is surely a text that has considerable credibility as a guide to spiritual practice. Certainly many yoga training organisations make it required reading for their students.

Yet the ultimate realisation in Patañjali's system, contra Wilber, is that the witness or seer (puruṣa/dṛśya) is ontologically distinct and separate from nature or the seen (prakṛti/draṣṭṛ). That realisation, called truth-bearing insight (ṛtaṃbharā prajñā) by Patañjali, in a state that he calls nirvicāra samāpatti in Book 1 and, perhaps, dharma-megha samādhi in Book 4, results in the experience of nirbīja samādhi (Book 1), which probably equates with kaivalya (isolation/aloneness – complete separation from prakṛti), when the seer abides in its own nature or own form (sva-rūpa) in Book 4. Patañjali is not alone in maintaining that the highest spiritual experience is *not* non-dual. Jains and many theistic mystics make the same claim, and Wilber's assertions that their experiences are on a 'lower' level than those of mystics who claim that the experience of non-duality is the highest insight does not negate their claims. They merely act as counter claims.

Moreover, although Wilber quotes a number of Buddhist writers he certainly seems to lack an understanding of the Pāli material, as his 'one (long) paragraph' summary of Buddhism on pp. 110–111 of *Integral Spirituality* makes abundantly clear. In that paragraph he claims that the Buddhist path 'includes right view, right meditation and right awareness'. Right view is obviously sammā diṭṭhi (the first item on the eight-fold, sometimes ten-fold list), right meditation presumably refers to sammā samādhi (the eighth item), but what is right awareness? The second item on the list is sammā saṃkappa (right resolve), the third is sammā vāca (right speech), the fourth sammā kammanta (right action), the fifth sammā ājīva (right livelihood), and the seventh sammā sati (right recollection or mindfulness). Perhaps sammā ñāṇaṁ (right knowledge), the ninth step in the ten-fold version of the path, is what Wilber has in mind? That, however, is knowledge of one's former births, of the causes of rebirth and of the destruction of the āsavas of kāma (lust), bhava (desire for existence) and avijjā (ignorance). None of these match Wilber's description of right awareness: 'nondual awareness, which unites subject and object, emptiness and form'.[115] His use of the term 'emptiness' here (= śunyatā?) suggests Mahāyāna sources. One's use of these needs to be careful as we find differences in the ways in which this and related terms are deployed in Mahāyāna texts. I am not a specialist in Mahāyāna Buddhist teachings, but my reservations about the uncritical use Mahāyāna material are rooted in observations such as the following.

There are clear continuities between early Buddhist usage of terms like śunya (Pāli – suñña = void or empty) and śunyatā *(voidness or emptiness)*. For example, in Sutta Nipāta 1118 the brāhman Mogharāja asks the Buddha 'How is any one to look upon the world that the king of death may not see him?' To which the Buddha replies:

> Look upon the world as void (suñña) O Mogharāja, being always thoughtful; having destroyed the view of oneself (as really existing), so one may overcome death; the king of death will not see him who thus regards the world.[116]

Similarly, in the Saṃyutta Nikāya the Buddha responds to Ānanda's enquiry about the meaning of the statement 'Void is the world' with the words 'because the world is void of self (attā) ... or of what belongs to self ... it is said 'Void is the world' (suñño lokoti)'.[117] The Mahāyāna teaching about emptiness then, is essentially a reiteration of the Buddha's emphasis on the dependently arisen nature of all phenomena. In terms of this analysis, the 'things' that we experience are mental constructs (vikalpa) and ultimately illusory (māyā). From the perspective of the Mādhyamaka school of Mahāyāna Buddhism, what we ordinarily call 'truth' is not, in fact, accurate. It is only conventionally true (saṃvṛtti satya) whereas the dharma of the Buddhas is actually true (paramārtha satya). 'Emptiness', on this analysis, is simply the absence of self-existence (svabhāva) in all phenomena, i.e. all phenomena exist only through their connections with other previously existing and concurrently existing phenomena. Nevertheless, the fact is that there was much debate and disagreement about these issues between different groups of Buddhists. Snellgrove offers a succinct overview in his *Indo-Tibetan Buddhism*.[118] Wilber just seems to pick his favourite position and assert that it is the most accurate.

Similarly, he also claims that Mahāmudrā and Dzogchen (rDzogs-chen) are 'the deepest Buddhist teachings'.[119] Well, for some maybe. Rawlinson categorises both as Cool-Unstructured. Dzogchen, according to Samuel, 'presented an alternative path to the attainment of the central liberating insight of the tradition, with its own specific methodology, and initially at least rejected most of the tantric techniques'.[120] Dzogchen is treated as a high-level practice in both the rNying-ma-pa and Bon traditions of Tibet, though some Tibetan adherents of the tantric practices found in texts that have been called Supreme Yoga Tantras (anuttara-yoga-tantra) might disagree, as did Tibetan monks such as Zhi-ba-'od, who claimed that those who practise rDzogs-chen 'will be led into evil rebirths'.[121] This term, anuttara-yoga, is, according to Samuel, reconstructed, i.e. not found in Sanskrit sources, and is 'apparently based on a Tibetan misunderstanding'. Nevertheless, the tantras that were collected under this rubric, the mahāyoga and the yoginītantras (also known as bhaginī [sister] or prajñā [insight] tantras[122]), do contain teachings that those who wished to denigrate certain tantric ritual practices could use for that purpose – by, for example, dubbing them as 'left-hand' or claiming that they are merely 'symbolic' or by taking them out of the ritual context and locating them within the human body (what James Mallinson calls 'corporealisation').[123]

Likewise with mahāmudrā. The interpretation of many tantric texts depends significantly on how one understands the deployment of 'twilight' or 'enigmatic' language (sandhabhāṣya). Do the distinctive and often obscure terms make symbolic meditations sound like they refer to sexual or taboo activities, or do they make sexual/taboo rituals sound symbolic? The 'right-hand', 'clean' version of tantra stresses the 'symbolic', e.g. 'mudrā' is often understood as a hand-gesture or as a symbol. In the left-hand version, mudrā is a female partner. In his comments on tantric 'consecrations' (abhiṣeka) Snellgrove explains that in the Supreme Yoga Tantras (anuttara-yoga-tantra) 'the four main consecrations consist of ritualized performance of the sexual act of union ...'[124] For the consecrations detailed in the Hevajra Tantra, 'the feminine partner, known as the *mudrā* (symbol) is required'.[125] When read from this perspective the following passage seems pretty clear:

> The sixteen year-old Wisdom (*prajñā* [= female]) he clasps within his arms and from the union of vajra and bell we understand the Master Consecration. She is fair-featured and wide-eyed and endowed with youth and beauty. With thumbs and fourth finger he lets (the drop) fall into the pupil's mouth. The taste of universal sameness is thereby brought within the pupil's range. (This is the Secret Consecration.)
>
> Then having honoured and worshiped the Wisdom [prajñā/female], the master should consign her to the pupil, saying: 'O great one, take thou this *mudrā* who will bring you bliss,' and knowing his pupil to be fully worthy and

free of envy and anger, he further commands him: 'Unite, O Vajra-Holder!' (This is the Consecration of Knowledge and Wisdom.)

Moreover, as Snellgrove points out, in tantras such as this the feminine partner is also referred to as Mahāmudrā, a term that also refers to the truth realised through her and to the central artery (avadhūti) in the nāḍī-cakra system.[126]

So, rDzogs-chen and Mahāmudrā may be regarded as 'the deepest Buddhist teachings' by some Buddhists and some Western interpreters of Buddhism, but not all Buddhists would agree, and the nature of the systems labelled by those terms a matter of some debate. If it were demonstrated that the literal, actual engagement in sexual and taboo rituals was, in fact, what they originally referred to would those who claim that they are 'the deepest' still maintain that view? I suspect that many would not, though, personally, I see no valid reason why they should be denigrated. In short, Wilber's assertions on these and other topics may be correct, though I believe that many of them are not. What does seem to be clear, though, is that he is inclined to pick and choose interpretations that suit his own ideas rather than acknowledging that in many of the areas with which he is concerned there is considerable debate and disagreement. In this case, he really does seem to be guilty of recreating Buddhist teaching in his own imagination's image.

With regard to (b) above: Wilber's claim that Underhill's stage scheme is an 'almost perfect' representative of a phenomenological approach to spiritual state development, my treatment of mystical experience in Part 1 demonstrates, I think, that while it might serve as an overview of mainly Christian mysticism it is far from being an accurate guide to mystical schema in other traditions. As far as I am aware, none of the major traditions of Indian mysticism include a 'Dark Night' phase in their descriptions of mystical progression. So, for example, the brāhmanical Maitrī Upaniṣad (6.18) gives the six stages of progress in yoga as consisting of breath control (prāṇāyāma), sense withdrawal (pratyāhāra), concentration (dhyāna), deeper concentration (dhāraṇā), contemplation (tarka) and absorption (samādhi). The quasi-brāhmanical *Yoga Sūtra* of Patañjali offers a similar scheme: restraint (yama), observance (niyama), posture (āsana), breath control (prāṇāyāma), sense withdrawal (pratyāhāra), concentration (dhāraṇā), deeper concentration (dhyāna), and absorption (samādhi). The eighth and final stage of samādhi is further divided by Patañjali into two types: with [karmic] seeds (sabīja) and without [karmic] seeds (nirbīja), the first of these having four stages called coincidences (samāpattis), namely with reasoning (savitarka), without/beyond reasoning (nirvitarka), with reflection (savicāra) and without/beyond reflection (nirvicāra). The Buddhist eight-fold/ten-fold path divides the practitioner's progress into right view (sammā diṭṭhi), right resolve (sammā saṁkappa), right speech (sammā vāca), right action (sammā kammanta) right livelihood (sammā ājīva), right recollection or mindfulness (sammā sati), right concentration/absorption (sammā samādhi), right knowledge (sammā ñāṇaṁ) and right release (sammā vimutti). The eighth step, sammā samādhi, is divided into a number of stages, called jhāna. The most common list of these has four of them before the acquisition of that right knowledge (sammā ñāṇaṁ) which leads to right release. There are, however, also lists of eight and nine jhānas (called coincidences – samāpattis), and nibbāna can be attained from the ninth.

Nowhere in these quite detailed schemes is there any notion of a 'dark night' phase, and only in the brāhmanical Maitrī Upaniṣad is the outcome of the practice an unambiguous 'unification'. Patañjali, as outlined above, does not seek unification but separation of spirit from nature/matter. The Buddhist material, particularly the earliest, is more ambiguous on this point, though a number of scholars have drawn attention to parallels between early Buddhist spirituality and that presented by Patañjali in his *Yoga Sūtra*[127]. Moreover, the early Buddhist contrast between the permanent, non-mortal, unconditioned, and sorrowless nibbāna and the impermanent, mortal, conditioned and sorrowful saṁsāra cannot help but evoke in the minds of many of us the contrast in both the *Yoga Sūtra* and the *Sāṁkhya Kārikā* between the seer/puruṣa and the seen/prakṛti, especially when we remember that nibbāna does not do anything and is sometimes described as a radiant or brightly shining mind (prabhāsvara citta) and that puruṣa does not do anything, is conscious (cetanaṁ), and a mere witness and spectator.[128] Underhill's scheme is *not* an 'almost perfect' representative of a phenomenological approach to spiritual state development. Again, Wilber seems to have adopted it more because it fits nicely into his 'integral spirituality' model than because it offers an accurate phenomenology of mystical experience.

Types

Types, claims Wilber, 'are as important as quadrants, levels, lines and states',[129] yet, unlike those components of his integral map, they do not get a listing in the index of *Integral Spirituality*. Their coverage in the text is pretty thin too. Types are the least salient elements of the model presented in that work. Wilber's prime examples of types are masculine and feminine, though there are 'numerous other "horizontal typologies" that can be very helpful when part of a comprehensive IOS' (integral operating system).[130] The only 'horizontal typology' besides masculine – feminine that he mentions is the Myers-Briggs Type Indicator (MBTI), which he refers to simply as Myers-Briggs, and states that its main types are feeling, thinking, sensing and intuiting. This is over-simplistic. In fact, the MBTI yields 16 types, which are determined by combining questionnaire results on four bipolar dimensions: introversion-extraversion; sensing-intuition; thinking-feeling and judging-perceiving. Each type combines four elements from each of the dimension combinations, e.g. extravert–sensing–thinking–perceiving (ESTP), or introvert–sensing–thinking–judging (ISTJ), or introvert–sensing–feeling–judging (ISFJ). It was created by Isabel McKelvey Myers and her daughter Katherine Elizabeth Briggs in 1943, based on the personality studies of C.G. Jung as set out in his *Psychological Types*.[131] This work was first published in 1921 and translated into English by H.G. Baynes in 1923. According to Wilber, each type has a healthy and an unhealthy version.

Two questions immediately come to mind: how robust are these type classifications and how useful are they? With regard to the first question, I will offer an anecdote and then some evidence-based comments. Many years ago I participated in a psychology summer school where one of the team had devised a playful yet relevant ice-breaker activity for the opening session. First we all completed a MBTI questionnaire to determine our type. Then we formed a group with everyone who had the same type and started to 'get to know' each other. After 10–15 minutes we were instructed to make a mental note of how much we felt we had in common with the other members of the group. Then we were told to join a group composed of other people who shared our astrological sun sign, and get to know each other for 10–15 minutes. At the end of that time we were instructed to make a note of how much we felt we had in common with the other group members. After that, in an open session, we had to declare whether we felt we had more in common with our MBTI group or our astrological group. Astrology won hands down. This result could be due to many factors, though I doubt that the principles of astrological categorisation had much to do with it. It does, nevertheless, raise a few questions about the status of the MBTI.

Modern personality psychologists rarely use the MBTI, preferring others of their own devising. This is partly because the methods for measuring personality have advanced considerably since 1943. The statistical technique of factor analysis has enabled researchers to connect or disconnect, i.e. measure the correlations between, large numbers of personality descriptions, e.g. energetic, modest, gregarious, helpful, active, compliant, risk-taking, trustworthy, assertive, soft-hearted, into clusters or traits, which can then be used to create personality profiles. Psychologists using factor analysis tend to group the personality descriptions listed above into two clusters/traits: extraversion and agreeableness. Would you concur? Can these words be arranged into two coherent columns? Different theorists aim for different levels of generality. So Raymond Cattell clustered his data into 16 factors to create personality profiles for individuals. Other researchers have sought to identify higher-level, i.e. more general and simple, clusters. Paul Costa and Robert McCrae developed a model with five factors: extraversion, agreeableness, conscientiousness, openness and neuroticism, each of which was constituted or indicated by particular clusters of traits.[132] Lewis Goldberg produced a five factor model that he hoped would apply across all human cultures, though only three of his five, the three he shared with Costa and McCrae (extraversion, agreeableness and conscientiousness), seemed to pass this test.

I am unsure what the implications of these partial overlaps are. Perhaps some personality factors are culturally created, or perhaps some cultures do not have the concepts that enable them to make the kinds of distinctions that researchers such as Cattell have identified. Despite the progress that personality psychologists have made since Carl Jung wrote *Psychological Types* there is still a long way to go before we will have a comprehensive understanding of human personalities. As Colin Cooper concludes, 'psychometricians do not yet have the measure of man'.[133] With regard to the second question, it is far from obvious how one would use all the 'numerous other "horizontal typologies" that Wilber claims are useful to people with an interest in spirituality. But what does he have in mind here? In the first place, the MBTI, Cattell's, Costa and McCrae's, Goldberg's and other psychometric tests such as the Eysenck Personality Inventory or Belbin's Team Role inventory are either expensive or restricted. As Cooper explains, 'In the UK, the British Psychological Society oversees a three-tier system of licensing test use in psychology ... [and] test publishers will only supply tests to properly qualified individuals'.[134]

The implication of this state of affairs is that most readers of *Integral Spirituality* will be unable to access this material. They might then fall back on something like Louis Janda's *The Psychologist's Book of Personality Tests*.[135] Janda offers these tests as reasonably accessible ways of improving one's self-understanding. They are all self-report or self-administered tests and do not include the kinds of checks against self-deception that psychological tests often contain, such as a lie scale:

> a list of common but socially undesirable peccadilloes embedded in the personality questionnaire, for example 'Did you ever cheat at a test in school?' Someone who admits to few of these is either a saint, out of touch with how they really behave or distorting their responses.[136]

They are, nevertheless, genuine psychological tests and are all reprinted with the permission of the designers. Janda also provides a reference to the original source material for those who wish to contextualise whatever tests they might be thinking of taking.

So, a keen integral spiritualist could complete all the tests, give them to all his/her friends and acquaintances, and eventually develop an ability to spot certain patterns in other people and make inferences about their personalities. Integrating all that information is, however, a substantial task. It may offer benefits in terms of improved communication with others, and that might help a person to make progress on their own spiritual path. But it also has the potential to create problems, especially if one starts to classify people's scores as indicative of a healthy or unhealthy type. Wilber tells his readers that 'Pointing to an unhealthy type is not a way to judge people, but a way to understand and communicate with them more clearly and effectively.'[137] Perhaps, though the temptation is there, and few of us would always be able to resist it, especially if we are employing type classifications on a regular basis.

Finally, I think the limitations on the use of 'type' information impose significant constraints on anyone who seeks to employ it to enhance their own spirituality or understand that of others. The type distinction that Wilber uses to illustrate the concept of masculine–feminine is not quite as simple as his 2 × 2 description implies:

	Masculine	Feminine
Healthy	MH	FH
Unhealthy	MU	FU

Although we can apply the basic biological criterion of dividing humans into egg carriers and sperm carriers to determine sex (I am not aware of any humans who carry both), our gender identities are shaped by a number of other factors, so much so that it might be better to conceptualise masculinity and femininity along a kind of sliding scale. These factors include *the effects of hormones* (people vary in the balance of male and female hormones in their bodies); *genotype* – most women have XX sex chromosomes and most males have XY, though some people have XXY (Klinefelter's syndrome) or have XY but look like women (androgen insensitivity syndrome), and even, in complex ways, *environmental influences*: 'girls with a boy twin might, some claim, have larger teeth and a more audacious attitude to life than those who share a prenatal home with a sister'.[138] In short, just understanding the dynamics of masculine and feminine identities is a complex task.[139] If we add healthy and unhealthy variants into the mix we are confronted with a challenge that has still not been adequately met by our best researchers in the fields of sex and gender, and it is far from clear how spiritual cartographers or Integral Spiritualists can best understand never mind use the information that is currently available.

Overall evaluation of Wilber's model

The integral map is an attempt at a grand synthesis of all knowledge pertaining to spirituality. One of the reviewers of *Integral Spirituality*, Roshi Dennis Genpo Merzel, describes it as 'possibly the most important spiritual book in postmodern times', and another, Rabbi Zalman Schachter-Shalomi, claims that it is 'One of the most important books on spirituality written in the postmodern era'. Wilber's own assessment of his work is that the integral map 'is the most comprehensive map that we possess at this time'.[140] My own judgement serves as a counterpoint to these claims. While Wilber's work has value in attempting to bring multiple perspectives and areas of knowledge into complementary relationships so that the field of 'spirituality' can be investigated more thoroughly and comprehensively than has previously been the case, its lack of rigour and critical evaluation of source materials, along with its embrace of some highly speculative and imaginative ideas that are presented as having epistemological equivalence with much more grounded material place it on the border zone between scholarship and science fantasy. My comments on each of the five primary components of the integral map offer some support for this judgement.

A few other reasons for that judgement are:

1. *His tendency for phenomenological distortion.* A catch-all category that he likes a lot is 'the Great Wisdom Traditions'. Examples of these that are found in the text of *Integral Spirituality* are 'Christian Mysticism, Vedanta Hinduism, Vajrayana Buddhism and Jewish Kabbalah'.[141] He seems to assume, in typical perennialist fashion, that they all teach the same thing, e.g. 'the wisdom traditions maintain that each of us … has 3 bodies, which are often called the gross body, the subtle body, and the causal body'.[142] This is simply false. This three-body idea is drawn directly from the Vedānta tradition, and, as far as I am aware, Christians do not subscribe to it.

2. *Exaggerated epistemological language.* In many places throughout *Integral Spirituality* he employs terms that claim more than is

warranted by the currently available evidence. One favourite is 'truths'. The great Wisdom Traditions have preserved 'incredibly important truths' and 'verifiable evidence' to support them; the integral framework 'accepts the enduring truths of premodern, modern and postmodern realisations ...' ('realisations' is another of these terms. Why not just say ideas or notions or claims?). The Great Wisdom Traditions also have 'enduring insights' that are only deficient in their comprehensiveness, not in their substance. Integral Post-Metaphysics, Wilber claims, can salvage these 'invaluable and profound truths of premodern traditions', and it can '*reconstruct* the important truths of the contemplative traditions but *without the metaphysical systems* that would not survive modernist and postmodernist critiques ...'[143] Perhaps, though, in my view, not only do these 'Great Wisdom Traditions' not teach the same 'truths', the epistemological status of what they deem to be truths is rather flimsy. What he is actually writing about is 'truth claims', 'claimed realisations' and 'claimed insights'. Such claims may turn out to be true, and point to genuine realisations and insights, but they do not have that status at the present time, and, as argued above, many of these claims conflict with each other; they are mutually exclusive, so some of them cannot be true, and therefore cannot be genuine realisations or be genuine insights.

3   Finally, for now, because this does not exhaust my reasons, I find his blend of Hegelian and Śuddhādvaita Vedāntic metaphysics (in a chapter on 'post-metaphysics'!), with its notions of 'Spirit' evolving and playing, 'Spirit-in-action' and 'Spirit unfolding its own being' to be completely unwarranted by the evidence he deploys.

Wilber's *Integral Spirituality* is *not* a reliable guide for anyone who seeks to make sense of the many and varied accounts of religious/spiritual experiences that are available to the modern enquirer. It comes with too much baggage, too much obscurity and, ironically, too much metaphysics for anyone who seeks an evidence-based understanding.

Roland Fischer's cartography of ecstatic and meditative states

In his influential works *Shamanism: archaic techniques of ecstasy*,[144] and *Yoga: immortality and freedom*,[145] Mircea Eliade argues that while yoga and shamanism share a number of common features, the differences between them are far more significant.[146] These differences are highlighted by his choice of epithets to label and characterise the two systems: *ecstasy* for shamanism and *enstasy* for yoga. Both words come from the Greek term 'stasis', which includes among its meanings the notions of to stand, or of a place, or of a "state" of a person. So *ek-stasis* is a state of standing outside of oneself (what we might call dissociation), and the Greeks often employed it to describe states of astonishment or entrancement. By contrast, *en-stasis* (Eliade's translation of *samādhi*) can be taken to refer to a state of being 'in' or 'within' oneself, though the Greeks tended to use it for conveying the idea of a plan or a beginning. For Eliade, this contrast highlights what he calls a 'structural difference' between yoga and shamanism. He writes, 'Although the latter is not without certain techniques of concentration ... its final goal is always ecstasy and the soul's ecstatic journey through the various cosmic regions, whereas Yoga pursues enstasis, final concentration of the spirit and "escape" from the cosmos.[147]

For Eliade, then, *ecstasy* is not to be understood in its primary English sense of 'a state of exalted pleasure or happiness',[148] but as referring to trancelike states, during which the shaman 'is believed to leave his body and ascend to the sky or descend to the underworld'.[149] It is this out-of-the-body journeying of the soul, which, for Eliade, lies at the heart of what he calls 'the shamanic complex' and renders the descriptor *ecstatic* appropriate. This 'complex' includes trances and dreams that involve various kinds of magical flight, mastery over fire,[150] healing,[151] and special relations with spirits.[152] This 'complex' can be encountered in many parts of the world, from Siberia through Central and Southern Asia to Australasia, Oceania and America.

By contrast, the yoga 'complex' is unique to India, a creation of the Indian soil.[153] It is 'a living fossil, a modality of archaic spirituality that has survived nowhere else'.[154] The constituents of that 'complex' are not systematically listed or described by Eliade, though it is possible to discern something of what he had in mind when using the phrase from comments in various parts of *Yoga: immortality and freedom*. So, 'The word *yoga* serves, in general, to designate any *ascetic technique* and any *method of meditation*'.[155] More specifically, it has an initiatory structure: a guru is required; there is a *death* followed by a *rebirth*, a rebirth into an unconditioned mode of being, e.g. *kaivalya, nirvāṇa*,[156] which involves the yogin embracing 'the *opposite* of what life demands that he do'.[157] All the yogic techniques, he claims, are designed to prepare the way for 'that final withdrawal from the phenomenal world'.[158] So the yogin has to abandon both body and personality in recognition of the metaphysical 'truth' that his true identity lies not in everything that he thought was himself but in something that was hidden *by* that understanding of himself. Finally, whereas the shaman cultivates ecstatic experience largely for the sake of accessing benefits for a community, the yogin *can* be understood as pursuing goals that require the abandonment of community altogether.[159]

To my mind, this contrast between ecstatic and enstatic complexes is far less pronounced than Eliade seems to think, and my own inclination is to regard these two 'complexes' as closely related expressions of the same underlying psychological processes. Before I present my argument in support of that view, however, I would like to consider the output of another influential writer, Roland Fischer, whose work purports to offer a physiological and neurological basis for Eliade's phenomenological intuition about the differences between ecstasy and enstasy.[160]

Over a period of around 20 years, from the late 1960s to the late 1980s, psychiatrist Roland Fischer developed in stages what he has variously called 'a cartography of non-ordinary states of consciousness',[161] 'a cartography of conscious states',[162] and 'a cartography of the ecstatic and meditative states'.[163] His two primary assertions about these states are:

1. that they can be arranged on a continuum, with ecstatic states, such as 'mystical rapture' at one end, yogic sāmadhi (enstasis) at the other and normal consciousness in the middle; and

2. that these states are discontinuous with each other to the extent that our memory of events is tied to the state we were in when we first experienced them ('The greater the difference between these states, the more difficult it is to recall in one state specifics learned in another').[164]

Charles Tart calls Fischer's work 'an excellent example' of attempts to understand altered states of consciousness (ASCs) in neurological terms, though he goes on to qualify his approval by commenting that 'the conceptual gap between knowing that a certain neurological function changes during a given ASC, and understanding the experiential, psychological functioning of that ASC is enormous'.[165] Other writers are less circumspect. Robert Forman, for example, simply assumes the accuracy of Fischer's model and defines the nature of mysticism on the basis of it.[166] This model is, then, one that is worthy of careful scrutiny. The earliest version of the model was outlined in 1968 and is summarised in Figure 6.[167]

We may note, first of all, that the ten divisions on either side of the mid-point of the hemisphere indicate increasing or decreasing levels of arousal and movement away from what Fischer calls a state of equanimity or relaxation (number 1). Such movement is characterised, he claims, by 'the

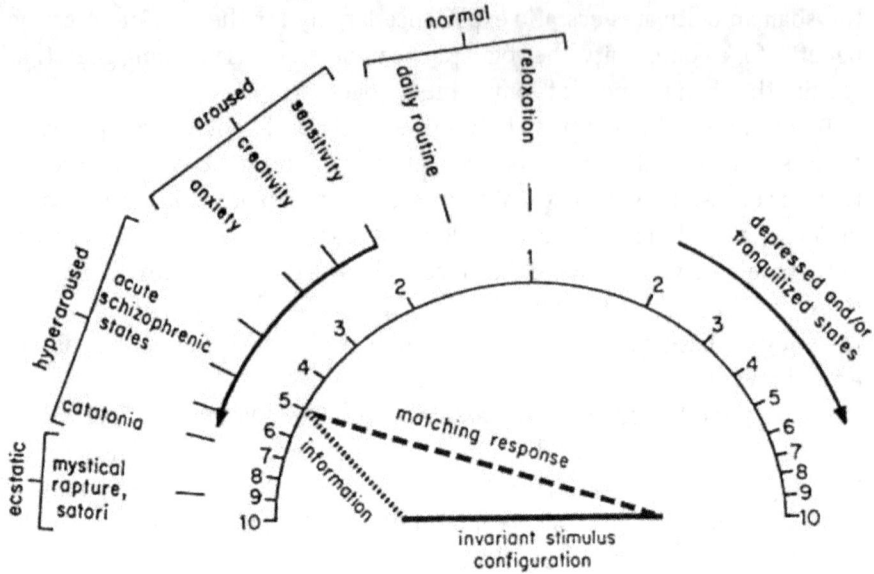

Figure 6 Roland Fischer's cartography of altered states.

gradual withdrawal from physical space-time to a combined sensory and cerebral space-time and finally at scale 10 to a cerebral space-time only', i.e. a switch from externally oriented to internally oriented attention.[168] We may also note that Fischer's main concern in the article from which the diagram is taken is to locate schizophrenic states on an arousal continuum which also embraces the experiences of people under the influence of a wide range of drugs and mystics having experiences of a rapturous or ecstatic nature. The connection between these groups is based primarily on the observation that all three demonstrated a pronounced invariability in their EEG profiles, that is, all were unresponsive to a range of external stimuli. He also noted that the schizophrenics and the drug users exhibited an increase in saccadic eye movements during their periods of reduced responsiveness to environmental inputs, along with a reduction in the extensiveness of their environmental scanning. In other words, they were 'hyperattentive to *selected* aspects of the visual field while minimally responsive to many ordinarily attended to aspects of the environment'[169]. Discussions with colleagues led him to conclude, however, that the experiences of Zen and Yoga masters are not accompanied by increases in the frequency of saccadic eye movements, which, in turn, meant that the schizophrenics and drug users were in a *non-alpha state* (i.e. not displaying alpha rhythms on their EEG outputs). By contrast, the meditators were in a *high alpha state.* Fischer's reflections on this separation of

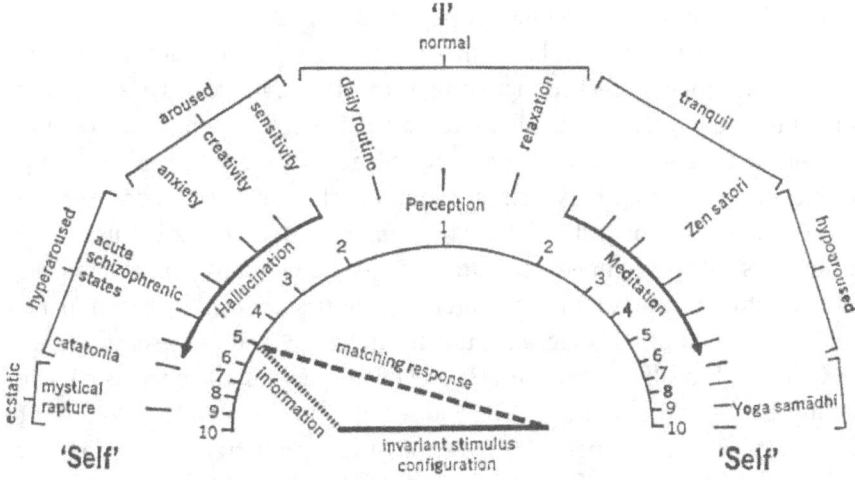

Figure 7 Fischer's model: version 2.

schizophrenics and drug takers from meditators led him to develop a second version of the model (Figure 7).[170]

Here we may note that the satori experience has shifted from the extreme left of the hyperarousal continuum and now occupies a position roughly halfway down the hypoarousal continuum on the right. This newly created hypoarousal continuum deletes the movement descriptors 'depressed and/or tranquillised states' and replaces them with 'meditation'. 'Hallucination is added as a descriptor to the opposite continuum and 'Yoga sāmadhi' becomes the end point of the meditation continuum.

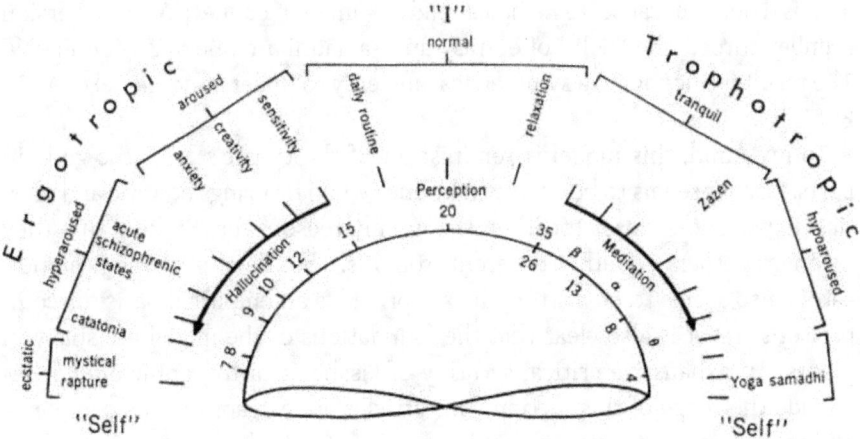

Figure 8 Fischer's model: version 3.

The third version of the model (Figure 8)[171] adds the terms 'ergotropic' and 'trophotropic' to the hallucination and meditation continua respectively. 'Ergotropic' refers to increasing sympathetic nervous system activity (accompanied by a reduction in motor activity) while 'trophotropic refers to increasing parasympathetic nervous system activity (again accompanied by a reduction in motor activity). The symmetry of the stage two model is broken, however, by the substitution of the hemispheric curve indicating movement from physical space-time to cerebral space-time with one that is composed of two different measurement strategies. The first, which is predominantly on the left side of the diagram, runs from 7 to 35 and represents changes in Goldstein's coefficient of variation – which specifies 'the decrease in variability of the EEG amplitude ...'[172] The second, numbers 26 to 4, 'refer(s) to those beta, alpha and theta EEG waves (measured in hertz) that predominate during, but are not specific to, these states'.[173] By 'these states' he presumably means Zazen (which replaces Zen satori) and Yoga Samādhi. The final change in this version is the addition of a figure of eight loop connecting the two ends of the hemisphere. This, he states, 'represents the rebound from ecstasy to samādhi, which is observed in response to intense ergotropic excitation'.[174] No mention is made at this point of the rebound from samādhi to ecstasy, though in later publications he describes this as the kuṇḍalinī experience.[175]

The final version of the model came in 1976 and remained stable for the next decade (Figure 9). There are few substantial changes here. The hemisphere pattern has been replaced by an almost circular one, the awkward EEG listings have been deleted and a number of Hindi/Sanskrit terms designating stages in yogic absorption according to Patañjali, author of the *Yoga Sūtra*, have been introduced to balance up the headings. Finally, the figure of eight loop is deleted because, as he had already claimed in connection with version number three, 'The "Self" of ecstasy and samādhi are one and the same'.[176] The result is once again a symmetrical and easy to understand model of ASCs. But is it accurate?

To my mind, this model is reminiscent of the curate's egg: it is good in parts. Fischer seems to be on the right lines when he brings ecstatic and mystical experiences closer together, though my reasons for thinking that they belong together are rather different from his. The use of physiological indicators also seems to be a strength as it provides an empirical basis for comparisons. Yet it is also clear that the foundations of the model are shaky in places. An exhaustive critical scrutiny of Fischer's cartographic efforts lies outside the scope of this section – his articles are extraordinarily complex – and indeed, is unnecessary for my purposes. My aim here is simply to show that there are sufficient problems with this model to make it an unreliable

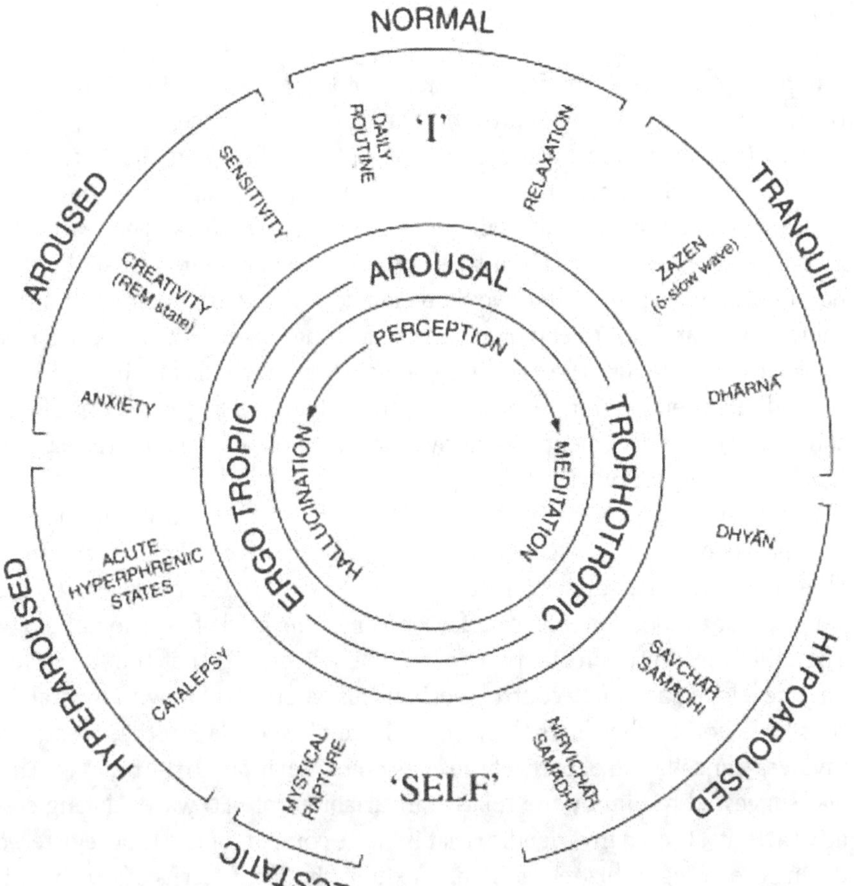

Figure 9   Fischer's model: version 4.

guide to the territory of ASCs generally and to the relations between ecstasy and enstasy in particular. To this end, I shall focus on four threads or themes running through his work:

1. the tendency to lump together phenomena without giving sufficient consideration of the differences between them;
2. the limitations of the continuum style of representation;
3. Fischer's knowledge of Buddhism and Yoga; and
4. problems with the relationship between the states at the ends of his continua, namely ecstasy and samādhi (= enstasy).

Lumping together

The perception–hallucination continuum of Fischer's model presents creativity, REM sleep, anxiety, schizophrenia, catatonia, psychedelic drug experiences (not displayed on the diagrams but significant in the texts) and mystical/ecstatic experiences as variants or intensifications of the same underlying processes. To my mind this is premature, to say the least. The postulated connection between these experiences has some plausibility but no more than that. Indeed, it would be fair to regard his first article on this subject as an attempt to explore the extent of that plausibility. The evidence he deploys to establish the feasibility of his continuum falls far short of what I would call a demonstration, however. Rather than developing a series of reasonably rigorous arguments Fischer weaves a net out of the tentative speculations of a number of writers.

One of the writers whose work is significant for Fischer is D.W. Mackinnon, who points out that the scores of many highly creative people on the eight clinical scales of the Minnesota Multiphasic Personality Inventory (MMPI) are very similar to those of people suffering from some kind of psychopathology. The difference between the two groups, he suggests, is that the 'creatives' have developed adequate control mechanisms whereas those with mental illness have not. Fischer links this with Goldstein's speculation that creativity involves 'cancellation of parts of the environmental input to the brain'.[177] This was suggested to him by the relative invariability of EEG waves during creative activity. It is an invariability that is 'quite comparable' to that registered during dreaming. Schizophrenics also exhibit similar patterns of EEG invariability, as, apparently, do Zen and Yoga meditators.

These commonalities are certainly suggestive, but they are far from being conclusive, as Fisher's own evidence clearly indicates. For example, people under the influence of LSD, psilocybin and mescaline also display highly selective attention and share with schizophrenics a high frequency of saccadic eye movements. On the other hand, the meditators, he claims, do not exhibit these eye movements. This discrepancy eventually led him, in version two of the model, to move the meditators off the perception – hallucination continuum altogether and locate them on one of their own: the perception-meditation continuum. But what about the creative thinkers, the dreamers, the anxious and the catatonic? Do any of them exhibit high frequency saccadic eye movements? We are not told. And what about the ecstatic mystics who were left behind at the end of the perception-hallucination continuum when the Zen and Yoga practitioners changed places? Did they, unlike their Zen and Yoga brethren, exhibit high frequency saccadic eye movements? Again, we are not told. Indeed, we are not even given a source for the claim that Zen and Yoga mediators do not exhibit these eye movements. This is still awaiting confirmation. There are certainly some similarities between these states, but there are differences too and Fischer does not supply the evidence to demonstrate that the former are more significant than the latter; and it is surely inappropriate – on the basis of links like these – to claim, as Fischer does, that 'daily we experience during the transition stages from waking to sleeping, and vice versa, a complete range of psychopathology – the features common to all psychoses'.[178] Indeed, in his construction of the entire perception-hallucination continuum Fischer appears to have committed the simple but significant error of going beyond the evidence.

The continuum pattern

For Fischer, not only are creativity, dreaming, anxiety schizophrenia, catatonia and ecstasy related states, they are related in a particular way. They constitute stages on a continuum of hyperarousal and hallucination. Given the nature of the evidence this is an amazingly bold claim to make. If the people experiencing creative thinking, dreaming, anxiety, schizophrenia, psychedelic drugs and mystic rapture all had their physiology measured in the same way, and there was a clear indication of directionality in the results then there might be ground for constructing a continuum. The foundations for Fischer's continuum are rather different, however. No one measurement runs all the way through. In his 1969, 1971 and 1986 versions of the model Fischer claims that the hyperaroused states are characterised by:

1. an increase in muscle tone;
2. a decrease in skin resistance;
3. fast habituation to alpha blocking;
4. mydriasis – extreme dilation of the pupil of the eye;
5. hyperthermia – an increase in body temperature;
6. piloerection – erection of head and/or body hair;
7. hyperglycaemia – increase in blood sugar; and
8. tachycardia – an increase in heart rate.

If the states on the perception–hallucination continuum could be shown to display increases in these measures as they move towards the extreme then the case for the existence of a continuum would be a strong one. But Fischer does not show that they do. For many of the states that he locates on this continuum, which include glossolalia (speaking in tongues), automatic or mediumistic writing and the trance dance of the Shaker religion, no sources of information are provided.[179] Where they are provided it is clear that not all the states were monitored for all the phenomena. What seems to have happened is that Fischer became so convinced of the validity of his model that he simply extrapolated findings about one or perhaps two states to all the rest.

We may note in this context that some of the writers who have studied the phenomena of glossolalia in considerable depth, Felicitas Goodman for example, argue that they are simply variants of a single trance state that she calls the ecstatic religious trance, which also embraces experiences of possession by a spirit or deity.[180] On Fischer's continuum this state would probably have to be located after anxiety but before catatonia as it involves a considerable amount of movement. Yet it is strange to think, as Fischer invites us to do, that someone who is moving around and speaking in the voice of a deity is in a less aroused condition than a catatonic or a mystic sitting quietly while experiencing hallucinations.

Buddhism and Yoga

The measurements which differentiate the states on the perception-meditation continuum present us with a different kind of problem. Apart from a few small-scale studies of Zen and Yoga meditators, mainly with the EEG, Fischer's sources for the construction of this continuum are scholars seeking to describe the contents of some Hindu and Buddhist religious texts. They are not always reliable, and Fischer's statements about the relationship between Buddhism and Yoga are clearly based on misunderstandings. For example, he claims that 'The jhāna of early Buddhism ... was not yet identified with meditation, contemplation or yoga. Jhāna represented loneliness as a spiritual process ...'.[181] The fact is that 'jhāna' *was* understood as a form of what we would call meditation or contemplation as can be seen, for example in the account of the Buddha's enlightenment in the *Mahā-saccaka-sutta* of the *Majjhima Nikāya*.[182] Moreover, this and other early descriptions of the jhāna states divide them into stages or levels which closely parallel Patañjali's later accounts of the stages of yogic samādhi. Fischer also claims that 'śunyatā implies a philosophy of zero, which contains nothing in itself ... the mystical self and the concept of zero thus share a common meaning that may be infinitely enlarged or diminished as a function of place value'.[183] This idea, that the Buddhist notion of śūnyatā (emptiness) can somehow be equated with 'the mystical self' is completely misguided. For Buddhists 'the mystical self' has no reality, and śūnyatā means the absence of self-existence (svabhāva) in all phenomena, not nothingness. The perception-meditation continuum is, then, constructed out of quite different materials from the perception-hallucination one and is substantially based on what is obviously a rather superficial acquaintance with the traditions to which he refers.

The ends of the continua

The people whose experiences are taken by Fischer to exemplify the state of ecstatic mystical rapture include St Theresa of Avila, St Francis of Assisi, Blaise Pascal, Sri Ramakrishna,[184] and St Catherine of Sienna.[185] These mystics are contrasted with the Zen and Yoga masters. Unlike these masters the experiences of the mystics are non-alpha states and are accompanied by an increase in saccadic eye movements. The obvious question here is 'who measured them?' and the answer is, of course, 'no one'. No measurements support his location of these mystics at the end of the perception-hallucination continuum. He seems to have simply noted that they report having visionary experiences and decided that this is where they belong. Moreover, as Fischer himself observes, these ecstatic mystics have much in common with Buddhist and Yogic meditators. In one of his earliest articles on this subject he suggests that the descriptions of mystical rapture provided by St Theresa are 'well in line' with the results of EEG studies of Indian yoga practitioners,[186] and in a later piece he argues that St Theresa, the teachers of the Upaniṣads, Jacob Bohme and Al Ghazzali all describe their experiences in a way that makes it 'very difficult to distinguish one from another'.[187] Later in the same article he also claims that Ignatius of Loyola 'provides methods of procedure that are for all practical purposes identical with some of the Eastern meditation practices ...'.[188]

Fischer's method for dealing with the fact that highly similar experiences occupy the two poles of his combined continuum is to employ the concept of 'rebound' and to bring them to a point of seeming unity in the idea of a deep or transpersonal self. This solution is, however, unsatisfactory – for a number of reasons. In the first place he is introducing the concept of rebound into accounts that have no place for it. For example, in the early Buddhist texts of the Pāli Canon the attainment of right concentration (sammā samādhi) leads on to right knowledge (sammā ñāna) and right release (sammā vimutti), not a kuṇḍalinī experience. Similarly, in Patañjali's *Yoga Sūtra* – from where

Fischer takes his Sanskrit terminology – the experience of nirvicāra samāpatti leads to the arising of truth-bearing insight (ṛtambharā prajñā), which, in turn, facilitates the experience of samādhi without seed (nirbīja samādhi), and again there is no mention of a kuṇḍalinī experience. In short, the texts on which Fischer relies simply do not support his idea that pushing at the limits of the experiences he has placed at either end of his continuum produces a shift into the experience characteristic of the opposite pole.

A second reason for rejecting Fischer's solution lies in the fact that the mystics and meditators to whom he refers are far from unanimous in proclaiming the experience of a mystical or transpersonal self as the pinnacle of their endeavours. St Theresa, for example, describes the final stage of her mystical path as an experience of union with God, the consummation of her Spiritual Marriage, 'it is like rain falling from the heavens into a river or a spring; there is nothing but water there and it is impossible to divide or separate the water belonging to the river from that which fell from the heavens'.[189] This is certainly similar to the kind of account we find in the Upaniṣads but quite different from the radical separation of self from matter that we find in the Jain, Sāṃkhya and Classical Yoga traditions. The Buddha, mystic par excellence, would also reject Fischer's claim since his experiences of samādhi led him to a knowledge that everything, including the unconditioned nirvāṇa, was without self. The Self is a metaphysical entity, accepted by some mystics and rejected by others; it cannot, therefore, act as a common denominator for all mystical experiences. Nor can it be presented as the pinnacle of all mystical experiences without relegating those which lack it to a lower level – an unjustifiable metaphysical ploy from my perspective. How would one set about showing, for example, that the Buddha (who denied self) was less accomplished than Patañjali (who affirmed it)? As it stands, Fischer's model contains too many tensions, inconsistencies and speculations to function as a reliable map of the terrain of ASCs.

My model of ASCs and spirituality

If I were to attempt a revision of Fischer's model I would, first of all, take the category of mystical rapture from the end of the perception–hallucination continuum and place it somewhere along the perception meditation continuum. The heading of ecstasy would also be moved across, though not attached to mystical rapture. This would place phenomena that are clearly similar to each other closer together on the map while, at the same time, distancing them from others with which they seem to have only a tenuous connection.

Then I would separate the two continua from each other. My comments on the perception–hallucination continuum will, of necessity, be rather brief as this is a technical field that lies beyond my competence; so I happily hand it over to those better qualified than I for such a task. Finally, I would rework the perception–meditation continuum as follows. The two poles are *normal consciousness* and *trance*.

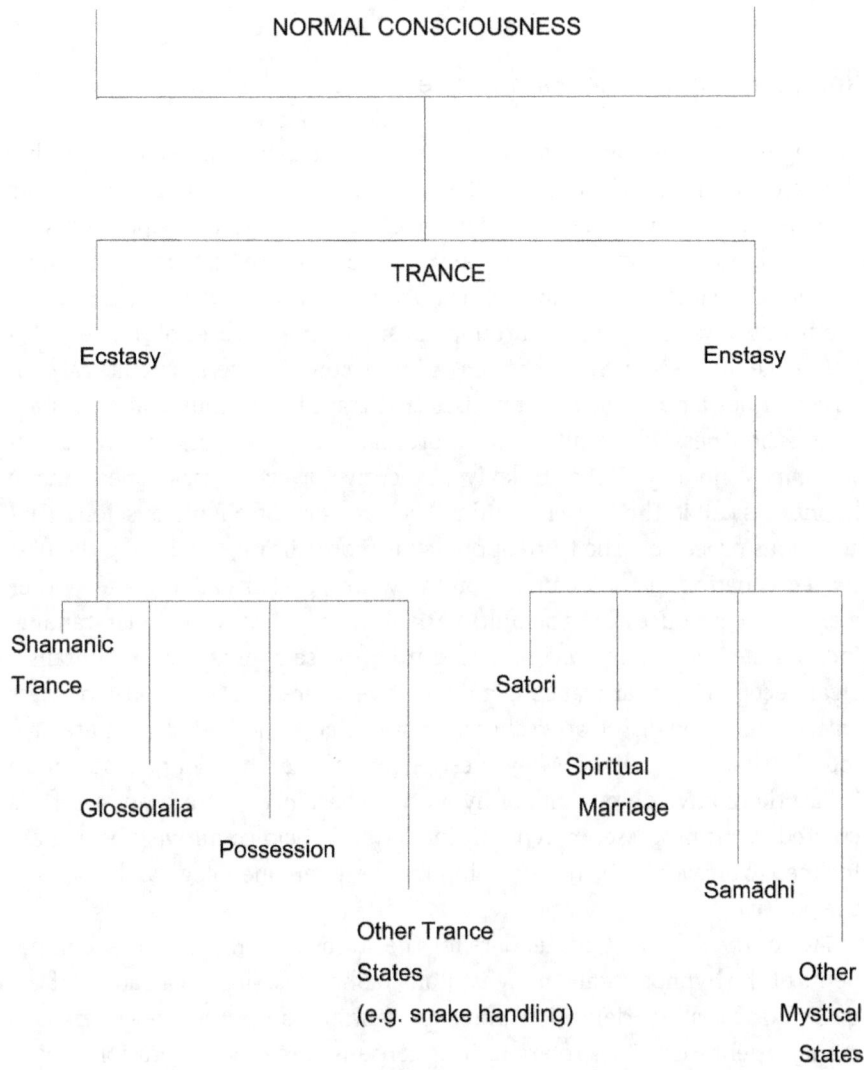

Figure 10 Spiritual experiences from the perspective of trance phenomena.

This arrangement does *not* constitute a continuum, a concept which, to me at least, suggests passing *through* the states closer to the centre in order to get to those at the extremes. Rather, this diagram attempts to show, first and foremost, that the experiences listed under the headings of *ecstasy* and *enstasy* (= samādhi) are all varieties of trance experience. Secondly, it indicates that some kinds of trance experiences are more closely related than others. The key question then becomes: 'can this way of representing these experiences be shown to be accurate?' I think it can.

Religious experiences and trance states

Among hypnosis researchers there are three broad approaches to explaining the nature of trance. The first is that which emphasises socio-cognitive factors such as role-play and imaginative involvement in suggested experiences. In short, this approach explains away any feature of trance that provide it with a distinctive character. This view would be compatible with what could be called the strong version of cultural artefactualism: all the features of trance states that make them seem different from ordinary consciousness are cultural constructs. Another approach emphasises that trance is a genuine altered state of consciousness which differs from ordinary consciousness in a variety of ways, most notably in that reflexive, executive or ego consciousness (many hypnotists call it 'the conscious mind') is dissociated from unconscious/subconscious processes. The third approach is more diffuse, combining the first two explanations and, depending on the writer, perhaps adding a few other elements to produce a kind of multi-variable theory.[190] My own understanding inclines me towards the second and third of these approaches and entails a clear recognition that trance is a distinctive altered state of consciousness with pronounced dissociative characteristics that is, nevertheless, quite profoundly shaped by culture. A key question for anyone who adopts this position is 'are there any components of hypnotic experience that are not artefacts created by the processes of hypnotic induction?' Socio-cognitive theorists are inclined to answer in the negative, interactive-phenomenological theorists in the positive.

Two of the strongest contenders for the status of non-artefactual components of the hypnotic state are what Ronald Shor describes as a 'fading of the generalized reality orientation' and experiential absorption. The generalised reality orientation (Tart refers to it as consensus reality orientation)[191] is 'a structured frame of reference in the background of attention which supports, interprets, and gives meaning to all experiences'.[192] It is what sociologist

Peter Berger would call our internalised socially constructed reality.[193] Many hypnotists use the rather vaguer phrase 'conscious mind' to refer to this orientation. Absorption is 'the sense of being caught up in the phenomena or content of the session or in the phenomena experienced'.[194] Fromm and Kahn found that the only structural and state-related common features of auto/self and hetero/other hypnosis were these two factors.[195] In different words they can be seen to form the core of Gilligan's definition of trance: 'a state of deep experiential absorption where a person can operate independently of the constraints of regulatory, error-oriented conscious processes'.[196] In short, the ability to experience trance is common to all humans, though some may have a greater talent for it than others, but cultures differ in the value they place upon it, the extent to which they cultivate it and the purposes for which they employ it.

There is also some intriguing research on the neurology of imagination in ordinary consciousness and after hypnotic induction. In 2008, the BBC, in conjunction with the Open University, produced a documentary programme on hypnotherapy.[197] One of the researchers interviewed by the presenter (Professor Kathy Sykes of Bristol University) was Professor Irving Kirsch, who was using fMRI scanning at the University of Modena in Italy to explore differences in brain activity when people were asked to 'see' colours in a black and white line drawing while in normal consciousness and then after experiencing an hypnotic induction. The results, from just a small sample, indicated that when the activity was undertaken in normal consciousness areas of what appeared to be the parietal lobes at the top of the brain lit up. By contrast, after hypnotic induction the same task lit up areas of the visual cortex at the back of the brain. In other words, after hypnosis the subjective experience of the participants seemed to be perceptual in character whereas in normal consciousness it seemed to be imaginative. Hypnosis, it seems, can make imaginative experience mimic perceptual experience.

The kinds of trance states most well known to inhabitants of the industrialised west are those usually associated with hypnosis or hypnotism (the terms are pretty much interchangeable). The term 'trance' is, however, preferable to 'hypnosis' despite the fact that it is difficult to avoid using the nomenclature of hypnosis when exploring trance phenomena. One of the main reasons for this is that the word 'hypnosis' is derived from the Greek 'hypnos' meaning sleep, and since hypnotic states have little in common with sleep states the term is actually a misnomer – though 'sleep' commands are remarkably effective during hypnotic procedures, especially in the context of stage hypnosis. There is, nevertheless, a growing body of evidence to indicate that the relaxation and sleep-like characteristics often associated with hypnotised persons are actually artefacts of the induction procedure rather than intrinsic features of the hypnotic or trance state itself.

The subjects of a stage hypnotist who perform a wide range of, often amusing, antics are in trance throughout the performance as are those people who engage in an action on the basis of post-hypnotic suggestion. In this latter case the cue they have been prompted to act upon re-induces the trance state.[198] As Robert Temple points out, it is active states of trance that are most commonly referred to in anthropological literature, some writers actually restricting the use of the term 'trance' to such active conditions. Hypnosis researchers have tended to go in the opposite direction and 'persist in believing that all trances must involve subjects drifting off to sleep-like states with suggestions of drowsiness'.[199] Things have begun to change, however.

Perhaps starting with W.R. Wells in the 1920s, a few researchers have been exploring the relationship between hypnotic trance, where participants are encouraged to relax, and what Arnold Ludwig and William Lyle call alert or hyper-alert trance.[200] These two types of trance have been found to be similar in terms of eliciting the characteristic hypnotic phenomena such as analgesia, perceptual distortions and involuntary movements, as well as in terms of subjects passing easily from one kind of trance to the other. As Bányai and Hilgard comment, in alert trance 'all the important characteristics of hypnosis occur except the resemblance to sleep'.[201]

Some notable differences have also been observed. In hypnotic trance subjects are physically relaxed whereas in alert trance they frequently display tension or rigidity. In hypnotic trance the experience of a blank mind is common during periods when the hypnotist is not making suggestions, whereas those who have experienced alert trance frequently report a cascade of thoughts and emotions. In hypnotic trance subjects often describe a deep sense of calm and mental tranquillity whereas in alert trance they tend to talk more about having ecstatic or peak experiences.[202] The method of induction can, then, shape subsequent experience in quite profound ways, and it is tempting to connect the mystical-numinous distinction with the hypnotic-alert one.

Another reason for preferring the term 'trance' to 'hypnosis' is that the latter is frequently understood to be something that one person does to another. Certainly trance states can be induced by one person talking to, touching or making passes over another. But they can be induced in other ways as well, not all of which involve another person. Individuals can put themselves into trances (auto-hypnosis) as well as have other people do it for them (hetero-hypnosis).[203] Many rituals link the two by providing a socially constructed context for the facilitation of auto-hypnotic strategies. Stephen Gilligan offers the following as a list of trance induction techniques:

rhythmic and repetitive movement (dancing, running, rocking, breathing exercises, etc.); chanting (meditation, prayer, group rituals, chants at rallies or sports events, the repetitive self-talk of depression, etc.); attentional absorption (on a mantra, the hypnotist's voice, an image, an idea, the television, etc.); and balancing of muscle tonus (via relaxation processes, massage, drugs such as alcohol or valium, rhythmic movement, etc.).[204]

We could add to this list factors such as exposure to stress,[205] extended periods of solitude, tension manoeuvres,[206] and loss of bodily equilibrium combined with a loud noise.[207] This last technique is frequently employed by revivalist preachers in the USA who invite people on stage to accept Jesus into their hearts. The person, already in a state of heightened arousal, is positioned with the preacher by their side. The preacher then places one hand on the person's lower back and the other on their forehead and, simultaneously, presses the lower back (causing the person to be off balance – loss of bodily equilibrium) while saying in a loud, commanding voice, something like 'accept Jesus' (the loud noise). This combination tends to have the effect of temporarily switching off the person's conscious processes and opens them up to suggestion. Such preachers often use 'catchers', who catch the person when he/she falls over as a result of the induction. The catcher is well placed to make suggestions while the person is in a highly receptive state, i.e. will tend to believe what is suggested. So, if the catcher says something like 'Jesus is in control of your life; just trust in Jesus and follow his commands', then the person will tend to go along with the suggestion. However, old habits and behaviour patterns will tend to re-emerge; so for this type of suggestion to have long-term effects follow-up sessions are often required.[208]

Whatever their means of induction one thing that all trances have in common, according to Gilligan, is that they 'tend to decrease the discontinuous, arrhythmic movements of deliberate conscious orientation, thus giving rise to a more unified mode of experience'.[209] At the heart of trance experience then is what we might call the displacement of the conscious mind, other terms for which are reflexive consciousness and ego. The conscious mind performs a number of important mental functions. It 'can be thought of as a blackboard available to all the various subsystems of the brain'.[210] It is thus a link between these subsystems and, as such, has an integrating function – particularly through memory which, as Peter Brown puts it, is 'the matrix of personal identity'.[211] It works, according to Gilligan, by 'structuring information into action frames or programs (mental sets) and sequencing and computing conceptual relationships'.[212] It is also highly sensitive to context, that is, it is realistic. It is the locus of what Ronald Shor calls the generalised reality orientation.[213] This makes it conservative rather than creative, more of a manager than an artist. Both yogic and zazen (mindfulness) meditations inhibit the activity of the conscious mind, though in different ways, and can thus be understood as forms of trance induction, one through the cultivation of focal attention and the inhibition of global attention; the other through the opposite.[214]

The conscious mind is permissive rather than initiatory. It can allow ideas emerging from the subconscious/unconscious to be implemented in behaviour or it can veto them. This power of veto enables the conscious mind to ensure that implemented ideas conform to the frame or map of the world with which it is operating. The way the veto functions is, in part, by the narrowing of attention to what Gilligan calls 'frame-relevant stimuli'. Such attentional control both arises from and is maintained by muscular tension patterns.[215] The conscious mind is not, however, an entirely unitary process. Ernest Hilgard, for example, distinguishes between what he calls the executive and the monitoring functions. He writes:

> Central executive functions are responsible for planning in relation to goals, initiating action commensurate with these plans, and sustaining action against obstacles and distractions.[216]

The monitor, by contrast,

> has a scanning function that includes alertness to all that is taking place, a recognition of the familiar, and a readiness for the unexpected ... In addition to scanning and selection the monitoring function includes a critical or judgmental role, based on feedback from initiated action as what is done is compared with intended goals and performances.[217]

The only really contentious point in this description of conscious processes is the claim that executive processes initiate action. Drawing on research carried out by Benjamin Libet during 1985, the year that Hilgard revised *Divided Consciousness*, Robert Ornstein argues that even when action appears to be initiated by conscious processes it is subconscious ones that are often the real driving force. Libet's work was concerned with what he called 'readiness potential' brainwaves. These occur only before movements we experience as being consciously willed whether they be calculated or spontaneous. They begin around a second before we become conscious of making a decision to act. It seems then, that even many of the activities which seem to be initiated by our conscious selves would appear to be generated subconsciously – albeit in response to a consciously thought out plan.[218]

When the conscious mind is displaced or dissociated subconscious processes are given a free rein as it were, guided only by the directions of the hypnotist, the social context or some goal determined prior to or during the induction procedure. Trance experience is thus significantly different from ordinary experience. Gilligan enumerates and describes its principal features. These include attentional absorption, involuntariness, immersion in experiential and symbolic rather than conceptual processing, enhanced suggestibility, perceptual flexibility, trance logic and a tendency to be amnesic for trance experiences on return to ordinary consciousness.[219]

One thing that emerges from a consideration of this list is that the experience of trance is rarely an end in itself. Usually it is a means to the attainment of some other end. It is something like the neutral gear in a car. Changing from one gear to another usually involves engaging or passing through neutral first. Another analogy might be the wood between the worlds in C.S. Lewis's story *The Magician's Nephew*. The wood was a place of transit. From there one could go to many other worlds. Such an understanding of trance is completely in accord with the term's Latin origins in the words *transitus* (a passage) and *transire* (to pass over). Trance states can thus provide the psychological conditions for the elicitation and exploration of a wide range of experiences.

In hypnotherapy a common distinction is that which is made between trance induction and trance utilisation. Induction refers to the methods employed for generating trance states, utilisation to the purposes for which they are employed and the techniques for achieving those ends. A trance state is relatively easy to elicit in a substantial proportion of the population by using standard induction techniques. What distinguishes the skilful hypnotherapist from the novice or the dabbler is the way in which the person is guided once in the trance state. Cultures employ trance for different purposes. In some it is employed to alleviate psychological and emotional distress, in others it is used to create memories and change identity and in yet others it is a means of facilitating possession by a deity, spirit or animal.[220]

Often, the method of induction will have a significant effect on the kind of experience a person has once they enter a trance state, i.e. on utilisation. As noted above, people who undergo traditional-style hypnotic inductions with suggestions for relaxation and/or sleep (which may be administered by oneself: auto-hypnosis, or by someone else: hetero-hypnosis) tend to describe a deep sense of calm or tranquillity and sometimes a state of complete mental blankness.[221] By contrast, people who undergo active-alert style inductions are more likely to report having ecstatic (in the everyday sense) or peak experiences. Dream images tend to be more joyous and benign after active-alert inductions[222] and post hypnotic amnesia more complete.[223] Maya Deren, an American convert to Voodoo (Vodun/Vodou/Vouduon), contrasts the experiences of hypnosis and possession as follows:

> the entire experience of possession is in the opposite direction from that of hypnosis. Hypnosis could be described as going inward and downward, whereas possession is accompanied by a sense of explosion upward and outward. One might say that hypnosis is the ultimate in self-negation, whereas possession is the ultimate in self-realisation to the point of self-transcendence.[224]

She, like Eliade and Fischer, seems to regard these experiences as opposites. However, as Ludwig and Lyle point out, both kinds of induction procedure produce essentially the same kinds of alterations in consciousness, alterations to which many researchers apply the label 'trance':

> Although the subjects' clinical state appeared opposite to that seen following standard hypnotic induction – i.e. relaxed and drowsy – subjects easily achieved all the hypnotic phenomena generally described for good hypnotic subjects and with the same degree of convincing behaviour.[225]

They also point out that 'subjects could be trained to pass easily from the hyperalert trance to the "sleepy" hypnotic trance, and vice versa ...'[226] Similar comments are made by other authors.[227]

Traditionally, the induction techniques employed for the creation of possession states (e.g. by shamans, healers and members of religious groups such as Candomblé and Voodoo) are typically those used to create a hyperalert/active-alert trance in the laboratory. And like some of the laboratory subjects practitioners of these traditional methods tend, when not amnesic, to report having ecstatic experiences.[228] For example, the experience of a Balinese Sang Hyang Jaran dancer, who dances on fire in trance, is described by Suryani and Jensen as follows:

> When he saw the fire, he felt that 'a power' had entered his body. He was happy to see the fire and he felt physically big and energetic. As the fire got bigger, he became happier and more eager to begin his performance. While dancing, his body felt light, his movements fluid, and he enjoyed touching the fire.[229]

In the course of describing her own experience of possession during a dance ritual, Maya Deren writes,

> So focused was I, at that time, upon the effort to endure, that I did not even mark the moment when this ceased to be difficult and I cannot say whether it was sudden or gradual but only that my awareness of it was a sudden thing, as if the pace which had seemed unbearably demanding had slipped down a notch into slow motion, so that my mind had time, now, to wander, to observe at leisure, what a splendid thing it was, indeed, to hear the drums, to move like this, to be able to do all this so easily, to do even more if it pleased one,

to elaborate to extend this movement of the arms towards greater elegance, or to counterpoint that rhythm of the heel or even to make this movement to the side, this time.[230]

We may also note that the preparation for the experience of possession has many parallels with the preparation a person would undergo for deep trance identification (DTI), in which the aim is to copy as fully as possible the behaviour of another individual. First of all, both sets of trainees have to become proficient in the induction and utilisation of trance experiences. For the initiate in Candomblé this usually involves about three months of training, which includes periods of intense learning such as three weeks complete seclusion.[231] Hypnotic subjects have to learn a range of hypnotic skills, one of the most important of which is becoming amnesic for their own identity. Another important aspect of the learning of both groups is the development of a rich internal representation of the person or deity with whom the identification is to be made. I'm not sure exactly how this is accomplished within Candomblé but in DTI it involves the trainee imaginatively, in trance of course, stepping into the other person's body and experiencing their mannerisms, behaviour, body posture and movement, feelings etc., from the inside as it were.[232]

One of the most effective techniques for facilitating DTI is the age regression of the person to childhood, where 'pretend realities' are more vivid and their adult identity suspended or displaced, and then go on to develop the identification. In the Candomblé tradition entry into and exit out of the state of possession involves the experience of 'ere'. As Gilbert Rouget describes it:

> the novice in a state of ere behaves in a wholly infantile manner ... the ere state is one of depersonalisation whose role in the initiation process is easily understood. For this process consists, in practice, as much in losing one's familiar personality as in acquiring a new one, and this loss is indeed a necessary condition for this acquisition process.[233]

To my mind the parallels between the preparations for DTI and possession by an Orisha are just too strong to be coincidental. The obvious conclusion is that, like dissociative identity disorder (formerly known as multiple personality disorder) and involuntary possession, deep trance identification and voluntary possession are simply different cultural variants of the same phenomenon.

Likewise, the activities of mystics and meditators are essentially the same as those employed in traditional hypnosis: stillness of body, attentional focus on a single outside point or internally, gradual absorption in inner experience and loss of awareness of the outside world. Most meditators do this for themselves, though usually according to the directions of a spiritual preceptor/guru, or according to some familiar set of instructions. In some instances, however, the experience is achieved under the direct influence of the teacher, who leads the practitioner through the journey with verbal instruction.[234] The results are also strikingly similar. The progressive experience in Buddhist jhāna and yogic samādhi is one of a reduction in the content of experience which brings with it a fading of the sense of personal identity, exactly the kinds of experiences reported by subjects in deep hypnosis.[235]

Consider the twelve 'phenomenological characteristics common in the experience of trance' described by Gilligan:

1. experiential absorption of attention;
2. effortless expression;
3. experiential, nonconceptual involvement;
4. willingness to experiment;
5. flexibility in time/space relations;
6. alteration of sensory experience;
7. fluctuation in involvement;
8. motoric/verbal inhibition;
9. trance logic;
10. metaphorical processing;
11. time distortion; and
12. amnesia.[236]

We can see that a number of them are particularly relevant for an understanding of mystical experience. *Experiential absorption of attention* means that entranced people can become 'fully immersed in one particular experiential context for a sustained period'. *Effortless expression* refers to the absence of a need to try to do anything or to plan 'ahead'. Experience 'just seems to happen' and 'flows quite effortlessly'. *Experiential, nonconceptual involvement* refers to the fact that entranced individuals 'usually are quite immersed in experiential, rather than conceptual domains. They are more able to directly experience "things as they are" and generally show little need to logically understand or conceptually analyze experience'.[237] *Flexibility in time/space relations* means that 'the hypnotized person becomes unbound from fixation to a single time/space co-ordinate (the "present") thereby making available an infinite number of potential realities'. Hallucinations and perceptual distortions in all sense modalities are also common, as is 'both–and' or 'trance' logic and highly symbolic or metaphorical processing. All of these characteristics are frequently found in accounts of mystical experience.

Like mystical experiences, trance experiences can also be content-less or content-full. With regard to content-less experiences, Charles Tart comments that 'Typically, if a deeply hypnotized subject is asked what he is thinking about or experiencing, the answer is "Nothing"'.[238] As noted above, such an experience, a state of empty-mindedness, which sounds rather like a pure consciousness event, is almost certainly an artefact of the induction procedure, especially when we remember the differences that Ludwig and Lyle observed between 'hypnotic' and hyperalert trances: 'In the hypnotic trance, subjects claimed that their mind was 'blank' whereas, in the hyperalert trance, they commonly stated that all sorts of thoughts and emotions were racing through their minds during periods of time when the experimenters chose to remain silent'.[239]

As regards content-full experience, Tart points out that the hypnotic state is 'characterized by greatly enhanced suggestibility, a greater motility of attention/awareness energy, so when a particular experience is suggested to the subject he usually experiences it far more vividly than he could in his ordinary d-Soc [discrete state of consciousness], often to the point of experiential reality'.[240] In a similar vein, Fromm and Kahn comment that when practitioners of auto-hypnosis gained some experience in the procedure 'internal events at times took on a quality of verisimilitude comparable to the way in which one experiences external reality itself'.[241] This also applied to self-suggestions that auto-hypnotists made to themselves, usually through actively planning the tasks they intended to undertake in trance.[242] The general point to be noted, therefore, is that in trance states people can experience mental creations being as real or even more real than ordinary waking experience. Trances can facilitate what Joseph de Rivera and Theodore Sarbin call 'believed-in-imaginings'.[243]

Three other points are worth mentioning at this juncture. The first is that trance states often develop spontaneously, they do not always have to be cultivated. Michael Yapko claims that people can spontaneously enter trance states during conversations, watching television, reading and making love and in many other ways, e.g. highway hypnosis.[244] The second and related point is that trance experiences often have a quality of involuntariness about them. 'Things just seem to happen' as Gilligan puts it. The phenomenon of post-hypnotic suggestion is interesting in this connection because when a person engages in an action or thought process in response to a trigger stimulus that had been suggested during trance the trance state is re-evoked.[245] Many of our everyday behaviours are actually responses to trigger stimuli and a little self-reflection will reveal that most of these behaviours are little sequences which, once triggered, need to run to completion (e.g. vaulting horse gymnasts in the Amicable Life advertisement, or even a simple handshake).[246]

When such behaviours are disadvantageous to us but we have been unsuccessful in removing them we often experience that 'Oh, here we go again' feeling every time they are triggered. Such sequences, often called conditioned behaviour patterns, have the involuntary character of many trance states and may even be kinds of trance states themselves. If this is the case, and it certainly seems that it might be, then our entire lives are filled with entries into and exits out of trance states. Now the most effective way to modify behaviours that were laid down during trance states or are maintained through trance states, as every hypnotherapist knows, is by utilising trance itself – because in trance states there is a loosening of previously conditioned patterns. Insofar as religious experiences have a trance dimension they have the capacity to evoke a sense of freedom and even eradicate some of a person's previous conditioning (= 'forgiveness of sins' or 'eradication of karma'?).

Trance states can thus exhibit all the characteristics that James uses to describe mystical experiences: they often have a passive quality, experience 'just seems to happen' as Gilligan puts it; they are transient – if the hypnotised person does not bring him or herself out of trance or someone else does not do it for them, sleep will intervene at some point and they will return to normal consciousness on waking; they also have a noetic quality – the vivid images and feelings sometimes experienced in trance are often taken to be realities. With regard to William James's ineffability characteristic I am not aware of any claims that hypnotic experiences are ineffable. What is clear, however, is that since trance states, as characterised by Gilligan, often involve non-conceptual processing, alterations in sensory experience and the experience of time, trance logic (akin to the paradoxicality often reported in association with mystical experience?) and metaphorical processing we would expect people trying to describe their experiences of trance to struggle when trying to put them into words. In short, mystical states and trance states have many characteristics in common, are induced by similar methods and show similarities in the variations of experience that they produce. Indeed, the parallels are so marked that a reasonable conclusion would seem to be that there is more than a *prima facie* case for regarding mystical experiences as varieties of trance experience.

Table 7 Parallels between mystical and trance experiences.

Mystical experiences	Trance experiences
All involve the inhibition or diminution of conscious processing	All involve the inhibition or diminution of conscious processing
All or most of them seem to share the qualities of attentional absorption and a fading of the generalised reality orientation	All or most of them seem to share the qualities of attentional absorption and a fading of the generalised reality orientation
They can be self-induced or induced by someone else	They can be self-induced or induced by someone else
They can be internally or externally oriented	They can be internally or externally oriented
They can be induced by many different methods or events	They can be induced by many different methods or events
They can generate a wide range of experiences, from a complete blankness or emptiness of mind to vivid, reality-like images	They can generate a wide range of experiences, from a complete blankness or emptiness of mind to vivid, reality-like images
They can be cultivated or arise spontaneously	They can be cultivated or arise spontaneously
They can be used to rework or remove existing mental sets and behaviour patterns	They can be used to rework or remove existing mental sets and behaviour patterns

Table 7 illustrates in brief the nature of the link between a range of seemingly very different experiences. They are types of trance experience that are induced in quite different ways and employed for purposes that are often also quite different. Moreover, given the continuity between active alert and hypnotic trance states it is surely legitimate to bring mystical, visionary, ecstatic, enstatic and hypnotic experiences together under the general heading of *trance*.

Myths, religious rituals and trance states

A common way in which cultures and religious traditions mould individual experience is through ritual. All societies have their rituals, many of which are to be found in a religious context. From a phenomenological perspective, a primary function of religious ritual is the setting up of a channel of communication between sacred and profane realms, as with the sacrificial rituals described in the Hebrew Bible and the Sanskrit Veda. Often religious rituals are carried out in conjunction with the narration of a myth, which supplies the cosmic context for the ritual activities. The frequency of this association led some earlier scholars to claim that myth and ritual always go together. Not surprisingly, they came to be known as The Myth and Ritual School.[247] Subsequent research has demonstrated, however, that not all myths have a ritual accompaniment and not all rituals are embedded in mythic structures. Even so, the close connection between the two is undeniable. It is less common for scholars to connect ritual activity with the generation of trance states, though that has begun to change in recent decades. Here I shall review some of the material that enables us to investigate these links.

This relationship between myth and ritual has been explored in some interesting ways by psychiatrist Eugene d'Aquili and anthropologist Charles Laughlin Jr.[248] According to these writers, the primary function of ritual is to reduce the sense of distance and separation between members of the same species whose survival depends on co-operation with their fellows.[249] The reason ritual is able to generate feelings of connectedness with others is that, in group contexts, ritual generally involves the repetition of rhythmic patterns which have the tendency to arouse the limbic system of the brain, the centre of control over the emotions.[250] In human beings, it appears to be the case that 'repetitive auditory and visual stimuli can drive cortical rhythms and eventually produce an intensely pleasurable, ineffable experience ...'[251] In group situations such rhythms are synchronised in all participants. Thus, participation in group rituals provides human beings with a biologically based method for creating group solidarity.

Such effects are mediated through the autonomic nervous system with its sympathetic and parasympathetic divisions. The former excites the organism, producing, as one of its outcomes, the fight or flight response, while the latter maintains the homeostatic balance in the body and is responsible for the baseline functioning of many organs. Normally, these systems are complementary. When one is active the other is dormant. Exposure to rhythmic stimuli, however, can eventually lead to both discharging electro-chemical stimuli into the body at the same time. It is this simultaneous high discharge that generates the pleasure. En route to this state a reversal phenomenon is often observed. This occurs when the active system starts to respond to stimuli that would normally trigger its counterpart.[252] Another, possibly related, kind of reversal phenomenon occurs in what Pavlov called the ultra-paradoxical phase of transmarginal inhibition. In this condition the brain's response to stress manifests as a reversal of conditioned behaviour patterns, e.g. affection might be replaced by aggression or an 'enemy' interrogator might become a 'friend'. According to William Sargant, all phases of transmarginal inhibition (which can be induced by a variety of means, including trance-generating dances) have one thing in common, it is that the activity of the brain exhibits characteristics similar to those observed in hypnotic conditions.[253]

Stories, if well told, can also cultivate hypnotic states of mind. Children seem to be programmed to copy their parents.[254] Such copying goes extremely deep. The posture of parents is frequently replicated in remarkable detail. Even emotional states are often reproduced with unnerving accuracy. Because children are so dependent on parents for their survival they seem to be neurologically receptive to all information coming directly from that source. Parents' opinions and beliefs are often taken as truths by children. Since parents and other family members also tend to act as transmitters of wider cultural values through social skills training and the sharing of stories with their children, it is not uncommon for such messages to be accorded some kind of absolute value. Stories take children deeply into internal experience where they remain receptive to the suggestions of the storyteller who led them there. Traditional cultural stories, myths, legends and folk tales usually embody sets of values to which a culture subscribes. In the trance state of inwardly experienced story images the listeners to the story – and traditional stories are ideally transmitted orally – unconsciously internalise those values. The structure of many traditional stories often amplifies the trance state and hence suggestibility in the listeners. To take one example, a common pattern in myths from many cultures is the embedding of one story within another story which itself is embedded in another story and so on. The *1001 Nights* collection uses this technique to great effect.[255] Eventually, listeners lose track of which story they are in and lose, thereby, the 'generalised reality orientation' that is provided by the conscious mind. One of the most powerful and elegant techniques for inducing hypnotic trance employs just this method. Bandler and Grinder call it 'stacking realities'.[256] It works by overloading the conscious mind, thereby enabling the hypnotist to communicate directly with the unconscious/subconscious mind, which is far more responsive to suggestion when freed from the constraints of conscious regulation.

For structuralist thinkers such as Claude Lévi-Strauss, myths are primarily concerned to explore and resolve antinomies and polarities in human experience such as those dealing with nature and culture, order and chaos, life and death, individual desire and social obligation. These polarities are reflected, according to d'Aquili and Laughlin, in the structure and functioning of the brain itself. Following the work of Lex, they argue that the two hemispheres operate according to a system of reciprocal inhibition. Perception is built up through rapid alternations of hemispheric dominance. At any time, the human subject experiences the world in two quite distinct ways. The left hemisphere functions in a logical, sequential and temporal fashion while the right hemisphere functions in an impressionistic, holistic and spatial one. The integration of the two is, not infrequently, problematic. Myths then, can be understood as narrative devices for addressing and resolving problems that typically arise out of the way our brains operate.[257]

Where d'Aquili and Laughlin part company with the structuralists is on the issue of resolution. Structuralists tend to argue that the cognitive resolutions contained within myths are adequate to human needs. d'Aquili and Laughlin, on the other hand, suggest that such resolutions lack 'existential reality', the emotional dimension. This, they suggest, is supplied by ritual. Humans who share in collective exposure to and participation in the rhythmic patterning of ritual activity will find themselves experiencing a sense of connectedness with fellow participants. The greater the number of vehicles promoting such participation the greater the sense of 'communitas' created. Combining rhythmic movement with rhythmic sound amplifies the effect, thus enhancing the sense of rapport between those involved. That state of rapport is, of course, one of heightened suggestibility. Involvement in the rhythmic patterns of rituals thus makes participants open to the suggestions about resolution of existential problems embedded in the associated myths. Myths and rituals then, offer religions and cultures powerful media for the promotion of group-specific supernaturalist beliefs, which, in various ways, shield human beings from the harsh realities of life and enable them to function in the world with a considerable degree of effectiveness.

The price to be paid for this security and effectiveness is, however, a high one. The most efficacious internal representations are usually those which are regarded as truths, that is, they are most powerful when the map is mistaken for the territory. But when groups seek to assert the infallibility of their own maps and, consequently, come into conflict, then, once again, the solution to one problem has generated another.

PART 3
LOOSE ENDS

In this final section I want to round off my exploration of religious experience by touching on what seem to be two closely related questions: 'what can neurological research contribute to our understanding of this controversial, influential and intangible dimension of human life?' and, 'are there any reliable ways of distinguishing 'authentic' (veridical) from 'inauthentic' (non-veridical) and healthy from unhealthy religious experiences?'

Neurological research

In 1950s Britain, conditioning theory was combined with studies on physiology to produce a new perspective on religion. After working with soldiers suffering from battle neurosis during the Second World War, psychiatrist William Sargant, who had grown up in a strongly Methodist family, encountered some of Ivan Pavlov's later writings on conditioned reflexes and psychiatry. In *Battle for the Mind* Sargant outlines Pavlov's explanation of how exposure to stress can have a profound effect on conditioning. Highly stressed individuals were frequently seen to have their recently conditioned behaviour patterns eradicated in the course of such exposures. They also became highly responsive to new sources of conditioning. The reason for this, suggested Pavlov, was that in stressful situations the brain becomes overloaded and breaks down to protect itself. Such breakdown, which Pavlov called 'transmarginal inhibition', exhibits degrees or stages of intensity. In the first stage, emotional response is flattened: strong and weak stimuli evoke the same level of response. In the second stage, weak stimuli evoke more intense responses than strong ones (probably because strong stimuli simply deepen the inhibition, they are too strong to respond to). In the third stage, previously conditioned patterns of behaviour are often reversed: a disliked food becomes liked; a liked person becomes disliked.

This third, ultra-paradoxical stage, as Pavlov called it, exhibits many of the characteristics normally associated with hysteria and other hypnoid conditions. In particular, the individual becomes highly suggestible and new patterns of conditioned behaviour can become established. Pavlov's dogs experienced this condition when the laboratory in which they were housed was flooded. Many dogs died and, thereafter, the survivors tended to respond to even a trickle of water with a degree of fear more suited to a life-threatening situation – a 'phobic' response. Sargant realised that the soldiers he had treated had been transmarginally inhibited and unable to clear the traumatic experience from their minds. The reason his abreactive therapy worked was that by getting a solider to relive the trauma again (with the help of emotion-intensifying drugs) he had recreated the fluid, suggestible state of transmarginal inhibition and this had allowed the conditioned patterns laid down during the trauma to be released. After a period of rest his patients started to become 'their old selves' again, i.e. their older patterns of conditioning became re-established.

The connection between this material and religion came when Sargant, seemingly inadvertently, was glancing through one of John Wesley's journals. He realised, almost in a flash, that Wesley's preaching strategy was a highly effective method for deconditioning and then reconditioning people. The hellfire and brimstone sermons created a state of acute stress in the listeners, suggestibility increased and then an escape was offered: conversion, the point at which conditioning is reversed:

> I will show you him that was a lion till then, and is now a lamb; him that was a drunkard, and is now exemplarily sober; the whoremonger that was, who now abhors the very 'garment spotted by the flesh'.[1]

Like the water in the case of Pavlov's dogs, exposure to symbols, behaviours, etc. associated with the original conversion experience would have the tendency to re-evoke and reinforce the change it brought about. Wesley was, understandably, keen to ensure that his converts underwent such reinforcing experiences and so he established follow-up procedures to keep them within the fold. Converts were divided into groups of twelve who met weekly under the guidance of a 'class leader', a person who also made weekly visits to their homes.

Sargant's recipe for successful conversion was, then, to create a hypnoid state, through stress induction, emotional arousal or some other means, suggest alternative patterns of belief and behaviour and follow up the experience with regular reminders. The decline of Methodism in modern times, according to Sargant, is largely due to the abandonment of this formula. It has not been entirely lost to the Christian world, however. The services of modern charismatic and evangelical groups would be immediately recognisable to Sargant, as would the activities of anti-cult deprogrammers – many of whom refer to Sargant's work as a kind of operational manual.

Already in *Battle for the Mind*, but in more detail in *The Mind Possessed*, Sargant extended his analyses of religious experiences to cover phenomena such as ritual trance and spirit possession. In so doing he recognised that exposure to stress was just one method of bringing about a state of heightened suggestibility or trance. Many traditions promote trance experiences through rhythmic drumming and dancing and, in the case of possession, states of dissociation as well.[2] Although he does not acknowledge Pierre Janet directly it is clear that Sargant had his concept of dissociation in mind when writing about these phenomena.[3] More recent studies have elaborated Sargant's generalisations in a number of ways (see 'Religious experiences and trance states' above). The fact that many of these practices are frequently employed in religious contexts will be immediately apparent to anyone familiar with the history of religions.

Clinical psychologist John Schumaker has woven this and other related material into what he calls 'a unified theory of religion, hypnosis and psychopathology'.[4] He proposes that religion and all other forms of 'reality distortion' arose as a direct response to the emergence of higher cognitive capacities in human beings. Possession of these capacities brought about two primary changes in the way human beings perceived the world. In the first place, we developed the ability to think of our own mortality; in the second, perhaps as a result of the cognitive transformations that led to the first, we experienced a need to perceive order in our world. As Schumaker puts it, 'At one stage [in our evolutionary history], our brains reached ... a "historical discontinuity", a developmental threshold wherein we became capable of recognising, and being negatively affected by, disorder.'[5] The way we dealt with distressing aspects of otherwise beneficial cognitive developments was to separate these higher cognitive faculties from other forms of mental processing. This, in turn, enabled the brain to 'dissociate itself from its own data'. The human brain, he claims, gained the ability to (a) selectively perceive its environment, (b) selectively process information, (c) selectively store memories, (d) selectively disengage from already stored memories, and (e) selectively replace dissociated data with more 'user-friendly' data. Ultimately, this empowered human beings, like no animal before us, to *regulate* their own reality.[6] The parallels between this description and what hypnotists call 'the conscious mind' are pretty obvious.

In Schumaker's view, at the cultural level, the regulation of reality has mainly been undertaken by religions, cumulative traditions of reality distortion whose purpose is to keep the spectres of mortality and chaos at bay. They are, to use theologian John Bowker's term, 'licensed insanities'.

Psychopathology also represents an attempt at reality distortion, but it is unlicensed (i.e. not culturally sanctioned) and individual.

The group distortions we know as religions exhibit, in most of their manifestations, techniques for inducing a trance state (dissociation) combined with reality-distorting suggestions. Usually the induction techniques are applied in a ritualised context which facilitates the autosuggestion of previously learned material (as in the case of meditation) or heterosuggestion from one or more leaders (as in the case of dances, sacrifices and other kinds of group activities). Although group and individual rituals might seem dissimilar on the surface both work by utilising the dissociative capacity of the mind. We can believe one thing with one part of our mind and something completely different with another.[7] For those with a talent for dissociation what Leon Festinger called 'cognitive dissonance' will rarely prove as problematic as he assumed.[8]

Schumaker's dissociative trance state exhibits many affinities with what Julian Jaynes calls 'bicamerality'.[9] According to Jaynes, the consciousness experienced by modern human beings is a relatively recent phenomenon, and it has much in common with 'the conscious mind' of the hypnotist.[10] The pre-literate cultures of the ancient world such as the Greeks of the Iliad and the Indians of the Vedas were not 'conscious' in the way we are.[11] Jaynes's understanding of consciousness is rather different from many commonly held notions. He distinguishes consciousness from what he calls 'reactivity' or responsiveness to environmental stimuli. When we are conscious of something we are directly aware of it, yet there is much that we do of which we are unaware. A pianist playing a piano is not conscious of his playing (he would probably make errors if he were), though he would probably use his conscious attention to learn a piece that he will later play fluently without being conscious of so doing.

Similarly, consciousness is not the opposite of unconsciousness in the sense of being knocked out. It does involve being aware, but in a special kind of way. In fact, Jaynes argues that consciousness

> need not be involved in speaking, writing, listening or reading. It does not copy down experience, as most people think ... It is not necessary for making judgements or simple thinking. It is not the seat of reason, and indeed some of the most difficult instances of creative reasoning go on without any attending consciousness. And it has no location except an imaginary one.[12]

Rather:

> consciousness is an operation rather than a thing, a repository, or a function. It operates by way of analogy, by way of constructing an analog space with an

analog 'I' that can observe that space, and move metaphorically in it. It operates on any reactivity, excerpts relevant aspects, narratizes and conciliates them together in a metaphorical space where such meanings can be manipulated like things in space. Conscious mind is a spatial analog of the world and mental acts are analogs of bodily acts.[13]

This consciousness, which most of us take for granted and many assume to have evolved when humans became a distinct species, first appeared, according to Jaynes, towards the end of the second millennium BCE. Prior to that most human beings were 'bicameral'. Decisions were made not by imagining what to do and what the likely outcomes might be but by a voice which had complete authority over an individual, the voice of a god (or an absent leader). The primary trigger for that voice was, according to Jaynes, the experience of stress.[14] The god's voice was, according to Jaynes, an auditory representation of society's values, regulations, etc., probably stored in the right temporal lobe of the cerebral cortex and communicated to the speech and comprehension centres in the left temporal lobe, primarily Wernicke's area, via the anterior commissure (a bundle of nerve fibres connecting the temporal lobes). The experience of hearing such a voice would have been very much an experience of total and commanding authority which automatically initiated behaviour. To hear really was to obey.

This pattern of mental functioning was a consequence of the development of language, which, Jaynes suggests, took place between about 70,000 BCE and 8,000 BCE. Bicameral processing began to emerge towards the end of this period and dominated human experience until the emergence of consciousness. These changes were not genetic, except in the sense that the human brain exhibits a plasticity which allows its functioning to change as a result of and in response to experience – particularly experience in infancy.

As consciousness emerged so too did religion, an attempt to maintain or re-establish communication with the gods – the sources of authority and guidance. Consciousness, with its mind space, analogue 'I' and personal narrative, inhibits such communication. Religions, therefore, employ methods for displacing consciousness, for re-establishing bicamerality. Hypnosis, for Jaynes, is essentially a method of achieving such a displacement or dissociation. In this he is in agreement with Schumaker. The emphasis is somewhat different though. For Schumaker, consciousness makes us aware of disorder from which we feel the need to escape; for Jaynes, on the other hand, it makes us aware that we have lost a sense of order which we desire to regain.

Both Jaynes's and Schumaker's accounts are rather speculative,[15] but they connect in some interesting ways with much 'harder' research in the field of neurophysiology. Michael Persinger, professor of psychology and head of the Neuroscience Research Group at Canada's Laurentian University, has been studying the neurophysiology of religious experiences for the last 30 years. His most significant finding is that the occurrences of religious experiences are highly correlated with brief activations of the temporal lobes of the brain. These patterns of activation he calls temporal lobe transients (or TLTs for short). Stimulation of the temporal lobes can produce subjective experiences of intense meaningfulness, profundity, conviction, depersonalisation, forced thinking and perceptual alteration. Often such experiences have a pronounced religious character, so much so that Persinger uses the term 'God experience' to indicate the general nature of experiences prompted by temporal lobe stimulation:

> a Catholic, for instance, is more likely to see Mary, a Protestant will see Christ, an Islamic, of course, Allah. Although more typically it's less a 'vision' exactly, more a sense of 'presence' – a presence, nevertheless, usually understood by subjects as supernatural.[16]

Indeed, Persinger comments that visions are not even the most common way of experiencing God, that honour goes to experiences of 'hearing God'.[17]

Apart from the kinds of electrical stimulations employed by Persinger and his colleagues (they developed a helmet to do this), Temporal Lobe Transients are most usually initiated by lack of oxygen, lack of blood sugar or reductions in blood flow. The kinds of behaviours and experiences producing such conditions include sojourns at high altitudes, low-level (yogic) breathing, fasting, illnesses of various kinds and stresses of various kinds, e.g. loss of a loved one, anxiety about anticipated death. There are also periods in the human life cycle when TLTs are more frequent: adolescence and old age (exactly what Edwin Starbuck and Carl Jung would have predicted had they known about TLTs). There are also connections between this research and that of Jaynes, Schumaker and Sargant in that Persinger recognises stress as a significant trigger for experiences of dissociation which allow processes generated in the right cerebral hemisphere to flood into the left, or, put another way, stress can displace conscious processing which, in turn, allows unconscious processing to become more prominent.

The involvement of the temporal lobes and the pronounced auditory component in the God Experiences studied by Persinger suggest significant links with the ideas of Jaynes. Indeed, Persinger himself recognises the parallels.[18] The role of the temporal lobes in many kinds of religious experiences has been investigated with some vigour since the husband and wife team of W.G. and M.A. Lennox published *Epilepsy and Related Disorders* in 1960.[19] The Buddha, Kierkegaard, Rasputin, St Paul, Socrates, were all identified as sufferers. Yet it is easy to go beyond the evidence with this kind of material. As Oliver Sacks comments:

> The danger is that we may go overboard in medicalising our predecessors (and contemporaries), reducing their complexity to expressions of neurological or psychiatric disorder, while neglecting all the other factors that determine a life, not least the irreducible uniqueness of the individual.[20]

That said, V.S. Ramachandran points to a very real relationship between temporal lobe epilepsy and religious experience that has been confirmed by a substantial number of studies.[21]

Using single photon emission computed tomography (SPECT) scans on Pentecostal Christians engaging in glossolalia (speaking in 'tongues') Andrew Newberg and his colleagues also found increased activity in the temporal lobes. This was not, however, prominent in the scans of Tibetan Buddhists meditating on an image and Roman Catholic nuns practising the 'centring prayer' from *The Cloud of Unknowing*. These groups showed increased activity in the frontal lobes, the parietal lobes, the hippocampus and the thalamus. Those patterns of activation prompted the hypothesis that 'prayer and meditation might be a way to make our brain experience certain beliefs as real'.[22] Normally, increases in the activity of the parietal lobes correlates with increasing activity of the thalamus. However, when the Buddhists and nuns were meditating, activation of the thalamus, which functions to create a sense of reality, was *not* accompanied by an increase in parietal lobe activity:

> when a person is meditating, ordinary perceptions of the world are being altered, yet the thalamus continues to create a lucid experience. The meditator remains fully conscious, but the brain is experiencing a very different sense of the world.[23]

When that lucid experience is communicated to the frontal lobes it tends to be understood within the framework of existing beliefs – in a manner reminiscent of the ways in which participants in stage hypnosis shows conjure of explanations for their behaviour: they make sense of it in terms of what they know since they do not have access to the actual cause (the suggestions of the hypnotist, for which they are amnesic):

> Thus, the nuns believed that they perceived or experienced the presence of God; the Buddhists felt that they had been in the state of absolute consciousness [whatever that is]; and as for nonbelievers – well, some might consider it an anomalous event, a neural quirk or hallucination. Each interpretation is based largely on belief systems the person had developed long before this experience.[24]

This, to my mind, comes pretty close to neurological support for, or even confirmation of, the argument developed by Steven Katz on phenomenological and philosophical grounds back in 1978: mystical experiences are more like neurological manifestations of religious teachings than insights into supernatural realities.

A significant implication of this line of research concerns spirituality in general. This is where the hippocampus kicks in: 'the hippocampus ... helps to embed the experience into long-term memory ... [and] the more a person meditates the stronger the memory of an event becomes ...'.[25] In other words, spiritual practice reinforces the beliefs that shaped the experience in the first place, and, contra claims by spiritual practitioners themselves, rather than rendering our cognitions and emotions more free and flexible it fixes them more firmly into well-established grooves.[26] What is more, and here we return to the psychology of homo religiosus, the asymmetry between the thalami that Newberg et al. found in the Buddhists, the nuns and some of the Pentecostals 'suggests that they have a unique perception of reality, which is continuously active whether they are meditating or not'.[27]

Finally, some of the differences between these groups provide a neurological basis for the distinction between mystical and numinous experiences. Firstly, both Buddhists and nuns showed increased activity (above normal) in the prefontal cortex (which functions to help us stay alert and attentive as well as assisting in the planning and executing of tasks[28]). By contrast, Pentecostals showed a decrease of activity in these areas ('With decreased activity in your frontal lobes, you would have the conscious experience that "something else" was running the show'[29]). Secondly, both Buddhists and nuns showed reduced activity in the parietal lobes (the orientation area of the brain) during meditation, which is connected with distortions in the experiences of space and time.[30] Pentecostals showed a slight increase in activity and did not report a feeling of oneness with God or the Universe as the Buddhists and nuns had done, but retained their sense of self: 'they simply give themselves over to the will of God. They remain in dialogue with God and thus God retains an aspect of otherness.'[31] The similarities between these Pentecostal experiences and the cases of lucid possession described by Oesterreich (see above) are plain to see. Thirdly, the nuns practising the centring prayer showed high activity in language centres and parts of the right hemisphere associated with meaning-making, whereas the Buddhists who were meditating on an image had lower activity in these areas but higher ones in the inferior temporal lobes (the visual processing area of the brain[32]).

As with hypnosis, the kinds of things one does to create an altered state (the induction) can have a profound effect on the kind of experience one has.

Different spiritual exercises create different spiritual experiences, substantially because they influence different parts of the brain or the same parts in different ways. In the future, connecting phenomenological typologies with neurological ones could be quite fruitful for mapping the finer contours of religious experience.[33]

At present, the exact relationships between left and right brain, conscious mind and unconscious mind, and experiences of dissociation are still being debated in psychological and neurological circles. What is clear, though, is that the outlines of a powerful explanatory paradigm are gradually being sketched out, and that it will not be long before all research in the psychology of religion has to become cognisant of it.

'Authentic' religious experience

The primary issue I shall address in this section is that of whether it makes sense to divide religious experiences into authentic and inauthentic types, a practice adopted by some of the writers whose work I shall examine. For example, according to Kevin Nelson, when investigating the neurophysiology of spiritual experiences, 'We must be sure that a person is having a genuine spiritual experience at the exact moment the MRI image is taken ...'[34] Similarly, Masters and Huston claim that the answer to the question of 'whether authentic religious and mystical experiences occur among the [psychedelic] drug subjects' must be 'yes'.[35] By way of contrast to these authors I shall argue that there is no robust basis for this distinction and that any experience of a supernatural realm is as 'authentic' as any other.

With regard to this issue of authenticity, many writers are content to follow a dictum attributed to William James: 'By their fruits ye shall know them, not by their roots',[36] i.e. the experiences are self-validating as long as the 'fruits' conform to some set of criteria that distinguish genuine religious experiences from counterfeit ones. What might those criteria be? James and others have offered their own lists, though all are problematic. In some ways, though, James is more aware of the potential for paradox than later writers who have addressed this issue. He writes, 'Mystical truth exists for the individual who has the transport, but for no one else', and 'No authority emanates from them [mystical experiences] which should make it a duty to those who stand outside of them to accept their revelations uncritically.'[37] Mystical (and, we may add, numinous) experiences are thus inherently subjective, yet authenticity requires some kind of public dimension, some kind of objectivity. For James the best candidate for determining objectivity is truth:

> Mystical conditions may ... render the soul more energetic in the lines which their inspiration favors. But this could be reckoned an advantage *only in case the inspiration were a true one*. If the inspiration were erroneous, the energy would be all the more mistaken and misbegotten.[38]

And here's the rub. The jump from subjective conviction to objective demonstration is huge, and James seems to have been fully cognisant of it.

The two main sources of doubt about the veracity of religious 'inspirations' that find their way onto the pages of the *Varieties* are the Janus-faced character of religious experience and what James called 'the pluralistic hypothesis'.[39] James recognises that 'religious mysticism is only half of mysticism. The other half has no accumulated traditions except those which the text books on insanity supply'.[40] Moreover, for James, both halves of mysticism arise from the same source, what he calls 'the great transmarginal region' or 'the unseen region' or 'the subconscious continuation of our conscious life'.[41] That region, he claims, 'contains every kind of matter; 'seraph and snake' abide there side by side. To come from there is no infallible credential'.[42] This is why, for him, the 'fruit' of these experiences is where we should look for their validation.

The other source of doubt about the veracity of religious inspirations, the pluralistic hypothesis, is the fact that different religious traditions teach, on the basis of certain religious experiences, quite different things about the natural world, the supernatural world and the relationship between them. His response to this is to seek common ground between religious traditions, and he claims to have found it in two areas. One is soteriology, which he presents thus:

> there is a certain uniform deliverance in which religions all appear to meet. It consists of two parts:
>
> 1. An uneasiness; and
> 2. Its solution.
>
> 1. The uneasiness, reduced to its simplest terms, is a sense that there is *something wrong about us* as we naturally stand.
> 2. The solution is a sense that *we are saved from the wrongness* by making proper connection with the higher powers.[43]

The other area where common ground can be discovered is what James calls 'feelings and conduct', for which he accepts James Leuba's label of 'faith-state'.[44] James writes:

> When we survey the whole field of religion we find a great variety in the thoughts that have prevailed there; but the feelings on the one hand and the conduct on the other are almost always the same ...[45]

Neither of these common elements can withstand critical scrutiny. I argued at the beginning of Part 1 that while diffused/communal traditions may incorporate soteriological elements, these are not their primary concerns and should not be understood as some kind of essence. That said, James's generalised characterisation would probably elicit some form of recognition in the adherents of such traditions, and even among those of traditions like Buddhism and Jainism, which do not understand the 'solution' in terms of a 'proper connection with higher powers'. However, even if this rather abstract and generalised commonality were granted it would do little to nullify the impact of 'the pluralistic hypothesis', for even if all religious traditions did accept that commonality they quickly differentiate themselves from each other through mutually exclusive claims on points of epistemology, ontology, soteriology and theology. Even if this were not the case, and all religions agreed in their characterisations of the supernatural realm, that in itself would demonstrate no more than a consensus among them. The hard work of demonstrating the existence of that realm would still need to be done.

What about feelings and conduct? Could they bolster the credibility of James's supernatural hypothesis? Rawlinson's work provides clear examples of profound differences in the ways that feeling states are judged. For example, 'hot' and 'cool' traditions have virtually inverted judgements about the role of feelings in spirituality. No consensus here.

In terms of conduct or behaviour, commonalities also evaporate rather quickly. An example of profound differences between traditions on just one issue, that of violence, will demonstrate the point. For Jains, all violence (in thought, word and deed) is to be abjured. In one of the earliest Jain texts, the *Ācārāṅga*, we read 'All breathing, existing, living, sentient creatures should not be slain, nor treated with violence, nor abused, nor tormented, nor driven away. This is the pure, unchangeable, eternal law which the clever ones, who understand the world, have proclaimed'.[46] That abjuration of all violence is the first of the five great vows made by all Jain ascetics. With this vow 'the ascetic rejects the act of killing any life-forms whatsoever and undertakes that for the rest of his life he will confess, repent of and avoid violence, whether performing it himself, compelling another to perform it or approving another carrying it out, mentally, vocally and physically'.[47] The medieval monk Hemacandra is unequivocal: 'Without the abandonment of violent activity, all religious behaviour, no matter how correct, is worthless.'[48] To paraphrase Sam Harris, as Jains become more extreme they become less violent.

The contrast with Islām could not be more stark, for that religious tradition allows, endorses and promotes many kinds of violence, both offensive and defensive. For example, Qur'ān 2.193:

> And fight them [disbelievers] until there is no more *Fitnah* (disbelief and worshipping of others along with Allāh) and (all and every kind of worship is for Allāh (Alone). But if they cease, let there be no more transgression except against *Az-Zālimūn* (the polytheists, and wrong-doers).[49]

Similar sentiments can be found in other parts of the text (e.g. 9.5, 9.29 and 9.123).

In the modern world there is much debate about the nature of Islāmic jihād (struggle/holy war). On one side of the debate we have, among others, scholars such as Chris Horrie, Peter Chippindale and Mir Zohair Husain.[50] On the other side we find writers such as Samuel P. Huntington, Jonathan Kirsch, Bernard Lewis and Steven Pinker.[51] Horrie and Chippindale claim that while many Muslims tend to agree that 'holy war' is a reasonable translation of 'jihād' they also tend to maintain that such war is always defensive.[52] Husain claims that 'holy war' is a translation error[53] and that in Islām the greatest *jihad* (*jihadi-i-akbar*) is the nonviolent spiritual struggle and the violent, lesser *jihad* (*jihadi-i-asghar*) 'is to actively defend oneself against tyrants, aggressors, and colonisers'.[54] Other scholars make similar claims, though Hugh Beattie does attempt to present alternative claims alongside these.[55] Nevertheless, the simple acceptance of the 'greater–lesser' nomenclature makes jihād seem to be primarily peaceful or defensive.

I tend to align with those scholars who reverse the 'greater–lesser' relationship. As Scott Atran comments, 'The idea of "greater jihad" as inner struggle appears to be a Sufi introduction from the Abbasid period.'[56] When I did a rough, quick calculation of Islām's history of offensive and defensive conflicts I found that Islām was broadly on the offensive from the seventh century to the eighteenth century. This was not, of course, all one-way traffic. Christian Europe mounted eight crusades between 1096 and 1270 in ultimately futile attempts to reclaim the lands of the Eastern Roman Empire that had been overrun by Muslim forces. Christian rule in the area was decisively ended in 1453, when the Ottomans captured and subsequently held Constantinople, now Istanbul. The Ottoman caliphs continued their attempts at military expansion into Eastern Europe until stopped at Vienna in 1529. After that the Balkans changed hands regularly until the First World War. Muslims were not expelled from Spain until the seventeenth century, though at that time Akbar was still extending Muslim rule over northern India.

From the eighteenth century to the twentieth, Islām tended to be on the defensive, and from the late twentieth century into the twenty-first it has been both offensive[57] and defensive.[58] If modern Muslims follow the exhortations of Ayman al-Zawahiri and engage in jihād until all lands that had at some time been under Muslim control are 'recovered' for Islām then we are in for a very protracted period of Muslim-instigated violence.

Reflection on such exhortations naturally raises the question of how those lands became Muslim in the first place, and in almost all cases it was by means of military conquest. Indeed, as Bernard Lewis indicates 'The overwhelming majority of early authorities ... citing relevant passages in the Qur'ān and in the tradition, discuss *jihād* in military terms'.[59] He goes on:

> the Christian crusade, often compared with the Muslim *jihād*, was itself a delayed and limited response to the *jihād* and in part also an imitation. But unlike the *jihād* it was concerned primarily with the defence or reconquest of threatened or lost Christian territory. ... The Muslim *jihād*, in contrast, was perceived as unlimited, as a religious obligation that would continue until all the world had either adopted the Muslim faith or submitted to Muslim rule. In the latter case, those who professed what Muslims recognised as a revealed religion were allowed to continue the practice of that religion, subject to the acceptance of certain fiscal and other disabilities. Those who did not, that is to say idolaters and polytheists, were given the choice of conversion, death or slavery.[60]

Muslims themselves disagree about this matter of greater and lesser; so it is not clear-cut, though there is a particularly Islāmic twist to it: taqiyya – concealment, deceit, dissimulation, dissembling – the guidance from the tradition that Muslims can mislead infidels about their true feelings or intentions without having any moral qualms. This is particularly troubling for phenomenologists, who tend to assume that 'insiders' are telling the truth about their traditions and aims. It's the same old conundrum for scholars investigating controversies: 'whom can we trust?' Even so, while the extent and character of the violence that is sanctioned and advocated by Islām may be disputed no one claims that the tradition abjures violence. James's hope that a common core of religions could be found in conduct is dashed by the obvious differences on this issue between Islām and Jainism.[61]

James, perhaps because he did not have access to or recognise the full implications of information that reveals a lack of consensus among religious traditions about everything except the mere existence of a supernatural realm, is optimistic about the fate of his hypothesis that such a realm does exist and that it has pragmatic effects on the natural world, though he does acknowledge his ignorance about what those effects might be:

> What the more characteristically divine facts are, apart from the actual inflow of energy in the faith-state and the prayer-state, I know not. But the over-belief on which I am ready to make my personal venture is that they exist.[62]

Although he does his best to present this jump into his 'over-belief' as a rational thing to do its evidence base is so flimsy that all it really amounts to is a statement of faith.

As he states in his 'conclusions' chapter, 'So far, however, as this analysis goes the experiences are only psychological phenomena ... What is the objective 'truth' of their content?' He admits that 'the world interpreted religiously ... must have, over and above the altered expression, *a natural constitution* different at some point from that which a materialistic world would have. It must be such that different events can be expected in it, different conduct must be required.'[63] Yes, there must be a difference in 'natural constitution' and there must be events that cannot be explained by materialists, but he never gets round to specifying what they might be. The closest he comes is the statement that the phenomenon of 'certain kinds of incursion from the subconscious region ... which in one sense is part of ourselves and in another sense is not ourselves, actually exerts an influence, raises our centre of personal energy, and produces regenerative effects *unattainable in other ways*'.[64]

This amounts to little more than a claim that religious experiences change people in powerful ways and that such changes express themselves in behaviour. The claim that those effects are 'unattainable in other ways' offers an interesting hypothesis, but no more than that. Moreover, it does not and cannot differentiate between 'fruit' that yields truth and 'fruit' that does not. As far as I am aware, no recorded religious experience has ever revealed anything that is counter intuitive about the world that has subsequently been demonstrated to be true by robust and publicly accessible methods. James's attempt to bridge the gap between the subjective and the objective and identify the criteria for authenticity has, therefore, to be judged as unsuccessful.

The same conclusion applies to similar attempts by subsequent researchers.[65] Here I will comment on just two: those by Masters and Huston in 1966 and by Grof in 1975/2009. Both works are frequently cited as authoritative guides to the spirituality of psychedelia and therefore warrant careful scrutiny. Masters and Huston's *The Varieties of Psychedelic Experience* makes an obvious (though unacknowledged) connection with James's *The Varieties of Religious Experience*.[66] Its contents are based on what the dust cover description dubs 'the laboratory induction of religious and mystical experiences'. Over a 15-year period they facilitated 206 sessions of psychedelic experience and combined information from these with that gleaned from interviews with 214 'persons who have been volunteer subjects, psychotherapy patients, or who have obtained or taken the drugs on their own'.[67] The main drugs employed in these sessions were LSD-25 and peyote, though DMT and psilocybin were also used.[68] LSD was used in 112 sessions, peyote in 85, mescaline in four, DMT in three and psilocybin in two. In their introductory chapter, Masters and Huston do not specify how many people were involved in the 206 sessions, though later[69] they indicate that that there were, in fact, 206 participants in their sessions, which implies that the sessions of these 206 volunteers were one-off and perhaps even first-time experiences.

In order to make sense of their participants' reports they devised a four-fold scheme that, in a loose kind of way, mapped out what they deemed to be 'levels' of profundity in the experiences. As the scheme was significantly influenced by psychoanalytic ideas 'progress' is represented by notions of increasing 'depth' rather than 'height', not a 'higher' state of consciousness but a 'deeper' one. Both sets of terms convey more or less the same value judgements: high is better than low; deep is better than shallow. They also suggest that our everyday consciousness is low or shallow or, indeed, both. The four 'levels' are:

1. the sensory;
2. the recollective–analytic;
3. the symbolic, and
4. the integral.

Approximately half of the book is given over to presenting and commenting on reports that Masters and Huston regarded as illustrative of each 'level'.

As I and many other experimenters with psychedelic drugs have found, there is a definite experiential shift when one closes one's eyes and 'goes inside', i.e. pays attention to and becomes immersed in experiences that are not of the everyday world outside one's body but of a universe that is revealed to or is a creation of one's own mind. Without such a shift one is denied the fullness of psychedelic experience. We could say, therefore, that there is probably a consensus among the users of these chemicals that the shift from 'outward' to 'inward' attention correlates with a sense of increasing profundity. So far; so good. However, once this shift has been accomplished, where does one find legitimate and robust criteria for determining progression through 'levels' of increasing depth and profundity?

Masters and Huston introduce their 'recollective–analytic' stage with the following statement: 'Possibly several hours into his session, and usually after he has spent some time in the sensory realm with its altered perceptions, the subject will pass on to a stage of his experience in which the content is predominantly introspective and especially recollective–analytic. Personal problems, particularly problem relationships and life-goals are examined. Significant past experiences are recalled and may be revivified ("lived through") with much accompanying emotion'.[70] Their descriptions of this 'stage' amount to little more than a catalogue of therapeutic benefits that might accrue from the changes in self-understanding precipitated by the effects of the drug. Readers are not informed about how many of the volunteers shifted from the sensory 'stage' into the 'recollective–analytic', nor whether any moved directly into symbolic or integral 'stages' without passing through the 'recollective–analytic'. Nevertheless, the language they use suggests a pretty clear-cut stage/level scheme:

> Sensory experiencing may, for example, lead the subject on to meaningful consideration of his place in the world; and this, in turn, may be the means of his 'descent' to a 'deeper' drug-state level ...[71]

> greater gains are possible when the subject uses this [recollective–analytic] level to effectively formulate his problems and goals and then 'carries' this material 'down' with him to the ... symbolic ...[72]

> unless he is able to participate directly in and respond emotionally to the mythic and ritualistic re-enactments [of the symbolic 'stage'] he will be unable to descend to the deepest level of the psychedelic drug state ...[73]

If many, or even just some psychedelic explorers shifted from the sensory into the symbolic or integral 'stages' without passing through the recollective–analytic then the notion that it is a 'stage' on the psychedelic 'journey' is, at the very least, called into question. Indeed, questioning the validity of the 'stage' notion becomes more pertinent when one reflects on the implications of obiter dicta such as 'at any stage of the experience, phenomena more characteristic of and predominant at another stage also may be present';[74] 'What we are dealing with here, then, is a level characterized by phenomena very familiar to the psychoanalyst, the hypnotherapist, and to practitioners of some other psychotherapeutic procedures';[75] and 'S, like many subjects who have been psychoanalyzed, went quickly to the recollective–analytic level ...'[76] If many of the volunteers who experienced the recollective–analytic 'stage' had been in psychotherapy or had issues that were amenable to psychotherapeutic interventions, then this 'stage' may well not be applicable to more psychologically and emotionally balanced people at all. Moreover, comments about conversations between the explorer and the guide suggest that processing at this 'stage' was being restrained by attention that is inevitably externalised or experienced during the period when the effects of the drug are beginning to weaken.

One of their comments about the integral stage/level is also revealing in this connection:

subjects who achieve this kind of experience are always very well prepared for the psychedelic drug state. ... All at the time of their sessions were comparatively very mature, developed personalities, who, at least in their public lives, would be generally regarded as functioning in a superior way in the world.[77]

The religious experiences reported by these eleven people, deemed by Masters and Huston to be deeper and more profound than 'deep' experiences classified as merely 'analogue' or 'pseudo' religious/mystical experiences, may well, given the similarity in their personality profiles, be simply manifestations of those profiles.

The separation of participants' experiences into symbolic level and integral level (with analogue and pseudo-religious experiences occupying some kind of liminal zone between the two) also seems, to my mind at least, to be rather contrived. Here I will comment on one example of each in order to demonstrate the arbitrary nature of the categorisation. At the symbolic 'level' subjects are reported to experience historical events and evolutionary processes, either from the perspective of a spectator or 'have the sense of being a participant in the event.[78] At a 'deeper' level within the symbolic stage lies a realm of symbolic dramas that 'is of a more profound and meaningful order than that of the historical and evolutionary sequences'.[79] One of these accounts reads like something that might have been appended to the biblical Book of Revelation. The guide, who often makes suggestions to participants, had just given the subject a cross to hold:

> I saw Jesus crucified and Peter martyred. I watched the early Christians die in the arena while others moved hurriedly through the Roman back streets, spreading Christ's doctrine. I stood by when Constantine gaped at the vision of the cross in the sky. I saw Rome fall and the dark ages begin and observed as little crossed twigs were tacked up as the only hope in ten thousand wretched hovels. I watched peasants trample it under their feet in some obscene forest rite, while, across the sea in Byzantium, they glorified it in jewelled mosaics and great domed cathedrals. My hand trembled, the cross glimmered, and history became confused. Martin Luther walked arm in arm with Billy Graham, followed by Thomas Aquinas and the armies of the Crusades.[80]

One feature of this account that Masters and Huston do not comment on is that the 'revelation' is quite clearly a product of the participant's imagination that has been amplified by the drug. It was never the case that Martin Luther walked arm in arm with Billy Graham and never will be, unless our best current understanding of how the world works is based on a deep and profound misunderstanding. In terms of religious experience, however, the grounds on which this or the experience described on pages 226–227 of Masters and

Huston's book can be distinguished from that of St John the Divine in the Book of Revelation are opaque. To deny that these are authentic religious experiences amounts to denying that ascription to many numinous ones that are preserved and cherished within established religious traditions.

In their final chapter, 'Religious and Mystical Experience', Masters and Huston do offer some criteria to differentiate what they deem to be 'authentic' religious experiences from those less authentic ones that emerge at the symbolic level. As will be shown, their arguments in support of both the distinction and the ranking are flimsy.

In their initial introduction to 'the integral level'[81] Masters and Huston inform their readers that all of the eleven people who 'reached the deep integral level' regarded their experience as religious, though they do comment that they see no reason why this level and its effects could not be experienced in other than religious terms.[82] Even so, their discussion of 'the integral level' is almost entirely devoted to issues surrounding the idea of authentic religious experience, for at this level there is

> the possibility of confrontation with a Presence variously described as God, Spirit, Ground of Being, Mysterium, Noumenon, Essence and Ultimate or Fundamental Reality. ... The experience is one of direct and unmediated encounter with the source level of reality, felt as Holy, Awful, Ultimate and Ineffable.[83]

If the encounter with such a 'source level of reality' is a core indicator of having reached the integral level then it is difficult to imagine havening an experience at that level that is not religious. Despite their qualification, the integral level seems to be intrinsically religious in character.

For Masters and Huston, however, some of the religious experiences reported by their volunteers were only pseudo religious or merely analogues of authentic religious experiences.[84] The process of distinguishing these from each other is based on three criteria:

1. encounter with the other on the integral level;
2. transformation of the self;
3. a process of phenomenological progression through the sensory, recollective–analytic and symbolic levels before passing into the integral.[85]

The first and third of these assume that their stage/level model is robust. If it isn't, then neither can serve as reliable criteria for making the distinctions that they do. The second criterion is independent of the others but hardly distinctive. For Masters and Huston such transformation has two aspects:

a subjective certainty that transformation has occurred and behavioural changes of a positive character supporting the certainty of transformation. The problem is that this transformation criterion is much too broad, for not only are most kinds of successful psychotherapeutic experiences rendered religious by it, so too, for example, are the experiences of workers in abattoirs who, sickened by what goes on around them and by their participation in it, decide to become vegetarian.

When faced with the challenge of creating a bridge between subjective experience and objective reality William James opted for truth as the most reliable indicator that the former involved a direct apprehension of the latter.[86] Masters and Huston give no indication that they even considered truth as a useful indicator of 'authenticity'.[87] Instead, they rely on what they deem to be parallels between their stage/level model and those found in traditional religious literature, and on William Stace's distinction between and judgement about the relative status of extravertive and introvertive mystical experience.

With regard to the former, they write:

> In our attempt to develop unbiased criteria for the authentic religious experience we have employed the usual measuring devices [and] ... have also found it important to place some emphasis on what we have termed the 'depth level' of the experience. The literature of nondrug religious and mystical experience *appears* to lend considerable support to this criterion. It is significant to note, for example, that in this traditional literature the writers repeatedly deal with and emphasize the stages on the way to mystical enlightenment and describe these with metaphors suggesting striking analogies to the psychodynamic levels hypothesized in our psychodynamic research.[88]

This statement indicates that Masters and Huston tend to regard what Rawlinson calls 'structured' traditions as paradigmatic here and that, mistakenly, they understand the mystical stage descriptions found in, for example, Pāli Buddhist texts and Patañjali's *Yoga Sūtra* as being similar to their postulated 'psychodynamic levels'. They are not. Moreover, the simple fact that 'mystical enlightenment' is described in ways that make many of the 'insights' gained by mystical methods incompatible with each other means that, as was argued in Part 1, no stage scheme can be taken as normative until robust criteria for determining which 'insights' are true and which false are available. Even if Masters and Huston's stages were paralleled by the scheme of some religious tradition, that, in itself, would do nothing to demonstrate that the stages were indicators of greater proximity to a deeper, more accurate understanding of the world than we have obtained by other means.

With regard to Stace's scheme, I argued in Part 1 that it suffers from a number of serious flaws. In particular, his postulated superiority of the introvertive over the extravertive experience is both unphenomenological – it is not found in the mystical literature of religious traditions – and, if Forman is correct, some traditions actually teach the opposite. My own analysis of religious and trance experiences suggests that rather than taking people closer and closer to an apprehension of the true nature of things these progressions in mystical absorption are merely deepenings of trance states in which imaginings can be clothed with the appearance of reality or can be deemed to be more real than real. In sum, the criteria employed by Masters and Huston to determine which, if any, psychedelic experiences are authentically religious are inadequate for that task. This is hardly surprising, for the notion of 'authentic religious/spiritual experience' is itself problematic. As I argued in Part 1, the only thing that all religious traditions seem to have in common is a belief in some kind of supernatural reality.[89]

If that argument is robust, then any experience of supernatural realms, beings or states is an authentic religious experience regardless of how it has been produced. One does not even have to resort to James's distinction between roots and fruits, for it is not just the 'roots' that are irrelevant, so too are the 'fruits'. Psychedelic experiences of the supernatural are, then, just as 'authentic' as those that arise spontaneously or through methods such as meditation, flagellation, dancing, chanting, fasting, or any other forms of asceticism. To claim that some of these experiences are superior to others is either an unwarranted epistemological leap of faith: a claim that they offer access to 'deeper' truths than others, or merely a claim that they have greater psychological and/or emotional benefits than the others. Indeed, once Masters and Huston's epistemological aspirations have been punctured (they offer no arguments in support of their claim that a number of their participants delivered 'remarkably accurate and sometimes esoteric historical descriptions' of events about which they would otherwise be ignorant[90]) there is nothing left that could legitimately divide religious experiences into authentic, inauthentic and pseudo categories.

Like Masters and Huston, Stanislav Grof divides the psychedelic experience into four 'levels' of profundity. His are:

(a) abstract and aesthetic;

(b) psychodynamic;

(c) perinatal; and

(d) transpersonal.

Like them, he also employs a mainly phenomenological approach to understanding psychedelic drug experiences. That approach involves categorising descriptions of LSD-induced experiences according to their content as well as their transformative effects on subjects' personalities, behaviours and sense of well-being. It is similar, in some ways, to the approach adopted by the American Psychiatric Association (APA) when compiling recent editions of its *Diagnostic and Statistical Manual of Mental Disorders* (DSM): identify symptoms/characteristics that cluster together and attach a label to the cluster. Here's an example from DSM-IV – '309.28 Adjustment Disorder with Mixed Anxiety and Depressed Mood':

A The development of emotional or behavioral symptoms in response to an identifiable stressor(s) occurring within 3 months of the onset of the stressor(s)

B These symptoms or behaviors are clinically significant as evidenced by either of the following

   1 marked distress that is in excess of what would be expected from exposure to the stressor

   2 significant impairment in social or occupational (academic) functioning

C The stress-related disturbance does not meet the criteria for another disorder

D The symptoms do not represent Bereavement

E Once the stressor (or its consequences) has terminated, the symptoms do not persist for more than an additional 6 months.[91]

The problems with this approach are easy to discern. In the first place, the labelled clusters become reified, i.e. treated as though they have an independent existence and are entities in their own right. Reification conceals the problem of validity. Clinicians may agree to label specific clusters of symptoms with disease-sounding names, i.e. they can reliably put patients into categories, but such consensus is no guarantee of validity: the extent to which a diagnosis describes an actual disease.[92] Like the APA, Grof inserts a number of disclaimers into his text that immunise him from the charge that he reifies his categories. The disclaimer in DSM-IV reads 'There is no assumption that each category of mental disorder is a completely discrete entity with absolute boundaries dividing it from other mental disorders or from no mental disorder.'[93] Here's a few of Grof's: 'I have not found a single symptom that would be an absolute component in all of them [LSD sessions] and could thus be considered truly invariant';[94] 'these levels can occur separately, simultaneously, or in an alternating fashion';[95] and 'individual responses to the same dosage level vary considerably'.[96] These disclaimers, which echo Masters and Huston's observation that 'at any stage of the experience, phenomena more characteristic of and predominant at another stage also may be present', also call the validity of Grof's 'levels' into question.

His first level, 'abstract and aesthetic', is quite similar to Masters and Huston's sensory level, and includes eyes open and eyes closed experiences. These range from heightened and distorted sensory experiences, through abstract and imaginary landscapes to optical illusions, auditory illusions and synaesthesias, all of which can be accompanied by emotional connotations. Grof characterises this as 'the most superficial level of the LSD experience'.[97] The second, psychodynamic, level also corresponds with Masters and Huston's second level, the recollective–analytic. Most of the people whose experiences are used to illustrate this level are psychiatric patients in psycholytic therapy[98] or other individuals 'who have considerable emotional problems'.[99] Grof claims that in order to understand such experiences one 'requires knowledge of the basic principles of the unconscious dynamics as described by Freud ...'.[100] As a sceptic about the insightfulness of Freud's theories and the effectiveness of psychoanalysis I am unwilling to allow such a claim to slip by without a comment. Much of Grof's LSD work was conducted in Czechoslovakia within a framework of psychoanalytically oriented psychotherapy.[101] In other words, psychoanalytic ideas were treated as veridical for the purpose of understanding what people were experiencing and to assist them in making therapeutic changes. In vernacular parlance, patients were 'shoehorned' into understanding their experiences in psychoanalytic terms. Indeed, psychoanalysis has something of a reputation for imposing its model on patients. Those who refuse to accept the analyst's interpretations of their experiences are labelled 'resistant'. Later in the book, after mentioning that he eventually concluded that many LSD experiences, particularly those he classifies as 'transpersonal', were not amenable to psychoanalytic interpretation and are unintelligible within a psychoanalytic framework, Grof even supplies an example of unsuccessful psychoanalytic 'shoehorning'. One of his patients had previously discussed his LSD experiences with a psychoanalytic therapist who made constant efforts to interpret the patient's 'mystical, religious and archetypal' experiences in Freudian terms: 'Where this was not possible he labeled them simply as psychotic ...'[102] When the patient refused to accept an interpretation 'the therapist spent many hours in frustrating attempts to analyze his alleged resistance'.[103]

Do we really need to embrace Freudian theory to understand people's experiences under the influence of LSD? I don't think so, even when they are of a kind that is, in Masters and Huston's characterisation of their recollective-analytic level, 'very familiar to the psychoanalyst, the hypnotherapist, and to practitioners of some other psychotherapeutic procedures'.[104] If therapists who use LSD for therapeutic purposes are seeking a conceptual framework within which to work then it is not difficult to find ones that are far superior to that provided by psychoanalysis. Readers will hardly be surprised that I would recommend hypnotherapy informed by hypnosis research as a more fruitful option.[105]

Grof's third level, the perinatal, covers experiences that engage 'the problems of biological birth, physical pain and agony, aging, disease and decrepitude, and dying and death',[106] though he does remind his readers that a 'causal nexus between the actual biological birth and the unconscious matrices for these experiences still needs to be established',[107] and that his basic perinatal matrices model 'should be considered at the present stage of knowledge only as a very useful model, not necessarily implying a causal nexus'.[108] Moreover, this 'level' cannot be clearly differentiated from the transpersonal one: 'some types of transpersonal experiences ... occur simultaneously with perinatal phenomena ...'[109] Typical of this level are what Grof describes as 'recollections' or 'memories'.[110] Also at this level are what he describes as 'insights'. They can be 'into the utmost relevance of the spiritual dimensions in the universal scheme of things' or into 'the essence of being and existence' or into 'Darwinian nature' or into 'human nature, society and culture'.[111] These 'insights' are typically 'accompanied by feelings of certainty that such knowledge is ultimately more real and relevant than our concepts and perceptions regarding the world that we share in a usual state of consciousness'.[112]

Grof's characterisation of these experiences as insights, recollections and memories seems, at the very least, premature, and quite possibly misleading. Indeed, his own descriptions of the overall experiences within which these 'insights', 'recollections' and 'memories' are embedded provide good reasons to be sceptical about the appropriateness of such terminology. A few examples will illustrate the point:

> A subject can experience himself as thousands of soldiers who have died on the battlefields of the whole world from the beginning of time.[113]

> Some individuals describe complex catastrophic events and scenes of havoc, such as the destruction of Atlantis, the end of Pompeii or Herculeum [=Herculaneum?], the annihilation of Sodom and Gomorrah, the Biblical Armageddon, or even an invasion from another planet ...[114]

> Subjects identify with Oriental harem owners, with participants in phallic worship or in unbridled fertility rites ...[115]

> Subjects may have very *authentic* feelings of eating feces, drinking blood or urine, or sucking on putrefying wounds ...[116]
>
> ... participating in Walpurgis Night, in a Black Mass, or in satanic sexual practices ... [which] usually results in *insights* into the psychology of the Inquisitors and witch-hunters ...[117]
>
> final destruction has on several occasions been experienced as coming from a powerful crushing step of Shiva the Destroyer ...[118]

Are these really 'insights' or 'memories'? If we incline to the view that they are not, perhaps preferring to use other terms employed by Grof, such as 'visions' or 'fantasies' or simply 'experiences', then we are faced with the task of determining whether any of them could be genuine insights or memories. Grof provides no criteria for making such a determination, and it may well be the case that he has been overly influenced by the subjective certainty conveyed by many of his informants about the actuality, facticity, reality, truth, veridicality of these experiences. Perhaps he had his own feelings of certainty about his personal LSD-induced experiences. Masters and Huston use similar terminology in their accounts, though, like Grof, they offer little by way of criteria that would enable us to separate experiences of genuine insight or memory from pseudo insights and memories that are created during the LSD sessions.

Grof labels his fourth level 'the transpersonal', which he defines as 'experiences involving an expansion or extension of consciousness beyond the usual ego boundaries and beyond the limitations of time and space'.[119] This rather bland description turns out to be a catch-all for an amazingly varied list of experiences, some of which I have had myself and many of which cross the boundary between Masters and Huston's 'symbolic' and 'integral' levels. He divides these experiences into two groups: those within the framework of 'objective reality' and those beyond the framework of 'objective reality'.[120] Two aspects of his treatment of these experiences are pertinent to an understanding of the relationship between religious and psychedelic experiences.

On the one hand, his notion of 'objective' is rather loose, for although he claims to restrict the phenomena in this category to those 'the existence of which has been generally accepted on the basis of consensual validation, empirical evidence, or scientific research', some of them clearly fall outside of these limits, e.g. past-incarnation experiences, precognition, clairvoyance and many others. Grof seems to accept many or most of these claims at face value, despite his occasional disclaimers such as 'the authenticity of recaptured intrauterine events is an open question...' and 'objective verification in this area can be particularly difficult ...'[121] Indeed, so persuaded is he of the veridicality of many of these 'transpersonal' experiences that he makes claims such as 'Their existence represents a serious challenge to accepted scientific paradigms'; 'Psychedelic research has generated an abundance of "anomalous phenomena" that – carefully examined – would lead to a radical revision of the current scientific worldview', and 'there are ... situations that are strongly indicative of genuine extrasensory perception'.[122]

Moreover, he claims that a range of new developments in science are 'in irreconcilable conflict with traditional science' though 'compatible with the findings of psychedelic research and with transpersonal psychology ...':

> Salient examples of this development are philosophical implications of quantum-relativistic physics (Capra 1975, Goswami 1995, Wolf 1981), David Bohm's theory of holomovement (Bohm 1980), Karl Pribram's holographic theory of the brain (Pribram 1971), Ilya Prigogine's theory of dissipative structures (Prigogine 1980), Rupert Sheldrake's theory of morphogenic fields (Sheldrake 1981), Gregory Bateson's brilliant synthesis of systems and information theory, cybernetics, anthropology, and psychology (Bateson 1979), and particularly Ervin Lazlo's concept of the PSI field (akashic field), his connectivity hypothesis, and his integral theory of everything (Lazlo 1993, 2003, 2004).[123]

I note from the vantage point of 2017 that this 'new scientific paradigm' has, so far, failed to materialise. Morphic and akashic fields, for example, remain and look likely to remain on the fringes of scientific enquiry.

The kinds of phenomena that Grof presents as 'insights' experienced at this level include 'hereditary, spiritual and cosmic factors *codetermining the development* of the embryo; they involve an awareness of genetic influences, cosmobiological and astrophysical energy fields, metaphysical forces, archetypal constellations, and the operation of karmic law'.[124] In addition, many difficult constructs of modern physics and mathematics, such as 'non-Euclidean geometry, Riemann's geometry of an *n*-dimensional space, Minkowski's space-time, and Einstein's special and general theories of relativity' were 'on occasion understood and actually subjectively experienced in psychedelic sessions'.[125] Some experiences are 'strongly indicative of genuine extrasensory perception', some individuals can acquire an ability to speak in a foreign language or *discover* deeper meaning in systems such as astrology, alchemy, I Ching and tarot.[126]

In addition to his use of terms such as *authentic, discover, genuine, insight* and *memory*, Grof makes a number of claims about verification, such as 'I was able to get surprising confirmations by independently questioning the mother or other persons involved [in intrauterine events]'; 'the attempt at objective verification brought positive results; experiences of 'the collective and racial unconscious ... can be considered important supportive evidence and *experimental confirmation* of one of the most controversial aspects of Jung's analytical psychology'; and 'Information communicated by these experiences is usually quite accurate and can be verified ...'[127]

Unfortunately, Grof's methods of verification are never specified in any detail, yet, as William James recognised, it is these verification processes that hold the key to the bridge that connects subjective experience with the universe outside of the subject. How were people's understandings of 'difficult constructs of modern physics and mathematics' or their foreign language abilities or their extra-sensory abilities tested? We are not told. How can a subjective experience of 'the collective and racial unconscious' be regarded as *experimental confirmation*? If Grof's notion of experimental confirmation is so loose and if his 'verifications' of mathematical understanding or ESP abilities are so unspecific how can he hope to persuade even mildly sceptical readers to regard claims about a law of karma, astrology and the tarot as credible?

All that is required for readers to take claims about knowledge acquisition during these sessions seriously is some demonstration that they have provided testable insights into some aspect of the external universe. Given the centrality of such verification for the credibility of drug-induced, numinously induced or mystically induced insights, discoveries and memories, one wonders why the presenters of such contributions to human knowledge never get round to undertaking and reporting the rigorous testing and verification processes that can provide the only means of demonstrating that these special and anomalous experiences really do offer a way to cross the bridge that separates the subjective from the objective. Surely they can understand the importance of those processes?

Like William James, Masters, Huston and Grof have been unable to build a bridge that will admit some kinds of subjective experiences, the psychedelic, into the list of reliable sources of information about the non-subjective universe. A similar point can be made about numinous and mystical experiences. According to Jain teaching, Mahāvīra and the other fordmakers (tīrthaṅkaras) were omniscient, that is, they had, 'in the most literal sense the ability to know and see everything in the universe at all times and in all possible modifications simultaneously ...'[128] All that would be needed for anyone interested in epistemology to take such claims seriously would be for Jain scriptures or any contemporary fordmaker (if there are any) to predict the discovery of something we do not yet know and for that prediction to be confirmed. For example, one of the early omniscient fordmakers would surely know that cholera is caused by the *Vibrio* bacterium, though he wouldn't necessarily use that name. He would also know that it has adverse effects on humans when it enters the small intestine, usually through the consumption of water inhabited by large numbers of the bacterium (between one and one hundred million according to Johnson).[129] Cholera infection can kill people in less than 24 hours, yet it is easy to cure, as I noted in Part 2 above:

> Cholera victims who are given water and electrolytes ... reliably survive the illness, to the point where numerous studies have deliberately infected volunteers with the disease to study its effects, knowing that the rehydration program will transform the disease into merely an uncomfortable bout of diarrhea.[130]

Surely, any omniscient and compassionate being, a fordmaker or a god such as Yahweh or Allah, would both know this and want to share it? Why then did a humanity that has been plagued by these bacterial and viral infections for its entire history never learn about them from their omniscient fellows or those who received revelations from supposedly omniscient and compassionate deities? The complete absence of any precise information about and guidance on how to deal with such sources of human misery is a good reason for doubting that religious experiences, however they are induced, do *not* provide reliable information about the universe outside of the experiencer. However insightful, illuminating or genuine such experiences might seem to those having them, in the absence of some kind of objectively testable insights they can never, and, in the current state of our knowledge, should never have authority for anyone else. Indeed, even the people who have religious experiences might well benefit from being aware of this epistemological deficiency when they reflect on the feelings of certainty that often accompany them. A subjective conviction of certainty does not guarantee knowledge, as we all know from reflecting on the certainty displayed by others about their false beliefs. The religious experiencer does, nevertheless, face a real problem. We rely on our subjective experience for determining what is real and what is not. Abandoning that reliance is no easy task.

The status of the 'insights' mentioned by Masters, Huston and Grof is not the only problematic element in the accounts of psychedelic experience provided by these researchers. Their schematic representations in terms of stages and levels is, as has been indicated above, also dodgy. To my mind, the safest and simplest way to think about the transformations of consciousness during psychedelic drug sessions lies along lines introduced by Kylie Cole for NeuroSoup.[131] It has four stages:

1. initial effects (coming up);
2. the peak (where most of the interesting stuff happens);
3. the come down; and
4. aftereffects.

The beauty of this scheme for the present enquiry is that it allows all psychedelic 'spiritual' experiences to be 'authentic' and does not grade them according to some predetermined notion of what is deeper, higher or more profound. All that remains for those who seek to rank psychedelic experiences, particularly the 'spiritual' ones, in relation to each other is the criterion of 'beneficial effects'. There is still, I suggest, quite a lot for researchers to work on in this area.

If the case I have presented above is a cogent one then it is clear that religious/spiritual experiences can be produced in many ways and that the only robust criterion for determining whether an experience is appropriately labelled as 'religious' or 'spiritual' is whether it is in some way 'supernatural'. Gods, angels, demons and spirits of various kinds are all 'supernatural'; so too are principles and processes such as 'the law of karma', the action of 'divine grace' and fate/predestination (e.g. kismet/qisma in Islām, 'election' in Christianity). Realms or states such as the Buddhist nirvāṇa, the Jain kaivalya, the Christian heaven and the Islāmic paradise are also supernatural. That is, their existence is not demonstrable by any robust method currently available and their characteristics contrast sharply with those that we can identify in any natural phenomenon, e.g. supernatural beings are often immortal whereas no natural beings are; supernatural processes produce effects that are inexplicable by any known causal mechanisms, and supernatural realms tend to be presented as unchanging or eternal, whereas nothing in the natural world has either of these characteristics.

Do supernatural experiences offer genuine insights into the way our universe works? No recorded religious/spiritual/supernatural experience seems able to offer a reliable bridge connecting the 'insights' of subjective conviction to objective demonstration, though there are many ways in which that the existence of that bridge could be established if it did exist. Unfortunately for religious people, none of the great prophets, divine incarnations or enlightened beings ever adopted any of them.

Finally, we might wonder whether supernatural experiences are good for people.[132] Much depends on how one determines what counts as flourishing, well-being, health or happiness for human beings. In this area there is scope for a great deal of further research; so I leave the final word to Kevin Nelson, who writes, following William James's claim that the transmarginal source of religious experience 'contains every kind of matter; 'seraph and snake' abide there side by side:

> It is sometimes impossible to tell where the healthy spirituality of the sage ends and spiritual psychosis begins. It's clear when a vision of Christ compels a husband to kill his wife in order to save the world from Satan, rather than inspires him to establish a monastery. But between the extremes, a difference between healthy and diseased spiritual experience isn't always clear.[133]

Notes

Introduction

1 Wallace (1966, ch. 2). My concern in this book is with supernatural belief systems, the experiences that inform them and their behavioural manifestations. Such systems, experiences and behaviours are usually described by native speakers of English as religious. If some writers wish to use the terms 'religion' and religion' to refer to systems, experiences and behaviours that do not have a supernatural referent that is up to them. What they are calling 'religion' and 'religious' is outside the scope of my definition.
2 For Huxley (1974, p. 17), that common core is the religion of unity.
3 For a critique of the perennialist position by an advocate of ranking see Zaehner (1957).
4 This term is used by different writers in quite different ways and carries the potential for a great deal of misunderstanding. Skim through any of the available 'companions' to philosophy and you will see that constructivism in mathematics differs from constructivism in ethics, though both are enmeshed in debates about realism, idealism and relativism. In the social sciences it is sometimes used interchangeably with 'constructionism', the idea that 'reality' is 'socially constructed', i.e. created by us rather than existing independently of us. Useful evaluations of constructivism/constructionism can be found in Pinker (2002) and Pompa (2003). John Searle makes an insightful shift of emphasis from *The Social Construction of Reality* (the title of a 1966 book by Peter Berger and Thomas Luckmann, who did not go as far as some of their successors and deny the existence of an 'objective reality') to *The Construction of Social Reality* (the title of his 1995 work on the subject – a sequel, *Making the Social World,* was published in 2010). Examples of full-blown constructionist claims would be 'Words do things like construct realities ...' and 'the social constructionist perspective ... views the world as constructed in language' (Miell and Pike 2007, pp. 267, 316).

My presentation of a constructivist perspective is largely taken from the work of Paul Watzlawick, e.g. *The Language of Change* (1978). This version derives significantly from Kant's distinction between phenomena (what we experience) and noumena ('objective reality', what is actually there). Accessing noumena is extremely difficult; some think it is impossible. Our most successful attempts have come via modern scientific research. One of the most outspoken advocates of the view that science can support a correspondence notion of truth, which is based on the idea that we *can* access 'objective reality', is Richard Dawkins, formerly professor of the public understanding of science at Oxford University. In a short and highly readable article entitled 'What is true?' he writes,

> It is simply true that the Sun is hotter than the Earth, true that the desk on which I am writing is made of wood ... forever true that DNA is a double helix, true that if you and a chimpanzee (or an octopus or a kangaroo) trace your ancestors back far enough you will actually hit a shared ancestor ... If scientific truth is open to doubt, it is no more so than common sense truth. (Dawkins 2003, pp. 17–18)

Dawkins argues that the road to knowledge through scientific enquiry is different from other routes. Although some notions in science are still open to modification, many are as well established as we could possibly hope for. In short, he claims that real knowledge does exist as a result of scientific enquiry, and when we express that knowledge in statements those statements can be true in a correspondence kind of way.

5 See Ramachandran and Blakeslee (1998, ch. 5) for a neurological exploration of the 'more real than real' phenomenon.
6 James (1902/1985, pp. 405, 422ff.).
7 Here I follow Karl Popper's use of the term. One of his many contributions to philosophy was a clarification of the problem of 'induction' in science. Induction is essentially reasoning from the particular to the general. For example, 'Everyone I've ever met speaks English; everyone my parents have ever met speaks English; therefore, everyone speaks English.' Another example is the turkey who becomes more confident with every day that it is fed that it will be fed tomorrow (though tomorrow is 25 December).

Induction was believed by philosophers such as Francis Bacon, and even some today (so it's a little more complex than I'm making out here), to be the basis of scientific method and the way we arrive at the universal statements that are often called 'Laws of Nature', i.e. the statements beginning with 'All'. This idea was challenged by Popper, who argued that scientific enquiry is not essentially inductive but hypothetico-deductive.

On this view, particular instances do not provide a springboard for inferring general laws or principles; rather they provide a context in which hypotheses can be generated. These hypotheses can then be tested, i.e. we try to prove that they are wrong. If we succeed then we have falsified the hypothesis, we have eliminated it as a contender for explaining whatever it is that we are seeking to understand. If we fail to falsify the hypothesis then we can have confidence in it, though we can never arrive at the point where we can be absolutely sure that our explanation is 'the truth'. Popper proposes the term 'corroborated' for hypotheses that have been tested but remain unfalsified.

8   I have taken this evocative phrase from the title of a book edited by Joseph de Rivera and Theodore R. Sarbin: *Believed-In-Imaginings: the narrative construction of reality* (de Rivera and Sarbin 1998).
9   Smart (1986, p. 196).
10 Op. cit., p. 197.
11 Op. cit., p. 198 (emphasis in original).
12 Connolly (2014).

Part 1: A critical phenomenology of religious experience

1   Yang (1967, p. 20).
2   Loc. cit.
3   Gombrich (1988, pp. 25–26). 'Soteriologies' are doctrines/teachings about salvation or liberation. They differ primarily on how the salvation or liberation is accomplished: by one's own efforts (self-power), by the grace/power of another being such as a god or bodhisattva (other-power) or by some combination of the two.
4   Op. cit., p. 26.
5   Op. cit., p. 27.
6   Sometimes such claims may be based on purely theological inferences rather than some kind of direct apprehension. In that case, an analysis of the reasoning can determine whether or not the arguments supporting them are sound.
7   See Introduction.
8   Otto (1950).
9   Smart (1958), especially chapter 5.
10 Ontology is the study of existence or being. Typically, it focuses on the ultimate level of existence. At the most fundamental level, how many existing things are there? If all matter is ultimately reducible to energy does that cover everything that exists, or is there something else, e.g. spirit? Epistemology is the study of knowledge and the processes by which it is acquired. Psychology is the study of 'mental' processes and their effects on behaviour.
11 Otto, op. cit., p. 6.
12 Op. cit., pp. 5, 175. Sui generis: of its own kind; distinct from anything else.
13 Loc. cit.
14 Op. cit., p. 7.
15 Op. cit., p. 19.
16 Cavanagh (1978, p. 20).
17 Beattie et al. (2009, p. 32).
18 Cited in Smith (1998, p. 281).
19 Barnes-Svarney (1995, p. 124).
20 Wallace (1966, p. 52).
21 Smart (1969, p. 28).

22 King (1998, pp. 670–671). A note on 'spirituality': I understand 'spirituality' to refer to what religious people do in the pursuit of their religious/spiritual goals. That is, a person's spirituality is primarily behavioural, even though it is informed and perhaps motivated by their religious/supernatural beliefs. As Ursula King (1998: 670–671) notes, 'Spiritual exercises and disciplines undertaken to attain specific spiritual goals are found in all religions. Such practices can range from individual and communal prayer to the practice of silence, the stilling of the mind, meditation, contemplation, the reading or recitation of sacred texts and mantras, to fasting penances, pilgrimages and many others'.
23 Otto (1950, p. 28). We may note here that Otto has shifted from writing about a kind of experience to writing about that which is deemed to be the source of that experience.
24 Otto, op. cit., p. 13.
25 Op. cit., p. 19.
26 Op. cit., pp. 19–20.
27 Op. cit., p. 29.
28 Op. cit., p. 27.
29 Op. cit., p. 14.
30 Op. cit., p. 17.
31 Op. cit., p. 33.
32 Op. cit., p. 32.
33 Op. cit., p. 33.
34 Loc. cit.
35 Op. cit., p. 125.
36 Op. cit., p. 129.
37 Loc. cit.
38 Op. cit., p. 134.
39 Loc. cit.
40 For example Armstrong (1999, p. 3); Eliade (1959, pp. 15, 18 and passim).
41 Adaptations are characteristics that all or most members of a species possess. Examples among humans would include stereoscopic vision, an opposing thumb, vocal cords and a locking knee joint. Some adaptations, such as stereoscopic vision, are paralleled in other species; others, such as vocal cords, are unique to humans. Adaptations are created by selection processes, i.e. natural and sexual selection. They begin as changes or mutations in the genome, though we should note that most mutations do not evolve into adaptations, not least because the majority of them are deleterious to the organism. Every so often, however, a mutation provides the organism carrying it with an advantage in either or both of survival and reproduction. If an organism can survive better than its fellows then its chances of reproducing its genes are increased; if an organism can attract mates better than its fellows then its chances of reproducing its genes are increased; if an organism can survive better *and* attract mates better than its fellows then its chances of reproducing its genes are increased.

Over time, organisms possessing the enhanced survival/attraction characteristics will increase in the population until all or most of its members have them to some degree. At that point (or perhaps a bit earlier) those characteristics have become adaptations. Even a cursory examination of human anatomy and physiology reveals that many of our physical characteristics are adaptations that were created over time by selection processes in relatively stable environments. Rapidly changing environments tend to restrict the advantages bestowed by particular mutations, and that prevents them from spreading through the population, i.e. from becoming adaptations. An important point to note here is that it is not the organisms, what biologists call phenotypes, that are 'adapting' but rather that certain packages of characteristics enable individuals to survive and reproduce better than their fellows.

So, adaptations evolve by means of selection processes operating over time in relatively stable environments. Now is it likely that human bodies have evolved numerous adaptations while human minds have not? Evolutionary biologists and psychologists think not. The most likely scenario is that many of our cognitive and emotional tendencies are adaptations, that is, adaptations to the environment in which human species (homo) evolved: over 5,000,000 years in Africa and, for homo sapiens, around 60,000 years across the rest of the globe. Examples of psychological adaptations would be what psychologists call 'theory of mind' and 'reciprocal altruism' (see my *A Student's Guide to the History and Philosophy of Yoga* for an argument to support this claim: Connolly 2014, pp. 277–284). 'Human nature' is a convenient shorthand for 'all the evolutionary adaptations shared by most humans'. Is 'religion' an evolutionary adaptation?

42 For example, Ayala (2012, p. 122).
43 Dawkins (1991, p. 178).
44 See Zimmer (2001, pp. 316–317) and Mayr (1982, pp. 531–534) for overviews. Examples of such writers and their works are Koestler (1971, 1972) and Teilhard de Chardin (1961).
45 Mencken (1949/1982, pp. 95–98).
46 Otto (1950, p. 134).
47 Op. cit., p. 178.
48 On the positive side, psychologist Shelley Taylor (1989) found that the most mentally healthy people were not those who had a realistic understanding of their situation in the world but those who had an unrealistic optimism about it. These optimists believed that: (a) they were better than average at most things; (b) that they were, overall, in control of their lives; and (c) that their future would be a good one. Not only were the optimists mentally healthy, they also tended to be quite successful and their success validated their optimistic beliefs so that those beliefs became true, they worked. This is not to say that the healthy fail to perceive things accurately, for they are quite good at perceiving the nature of both physical and social situations. Rather, it is to note that such perceptions are far less salient for them than for depressives. In other words, the healthiest

people seem to be able to operate accurate and illusory conceptions of the world in parallel.

The reason why this ability helps to promote mental health is, according to John Schumaker, that the generally accurate perception of reality made available to us by our developed cognitive abilities (for example, the recognition of the inevitability of death) can be debilitating. Human beings require, therefore, something to counter-balance the sense of powerlessness, meaninglessness and futility that an accurate understanding of our existence can generate. This something, suggests Schumaker, is our capacity for reality distortion. Religion, in his view, is the traditional method employed by cultures to distort reality in a way that is deemed to be beneficial – by the promotion of meanings and values for example. It succeeds in this because of the brain's capacity for dissociation, the capacity to run different programmes at different times and even in parallel (Schumaker 1990, 1995).

On the negative side, reality distortion is not always beneficial. Individuals and cultures can create negative illusions, e.g. the need for human sacrifice, almost as easily as they can create positive ones. What is more, illusions seem to be more potent when they are given objective status, when they are taken to be realities. That, I would suggest, is exactly what we find when we examine human conceptions of value, meaning and the sacred. In contrast with the long-standing, dominant tradition of moral objectivism in western ethical philosophy a major strand in meta-ethical enquiry during the twentieth century has been to argue that moral principles are invented rather than discovered (see Mackie 1977). Likewise, recent psychological investigations into the attribution of meaning to situations and events suggest that it is constructive rather than perceptual (see Bandler and Grinder 1982 and Schumaker 1995, which present a strong case for understanding conceptions of the sacred in the same way).

From the pragmatic perspective of assessing their contribution to mental health value systems, meaning systems and religious systems would all seem to be on a par. They are often attributed with objective status though there are good reasons for thinking that they are all illusions, constructed by human minds with the aim of benefiting human lives. Whether they do so is a matter for well-constructed empirical enquiries to determine. To paraphrase one well-known religious teacher, 'By their fruits shall ye know them'.

49 Most of the material on possession is taken from my *A Psychology of Possession* (Connolly 2000A).
50 Oesterreich (1974).
51 Op. cit., p. 39.
52 From the television broadcast 'They Shall Take Up Serpents', *Everyman*, BBC Wales, 1984.
53 For further discussion of benefits deriving from involuntary possession see, for example, Lewis (1971), especially chapter 3; Spanos and Gottleib (1979).
54 Modern academics tend to prefer 'vodun' to 'voodoo'. I don't. See, for example, Goodman (1988B, pp. 108–110).

55 Hultkrantz (1978, p. 42).
56 Op. cit., p. 48.
57 Op. cit., p. 36.
58 Op. cit., p. 40.
59 Goodman (1988B, p. 109).
60 From the television broadcast 'Bahia of All the Saints', *Arena*, BBC2, 7 May 1994.
61 Op. cit.
62 Much of the material in this section is taken from my 'Mystical Experience and Trance Experience' (Connolly 2000B).
63 Smart (1980, p. 78). Smart, it should be noted, does acknowledge that these expressions of religiosity are often found intermingled.
64 James (1902/1985, p. 309); Stace (1961, p. 60).
65 Stace, op. cit., pp. 61–62. Although I am here simply quoting Stace's general descriptions of these experiences readers should not infer that the distinction he makes lacks phenomenological grounding. His treatment contains numerous extracts from religious texts that illustrate the points he is making.
66 Op. cit., p. 60.
67 Nelson (2011, p. 28).
68 James, op. cit., p. 385.
69 Forman (1990, p. 8).
70 James, op. cit., pp. 380–382.
71 Stace, op. cit., p. 132.
72 Smart, op. cit., p. 82.
73 Op. cit., p. 83.
74 Katz (1978, p. 26).
75 Cf. Newberg and Waldman (2007, pp. 207–209).
76 Loc. cit.
77 Op. cit., p. 57.
78 Forman (1990, p. 8).
79 Bernhardt (1990, p. 232).
80 Forman (1990, p. 8).
81 Horner (1954/1976, p. 302).
82 Masefield (1986B, p. 63).
83 Masefield (1986A, p. 167).
84 Sinh (1975).
85 Vasu (1976).
86 Muktananda (1978, pp. 21–23).
87 Argyle and Beit-Hallami (1997); Hood et al. (2009); Nelson (2009); Paloutzian and Park (2013); Wolff (1996).
88 Eliade (1959, p. 100).
89 Op. cit., p. 14.
90 Op. cit., pp. 17–18.
91 Op. cit., p. 23.
92 Op. cit., p. 24.

93 Op. cit., p. 31.
94 Op. cit., p. 47.
95 A storyline that immediately invites parallels with the abduction of Helen by Paris.
96 Klostermaier (1989, p. 88).
97 Doniger (2009, p. 23).
98 Bronkhorst (2013, pp. 4–8).
99 Doniger and Smith (1991).
100 Zaehner (1969, p. 393).
101 Edgerton's translation. Compare Plato's use of Hesiod's story of how the gods created the demigods and the four races of men, each from a different metal: gold, silver, bronze and iron (*Works and Days* 105–201) in *The Republic* 415–418; 433ff.; 546ff., and Aristotle's discussion of 'natural slavery' and the inherent inferiority of women in *The Politics* (1.4–7).
102 Eliade (1959, p. 163).
103 Op. cit. e.g. pp. 11–12, 24ff.
104 Op. cit., p. 183.
105 Op. cit., p. 166.
106 See, for example, Harrington (2008); Benedetti et al. (2011, pp. 339–354); Zubieta and Stohler (2009, pp. 198–210).
107 Eliade (1959, p. 166).
108 van Gennep (1960).
109

The liturgical year

Christian churches divide every year into a number of elements that remind their adherents of events in the life of Jesus and connect them with those events through rituals. The pivotal points are Easter, when Jesus is claimed to have risen from the dead, and Christmas, the date on which the birth of Jesus is celebrated. Since 1969 the Roman Catholic church has divided the liturgical year into six 'seasons': Advent, Christmas, Ordinary Time, Lent, The Easter Triduum, and Easter (http://catholicism.about.com/od/holydaysandholidays/tp/What-Are-the-Liturgical-Seasons-of-the-Catholic-Church.htm?utm_term=seasons%20of%20the%20liturgical%20year&utm_content=p1-main-2-title&utm_medium=sem&utm_source=msn_s&utm_campaign=adid-144f5369-f530-4e81-9f69-a864053afd36-0-ab_msb_ocode-28799&ad=semD&an=msn_s&am=broad&q=seasons%20of%20the%20liturgical%20year&o=28799&qsrc=999&l=sem&askid=144f5369-f530-4e81-9f69-a864053afd36-0-ab_msb, accessed 16 July 2016).

The Vatican website lists the six divisions of the liturgical year as Advent, Christmas, Lent, Easter, Pentecost and Ordinary Time. Various activities are encouraged in each. So, during Advent, a period of preparation, extending over four Sundays, before Christmas, Roman Catholics are encouraged to pray more frequently and to fast, either moderately, e.g. by refraining from eating meat during the period, or rigorously, e.g. by missing one or more of the day's meals. They are also encouraged to engage in symbolic activities, such as preparing and celebrating with an Advent wreath. The Advent wreath 'consists of four candles (three purple, signifying penance, and one rose, signifying joy), surrounded by evergreen branches. One purple candle is lit the first week, two the second, two purple and one rose the third, and finally all four in the last week of Advent. The light of the candles signifies the light of Christ, Who will come into the world at Christmas' (http://catholicism.about.com/od/adventactivities/p/Advent_Wreath.htm, accessed 16 July 2016). The wreath acts as a focus for religious thinking and action during those four weeks, and Roman Catholics are encouraged to engage in rituals of blessing the wreath and reading selected Biblical texts as a family group. Similar guidelines are provided for each of the other six seasons.

Through activities such as these are the lives of everyday Roman Catholic people 'sacralised' on a daily basis. They are constantly reminded of the doctrines, stories and spiritually transformative powers of the church. They engage in actions that turn them into participants in the cosmic drama described by their religious tradition. And they experience structured emotional encounters with key events in the religious narratives of their tradition. For example, during Lent Roman Catholics are encouraged to perform the 'stations of the cross': 14 incidents leading up to the entombment of Jesus. They are commonly represented in pictorial form around the walls of Roman Catholic churches, though some are outdoors, where they create a kind of processional route. A fine example of this can be found on the hills above the Italian town of Sorrento. The events usually depicted in the stations are: (1) Christ is condemned to death; (2) Christ receives the cross; (3) His first fall; (4) He meets His Mother; (5) Simon of Cyrene is made to bear the cross; (6) Christ's face is wiped by Veronica; (7) His second fall; (8) He meets the women of Jerusalem; (9) His third fall; (10) He is stripped of His garments; (11) He is nailed to the cross; (12) Christ dies on the cross; (13) His body is taken down from the cross; (14) His body is laid in the tomb. As the devotees reach each station they are encouraged to meditate on the event and reflect on what Jesus was undergoing for their benefit. ('The devotion probably arose out of the practice, attested from an early date, of pilgrims at Jerusalem following the traditional route from Pilate's house to Calvary and wishing to reproduce an analogous devotion at home'; from 'Stations of the Cross' in Cross and Livingstone 2005).

The sacraments: Roman Catholic rites of passage

Interspersed with the regular 'sacralisations' of the liturgical year are occasional ones that are usually connected to events within the life cycle of individuals. The seven sacraments of the Roman Catholic Church exemplify this well. A Sacrament, according to the church, 'is an outward sign instituted by Christ to give grace' (http://catholicism.about.com/od/baltimorecatechism/f/Question_136_BC.htm?utm_term=7%20Sacraments%20in%20Order&utm_content=p1-main-6-title&utm_medium=sem-rel&utm_source=msn_s&utm_campaign=adid-9c8bc261-90df-4dc5-9cfe-919bf1aaf70b-0-ab_msb_ocode-35469&ad=semD&an=msn_s&am=broad&q=7%20Sacraments%20in%20Order&o=35469&qsrc=6&l=&askid=9c8bc261-90df-4dc5-9cfe-919bf1aaf70b-0-ab_msb, accessed 16 July 2016). The sacraments are: Baptism, Confirmation, Holy Communion, Confession (Reconciliation or Penance), Marriage, Holy Orders, and the Anointing of the Sick (Extreme Unction/Last Rites) (Loc. cit.). Baptism is the initiation of an individual into the church. By this rite the stain of original sin is removed from the person's soul. Confirmation 'is regarded as the perfection of Baptism, because ... [the baptized] are more perfectly bound to the Church and are enriched with a special strength of the Holy Spirit' (http://catholicism.about.com/od/beliefsteachings/p/Confirmation.htm, accessed 16 July 2016).

Holy Communion is the only sacrament that Roman Catholics 'can (and should) receive repeatedly – even daily, if possible. In Holy Communion, we consume the Body and Blood of Christ, which unites us more closely to Him and helps us to grow in grace by living a more Christian life' (http://catholicism.about.com/od/beliefsteachings/p/Sac_Communion.htm, accessed 16 July 2016). Confession involves telling a priest the sins one has committed and receiving God's forgiveness for them. The Church requires its members 'to go to Confession once per year, in preparation for doing our Easter Duty; and we must, of course, go to Confession before receiving Communion whenever we're conscious of having committed a grave or mortal sin. ... [moreover] Monthly Confession, even if we're only aware of minor or venial sins, can be a great source of graces and can help us to focus our efforts on neglected areas of our spiritual life' (http://catholicism.about.com/od/beliefsteachings/p/Why_Confession.htm, accessed 16 July 2016).

The 5th and 6th sacraments are, to all intents and purposes, alternatives. Laymen and laywomen are encouraged to marry, but men who feel themselves to have a spiritual vocation may take Holy Orders and become a priest. 'At its most basic level, marriage is a union between a man and a woman for the purpose of procreation and mutual support, or love ... It is a union of opposite sexes. It is a lifelong union, ending only with the death of one spouse. It excludes a union with any other person so long as the marriage exists. Its lifelong nature and exclusiveness are guaranteed by contract.' Moreover, in the Catholic Church 'marriage is more than a natural institution; it was elevated by Christ Himself, in His participation in the wedding at Cana (John 2:1-11), to be one of the seven sacraments. A marriage between two Christians, therefore, has a supernatural element as well as a natural one' (www.thoughtco.com/what-is-matrimony-542851?_ga=2.111675460.1304738479.1495185138-609872486.1495185138, accessed 16 July 2016). Holy Orders 'is a Sacrament by which bishops, priests, and other ministers of the Church are ordained and receive the power and grace to perform their sacred duties'. (http://catholicism.about.com/od/baltimorecatechism/f/Question_278_BC.htm, accessed May 2017).

Finally, Anointing of the Sick (Extreme Unction or Last Rites). 'The essential rite of the sacrament consists in the priest (or multiple priests, in the case of the Eastern Churches) laying hands on the sick, anointing him with blessed oil (usually olive oil blessed by a bishop, but in an emergency, any vegetable oil will suffice), and praying: "Through this holy anointing may the Lord in his love and mercy help you with the grace of the Holy Spirit. May the Lord who frees you from sin save you and raise you up." ... Only priests (including bishops) can administer the Sacrament of the Anointing of the Sick, since, when the sacrament was instituted during Christ's sending out of His disciples, it was confined to the men who would become the original bishops of the Church' (http://catholicism.about.com/od/beliefsteachings/p/Sac_Anointing.htm, accessed 16 July 2016).

Thus, not only is every year of a Roman Catholic's life punctuated by regular rites and rituals that immerse the person in the tradition's supernatural and sacralised cosmos, so too are most of the significant changes in each of those lives. The Hindu tradition, though much less centralised in its organisation, exhibits a similar pattern.

Hindu festivals

Spread across the year are numerous festivals (utsava), occasions for joy and merriment. Some of these are almost national though many are merely local. Some, such as Dīvalī, function to promote a common Hindu identity, while others, such as Holī, act as pressure valves that, temporarily, release people from pervasive straightjacket of brāmanical dharma regulations. The dates of these tend to be determined locally and in dependence on astrological calculations (auspicious times must be sought; inauspicious times must be avoided) and the kind of calendar being used. In addition to the solar calendar, which is quite similar to the 'Gregorian' calendar familiar in the West, two lunar calendars are used: one is calculated by reference to the beginning of the moon's 'dark fortnight' and the other by reference to the beginning of its 'light fortnight. The former is common in Northern India; the latter in Southern India. Full moon and new moon days are auspicious and commonly used for holidays. The website www.about.com produces a yearly list of major festivals (see http://hinduism.about.com/od/festivalsholidays/a/hindunewyear_2.htm, accessed 20 July 2016).

Festivals that are popular and widely celebrated include:

- *Makara Saṃkrānti* (the Winter Solstice) is held on the eve of the full moon in the month of Magha (Aquarius). The work of the god Śiva in creating and destroying the universe is often celebrated at this festival and women often pray for the welfare of their menfolk or a good husband.

- *Holī* is celebrated in the month of Phalguṇa (February/March). It is a Spring festival with an emphasis on fertility. Caste differences are often relaxed and lower castes can be allowed to wreak a little vengeance on their higher caste neighbours for the discrimination that operates during the rest of the year, e.g. by emptying piss pots on them or, in more restrained environments, plastering them with coloured powder or paint.

- *Meṣa Saṃkrānti* is celebrated in the month of Caitra (March/April). It is known as Vaisakhi/Baisakhi in Northern India). In the North people often 'clean and decorate their houses and invoke Goddess Lakshmi, the bestower of wealth and prosperity. All new enterprises begin on this auspicious day, as businessmen open their fresh ledgers with "Haal Khata" – a ceremony in which Lord Ganesha is summoned and customers are invited to settle all their old dues and offered free refreshments' (http://hinduism.about.com/od/festivalsholidays/a/hindunewyear_2.htm, accessed 20 July 2016). In the South people often distribute coins to the poor, don new clothes, light fireworks as well as cleaning and decorating their houses (loc. cit.).

- *Kṛṣṇa Jayānti/Janmashtami* (Śrāvana = July/August) is a celebration of Kṛṣṇa's birth that is almost pan-Indian. 'Krishna's birthplace, Mathura, and Vrindavan [where he spent his youth] celebrate this occasion with great pomp and show. Raslilas or religious plays are performed to recreate incidents from the life of Krishna and to commemorate his love for Radha. Song and dance mark the celebration of this festive occasion all over northern India. At midnight, the statue of infant Krishna is bathed and placed in a cradle, which is rocked, amidst the blowing of conch shells and the ringing of bells. In the south western state of Maharashtra, people enact the god's childhood attempts to steal butter and curd from earthen pots beyond his reach. A similar pot is suspended high above the ground and groups of young people form human pyramids to try and reach the pot and break it' (http://hinduism.about.com/od/festivalsholidays/a/janmashthami.htm, accessed 21 July 2016).

- *Dassera* (Aśvina = September/October) is another pan-Indian festival, or rather, clutch of festivals, that includes Durgā Pūja (worship of the goddess Durgā), especially in Bengal, and various Rām Līlās (celebrations of Rāma's victory over Rāvaṇa) in the North.

- *Divalī/Dīpavalī* (also in Aśvina = September/October) is a four-day festival of lights which contains other festivals that link to a variety of myths and stories, many of which are celebrated in just one or two regions of India (http://hinduism.about.com/od/diwalifestivaloflights/a/diwali.htm, accessed 21 July 2016).

Like the liturgical year of Roman Catholicism the frequent festivals of Hinduism ensure that the population is almost constantly exposed to supernatural stories and myths that, largely through presupposition, bestow life and reality upon them. I remember a friend returning from India with what was, ostensibly, a geography book on Mount Kailash and Manasarovar, one of the highest freshwater lakes on Earth. It included material on myths related to the site as though they were geographical facts, a fine example of Eliade's claim that for *homo religiosus* 'life is lived on a twofold plane; it takes its course as human existence and, at the same time, shares in a transhuman life, that of the cosmos or the gods' (Eliade 1959, p. 167). For the devout reader of such books there is no incongruity between the geography and the mythology.

The Saṃskāras: Hindu rites of passage

Like many Hindu practices, who does what in terms of transformative rituals/sacraments (saṃskāras) is determined by caste. The main focus is twice-born males. 'Twice-born' (dvija) refers primarily to the 'second birth' that a male of the upper three varṇas (literally 'colour' but here referring to social group/class, each of which has its own symbolic colour) experiences at his initiation into adulthood at the sacred thread ceremony (upanāyana). The most influential of the traditional textbooks on dharma, the Laws of Manu (*Mānavadharmaśāstra*), lists twelve of these, though not all are commonly practised. The index of Wendy Doniger's translation lists all twelve 'transformative rituals' along with their locations in the text of the *śāstra* (Doniger and Smith 1991). They are: conception; bringing forth a male child; parting the mother's hair; birth; name-giving; going out; first food; tonsure; initiation (upanayana); final haircut; student homecoming, and marriage (vivāha). Subsequently, the last rites (antyeṣṭi) were added to this list and are now performed by almost all Hindus. However, as Simon Weightman notes, 'The pre-natal rites have nowadays fallen from use and the first obsevances are those attending birth' (Weightman 1998, p. 287). Conception is a particularly important time as a person's horoscope is based upon the exact time. Astrology also plays an important role in determining the times at which other saṃskāras are performed. Where astrology is employed within religious traditions it can be seen to facilitate what Eliade called the process of 'cosmicisation', essentially, connecting people with postulated supernatural realities.

For members of the brāhman castes the upanayana ceremony is still highly important. This is the second birth and initiation into adulthood that separates males from females and the twice-born from the once-born (śūdras and untouchables). For all castes it is marriage (vivāha) that is the most important saṃskāra, for marriage leads to reproduction, and reproduction lies at the heart of societal continuity. Hence the couple are deemed to be at their most ritually pure (an intrinsically supernatural concept) at this point in their life cycles.

Marriage ceremonies tend to be the most elaborate of all transformative rituals and often last for a week or even longer. Finally, it is the last rites that provide the most powerful supernatural element in the cosmicisation of the Hindu *homo religiosus*. Traditionally, they accomplish two things: first, enabling the spirit of the departed to avoid becoming a ghost and join the ancestors, and second, cleansing the family of the ritual pollution that is believed to be generated by a death. The eldest son plays an important role in these ceremonies as males are believed to be necessary for the rites to be effective.

The liturgical year/festival cycle and rites of passage are just two of the ways that the everyday lives of religious people are turned into religious experiences. The changes in the year are cosmicised and celebrated through supernaturally informed rituals. Significant points in the lives of individuals are cosmicised by rituals that, in a variety of ways, touch people's experiences with a supernatural caress or jolt. There are also a number of other voluntary activities that religious people can undertake to deepen their sense of cosmicisation, one of the most popular being pilgrimage.

Pilgrimages

The practice of going on pilgrimage is found in all major religious traditions (see Hinnells 1998, p. 886 for references). In all, except for Islām, it is a voluntary or optional form of spirituality, and even in Islām the great pilgrimage (hajj) 'is required of all Muslims at least once in a lifetime [only] *if* they are physically able to make the trip and can afford it ...' (Welch 1998, p. 193; emphasis mine). More specifically, men 'must be sane, free from serious physical infirmity and – most importantly, able to provide for their dependants while they are away ... Muslim women may take part in the *hajj*, subject to certain restrictions. During it each must be accompanied by a male chaperon (*mahram*), who must be a man she is legally unable to marry – for example her father or brother' (Horrie and Chippindale 2007, p. 42). A detailed survey of pilgrimage traditions is unnecessary for my purposes here, for I simply want to illustrate how the practice of going on pilgrimage can be a source of everyday religious experience and, on occasion, result in something more profoundly numinous or mystical. Hence I shall concentrate on pilgrimage within the Hindu tradition. My treatment will be divided into five sections: reasons for undertaking a pilgrimage; the journey itself; pilgrimage sites; appropriate times for undertaking a pilgrimage, and activities engaged in at pilgrimage sites.

Reasons for undertaking a pilgrimage

Often a pilgrimage is undertaken as the fulfilment of some particular vow, which could have been made for a variety of reasons, ranging from curing sickness to the granting of wealth or offspring. Some pilgrims will be seeking to appease deities that they feel are responsible for their misfortunes or whom they think will help them to overcome misfortunes. Yet others go on pilgrimage simply to acquire religious merit and obtain a better rebirth. For the very devout it can simply be an expression of their devotion to a chosen deity. It also needs to be recognised that for many people a pilgrimage can be a kind of holiday.

The pilgrimage journey

'In the most general terms a pilgrimage represents a person's journey from the world of the profane, or ordinary, to the world of the sacred, and as such is often marked by the characteristics of a rite of passage in which the participant undergoes a three stage process of separation, threshold and incorporation' (Kinsley 1982, p. 108). Before the journey, in the stage of separation, from ordinary life, the pilgrim often engages in actions that symbolise a transition such as shaving the head (symbolic of new birth) and donning new/clean clothes (symbolic of moving from the old, tarnished life into one that is more pure). On the journey, in the stage of threshold (liminality: a condition of being between two states) the pilgrim abides in a kind of identity limbo, neither the person (s)he was nor the person (s)he is to become. This, perhaps, goes some way towards explaining why caste differences, so meticulously observed in the village context, are often less in evidence during pilgrimages.

The journey also provides opportunities to engage in other religious activities. One of the most popular is penance, which can help the pilgrim to dissociate from their former life and identify with the soon-to-be-transformed one. There are many acceptable penances. One is for the pilgrim to observe a vow of silence for the entire journey. To facilitate this many wear a handkerchief over the mouth while the more devout/extreme employ a mouth lock: a silver band placed over the mouth and held in place by a skewer that pierces the cheeks and connects the two ends of the band. Another is to cover either the whole journey or a section of it by successive prostrations, a practice also adopted by Buddhist pilgrims. Some pilgrims even go so far as to complete the entire journey by rolling sideways, i.e. not head over heels. (e.g. Lotan Baba in the film *Sadhus*). The more enthusiastic pilgrims can often be identified by the symbols they display. A white conch shell indicates a successful pilgrimage to Rāmeśvara, iron bracelets a pilgrimage to Paśupatināth, brass ones to Kedarnāth and copper ones to Badarīnāth. In the past pilgrims to many sites were branded with the symbol of the deity worshipped at there. Nowadays it is more common to make the deity's mark with moistened clay, though some South Indian monasteries (maṭha) still retain the older practice and festival celebrations at many sites still host a variety of ascetic activities ranging from firewalking to being strung up from hooks inserted into the flesh of the devotee's back and legs.

Pilgrimage sites

On arrival at a sacred site the pilgrim usually participates in a number of standard activities that are organised by the resident priests. Such sites tend to be of two kinds. One is the naturally 'sacred' site, a place of geographical distinction and transition (liminal qualities) such as a river bank, the junction of two rivers, mountains and places where unusual rocks, trees or caves can be found. The other is the site that is made sacred through association with a mythological event. Places that combine the two types are especially sacred, e.g. Ayodhyā, the birth place of Rāma (see Schwartzberg 1978/1992, p. 99 for a map of all the major Hindu, Buddhist, Jain and Sikh pilgrimage sites in this region).

Times for pilgrimage

In addition to the notion that certain places are sacred, i.e. have supernatural qualities, pilgrimage activities are profoundly influenced by astrological considerations. Sacred sites are believed to have greater spiritual potency at particular times, which are usually calculated by local astrologers. The role of astrology is especially evident in the timing of the great fairs (mela) that take place every twelve years at Allahabad, Hardwar, Nasik and Ujjain.

Activities at pilgrimage sites

In everyday discourse we often say that good fortune depends on being in the right place at the right time. In the case of Hindu pilgrimage this is not sufficient. Once people have arrived at the right place at the right time they also have to do the right things. These differ from site to site, though some general observations can be made about the more common ones. For example, certain sites have a particular connection with the cult of the dead. This tends to be based on ancient Vedic ideas that the spirits of the dead live on in heavenly realms rather than the more 'yogic' notion of transmigration. The most important sites for these cults are Vārāṇasī, Hardwar, Gayā, and Siddhpur. The primary activity at such sites is consigning the ashes of dead relatives to the holy water while a priest guides the relatives through the appropriate rites, which usually involve making offerings of milk and balls of rice. This kind of rite is restricted to members of the twice born classes. Members of other classes are restricted to local patterns of worship (pūja). With the development of the Indian postal system the sending of ashes to a priest at an appropriate site so that he may perform the rites without the relatives needing to be present has become quite popular.

For most pilgrims the activities at any particular site will involve some kind of veneration of a cult object, perhaps a sacred stone, tree or pool, or the image of a deity, which will be housed in a temple. At the simplest level the pilgrim may perform a circumambulation of the object, where he/she keeps the right shoulder towards it. Other activities increase in complexity and usually require the services of a priest who knows the appropriate mantras (chants) and texts.

Each religious tradition has its own variants on the elements of separation, threshold and incorporation. Each will emphasise different things at 'sacred sites', e.g. relics figure prominently in Buddhist and Christian pilgrimage destinations but are a minor feature at Hindu ones, and, of course, the stories, symbols and rituals performed will be distinctive in many ways. Nevertheless, even a casual observer of festivals, rites of passage and pilgrimage journeys cannot fail to notice that they all serve as vehicles for maintaining belief in a supernatural realm and the value of activities that promote an effective engagement with it. Each contributes, in its own way, to fostering modest religious experiences in those who participate in it, and, since these activities and events punctuate the lives of religious adherents with considerable frequency, the reinforcement of belief in the reality of the sacred is literally unremitting.

110 Eliade (1959, p. 23).
111 Op. cit., p. 203.
112 Davies (1996, p. 601).
113 Newberg and Waldman draw attention to some interesting data on this point:

> Many studies have attempted to correlate religion with health, but none has clearly shown that atheism is an unhealthy belief system. ... according to the research of Phil Zuckerman, a professor of sociology at Pitzer College, 'In sum, countries marked by high rates of organic atheism [i.e. not imposed by the rulers] are among the most socially healthy on earth, while societies characterized by non-existent rates of organic atheism are among the most destitute. Nations marked by high degrees of organic atheism tend to have among the lowest homicide rates, infant mortality rates, poverty rates and illiteracy rates, and among the highest levels of wealth, life expectancy, educational attainment and gender equality in the world.'
> (Newberg and Waldman 2007, pp. 238–240)

See also my 'Religion and Mental Health: an exploration of the relationship between the ineffable and the indefinable' (Connolly 1998).

114 Paulson (2006).
115 Loc. cit.
116 Loc. cit.
117 Loc. cit.
118 Rambo (1987). The other stages are: 'crisis', roughly corresponding to Clark's first stage of 'unrest'; 'quest', a searching for meaning or resolution of questions; 'encounter', usually with a proselytising group, or, in Collins's case, an 'awesome' phenomenon, and 'commitment', which corresponds to Clark's fourth stage. He subsequently expanded this model into seven stages, a summary of which can be found in Rambo and Farhadian (1999, pp. 23–34).
119 Momentum Pictures, 2008.

Part 2: A reductionist explanation of religious experience

1. In his booklet published by The British Wheel of Yoga, *Yoga: its beginnings and development*, Karel Werner describes yoga as being 'free from any particular religious or metaphysical affiliation – not only at the end of the journey, but right from the start'. He calls it 'a neutral method of training the mind for supersensory vision ...' More particularly, when writing about Patañjali's yoga, he claims that 'It is futile to wish to create a metaphysical system from this basic philosophical framework of the [*Yoga Sūtra*]. It is equally futile to try to interpret it as a summary of the Sankhya metaphysics. It is nothing more than an invitation to turn to practice and see the final truth directly' (Werner 1987, pp. 2–4). His position, in short, is that with regard to meditation, theory and practice are essentially independent of each other.
2. Carroll (1865/1927, pp. 94–95).
3. Goleman (1977). It is somewhat surprising that Goleman makes no mention of Naranjo and Ornstein's *On the Psychology of Meditation*, which presents a similar though more complex scheme and was published in 1971.
4. Thomas (1949, pp. 66–68). See also Horner (1954/1976). Another version of this account can be found in the *Bhayabheravasutta* (Horner, op. cit., pp. 21–30.) see also Vinaya 3.5 and Anguttara Nikāya 2.211; 4.179.
5. The term in Pāli texts is dhamma, a word with a variety of meanings. Here it may refer to the Buddha's teaching (dhamma) or to the phenomena of our experience (also dhamma, plural: dhammā).
6. EEG machines record the electrical impulses generated by the brain. Generally these range from 0 to 50 hertz (cycles per second). Frequencies from 0 to 3 hz are termed delta waves; those from 4 to 7 hz theta waves; those from 8 to 14 hz alpha waves; those above 15 hz are called beta waves. *Delta waves* are normally associated with deep sleep. *Theta waves* normally appear in the state of transition from wakefulness to sleep (hypnogogia). They are often associated with drowsiness. In meditators, however, these theta waves often appear in extended rhythmical patterns (trains), which differ from normal theta activity. Some meditators have been found to retain theta activity even in eyes-open, post-meditation states. *Alpha waves* are prominent when a person is in a relaxed, non-problem-solving state of mind. They also occur prior to sleep. *Beta waves* are associated with active attention to the outside world or the solution of specific problems. *Amplitude* is the distance from one side of a wave to the other. *Frequency* is the number of waves per unit of time. *Habituation* is the tendency to cease being aware of a stimulus.
7. McGilchrist, (2009, ch. 1).
8. Op. cit., p. 10.
9. Goleman (1977, p. xxv).
10. Naranjo and Ornstein (1971).
11. Op. cit., p. 94.

12   By way of an aside here, I would point out that both Goleman and Naranjo describe Patañjali's yoga as concentrative. In doing this I think they overlook something significant. *Yoga Sūtra* 1.12 states that the cessation of the mind's activities is accomplished through a combination of practice (abhyāsa) and dispassion/detachment (vairāgya). The latter is characteristic of the negative or mindfulness way. I would also argue that Patañjali gives the vairāgya aspect much more emphasis that most commentators allow, for it seems to me that the meditations on īśvara (the lord) are essentially undertaken for the cultivation of vairāgya. By meditating on īśvara the meditator becomes detached from the world of change, just like īśvara. We can therefore see parallels between the Buddhist combination of mindfulness and concentration in steps 7 and 8 of the eight-fold path and Patañjali's dual emphasis on abhyāsa and vairāgya.

13   See note 3 above for a brief explanation of self-power and other-power.
14   Rawlinson (1997, pp. 98–99).
15   Horner (1954/1976, section 36, 'Mahāsaccaka Sutta').
16   Yoga Sūtra 1.48.
17   Vivekananda (1912, pp. 74ff.).
18   Accessed on 14 September 2011 at www.ananda.org/meditation/support/articles/higher-guidance1.html.
19   Wilber (1993, p. 248).
20   Loc. cit.
21   Op. cit., p. 249 (emphasis mine).
22   Op. cit., p. 250.
23   Loc. cit.
24   See, for example, his comments on p. 247f. and p. 95.
25   Op. cit., p. 248.
26   Op. cit., p. 2.
27   Wilber (2007, p. 19).
28   Loc. cit.
29   See, for example, Dilts (1999, pp. 55–58).
30   Taken from Wilber (2007, p. 21).
31   Op. cit., p. 20.
32   See, for example, Tajfel (1981), Kelly and Breinlinger (1996), and Robinson (1996). A slightly different take on the in-group–out-group dynamic is provided by evolutionary biologist Robert Trivers (2011, pp. 279, 289). He noticed a strong and unexpected correlation between the number of religions in an area and the area's 'parasite load' ('roughly the degree of human loss due to parasites'). High parasite load correlates with high numbers of religions and vice versa. Why? Trivers's account is:

> An in-group member will generally have been exposed to the same set of parasites as the other members and will carry some of the same genes that give at least partial resistance to many of these parasites. But an out-group member will be subject to selection from a slightly different set of parasites and will carry a

subset to which it may be partly resistant but in-group members are not. From the standpoint of each group the other is a threat. ... In short, other things being equal, high parasite load is expected to increase ethnocentrism, within-group love and hostility towards strangers ... the higher the parasite pressure, the more religions, languages and ethnic groups per unit area. (Loc. cit.)

33 Wilber (2007, p. 19).
34 Op. cit., pp. 26–28.
35 Johnson (2006).
36 Op. cit., p. 40.
37 Op. cit., p. 51.
38 Op. cit., p. 45.
39 I came across the horse and canary pie metaphor in Torrey (1987, ch. 12). In the cholera example the emotions, psychological attitude, imagery, intentions and spirituality constitute the canary and hydration is the horse.
40 Barnes-Svarney (1995, ch. 5).
41 For details of the periodic table see Dan Green's superb introduction, *The Periodic Table in Minutes* (Green 2016), and Parsons and Dixon's *The Periodic Table: a field guide to the elements* (Parsons and Dixon 2013). For embryological development see Richard Dawkins's *The Greatest Show on Earth* (Dawkins 2009, ch. 8).
42 Wilber (2007, pp. 60, 68).
43 Op. cit., p. 60.
44 Op. cit., p. 53.
45 Op. cit., p. 59.
46 Op. cit., p. 65.
47 Op. cit., p. 60. The questions that are deemed to lie at the heart of these lines offer useful simplifications of the concerns of the related disciplines, though at a price. Each of the fields that he incorporates into his scheme as lines addresses important questions other than those he lists.
48 Op. cit., p. 68.
49 Op. cit., figs 2.4 and 2.5, pp. 68–69.
50 For a brief and reliable introduction to Piaget's work on these stages see the Appendix in Donaldson (1978). An accessible introduction to Jean Piaget's work, with comments on the contrasting approach of Lev Vygotsky can be found in Harré (2006). For a critical evaluation of the Piaget-Kholberg approach to 'moral development' see Hauser (2007, pp. 16–21), which also contrasts Carol Gilligan's reworking of Kholberg's ideas with the results from work by Lewis Petrinovich and John Mikhail. Hauser's conclusion on this matter: 'gender differences may play a role in performance, and the justifications that the sexes give. But when it comes to our evolved moral faculty – our moral competence – it looks like we speak in one voice: the voice of our species' (op. cit., p. 126) In short, Wilber's confidence in Gilligan as a guide to moral psychology is premature to say the least, and potentially misguided.
51 Op. cit., p. 68.

52 Janaway (2005).
53 Gardner (2003).
54 Beck and Cowan (1996).
55 Wilber (2007, p. 100).
56 See Fowler (1981) and also Fowler et al. (1991).
57 Cited in Slee (1991, p. 141).
58 Parks (1991, p. 105).
59 Fowler (1981, pp. 4–5). Emphasis in the first quotation is mine – the meaning of *moving into the force field of life* is pretty opaque to me, more opaque than the meaning of *faith*.
60 Op. cit., p. 5.
61 See Power (1991).
62 Fowler (1981, p. 11).
63 Gould (1999).
64 Fowler (1981, p. 9; emphasis mine).
65 Op. cit., p. 11.
66 Moran (1991, p. 150).
67 Wilber (2007, p. 65).
68 Fowler (1981, p. 200).
69 Hitchens (1995/2012).
70 Fowler (1981, p. 206).
71 Op. cit., pp. 206–207.
72 Op. cit., p. 207.
73 Op. cit., p. 208.
74 Op. cit., p. 209.
75 Parks (1991, p. 107).
76 Op. cit., p. 5.
77 Loc. cit.
78 Op. cit., p. 7.
79 Op. cit., p. 5.
80 Rangaswami (2012, p. 268).
81 Loc. cit.
82 Wilber (2007, p. 6). The equivalences that he claims for these terms, e.g. that the 'conventional stage of morality' is to be equated with an ethnocentric outlook and 'mind', where 'my identity expands from "me" to "us"', are certainly not self-evident, and his supporting argumentation is thin.
83 Op. cit., p. 13.
84 Here's what Ram Dass wrote in *Doing Your Own Being*:

> For most people in the Western universe, in fact most people in the world, almost all of the energy is located either in the first, second, or third chakras. The first chakra can be characterized crudely as being connected with survival and survival of the individual as a separate being. It's like we're in the jungle and there's one piece of meat and who's going to get it, you or me? It's a survival-of-the-fittest-type

model. It's a Darwinian assumption about the motivations of beings. When you're at that chakra, your motivation is to protect yourself as a separate being, your separateness. You can think of that as darkest Africa. And the channel up which this is all going is called the Sushumna – think of it as a big river. You go in the river from Africa and the next stop is like the Riviera. See, you've got your security under control and now you start to go into sensual gratification and sexual desires and reproduction. You can't be busy reproducing if you're protecting your life, but the minute your life's protected a little bit, then you can concern yourself with the next matter, which is reproducing the species. So the second chakra is primarily concerned with sexual actions, reactions, and so on – at the reproduction level. Procreative. Sex.

The third chakra ...that's like Wall Street and Washington and London. It's primarily connected with power, with mastery, with ego control. Most of the world that we think of is connected with those particular centers. All the energy's located there. People justify their lives in terms of reproduction or sexual gratification, sensual gratification, or power or mastery. And it's interesting that pretty much any act we know of in the Western world can be done in the service of any one of those energies. So that a man can build a huge dynamic industry and we can say, 'Aha, phallic,' meaning second chakra. Or a person can seduce many women in order to have mastery and power over them and we say, 'Aha, concerned with power and mastery,' meaning third chakra. Doing sex in the service of third chakra. Now it turns out -and this is the one that many of you will find hard sledding, but this is the way I understand it now, having been through this particular trip I've been through – that Freud is an absolutely unequalled spokesman and master of second-chakra preoccupation, that is, of those beings who were primarily involved in second chakra. So he could say quite honestly, because it is true at the second chakra, that religion is sublimated sex. Now it is true that in his generalized libido theories and the idea that all the body is erogenous ... there are a lot of ways in which he slips over the edge; but his system is primarily concerned with the second chakra. Adler is primarily concerned with third chakra. Jung is primarily concerned with fourth chakra. I would point out that there are still the fifth, sixth and seventh chakras. And these are in terms of other kinds of psychic spaces and ways of organising the universe and understanding what's happening. So that to the extent that you have 'uncooked seeds' of the second chakra and you have a Freudian analyst, he's going to help you cook those seeds. He's not going to do much about where you're stuck in the third chakra, particularly. And he hasn't much to say about the fourth chakra, which is what Jung pointed out about Freud. (Baba Ram Dass 1973)

85 Woodroffe (1973).
86 Eliade (1969, p. 243).
87 Varenne (1976, p. 170).
88 Hardy (1988, p. 117).
89 Dasgupta (1974). Dasgupta points out that the Buddhist equivalent of the sahasrāra is the usnīṣa-kamala (op. cit., pp.147–148).
90 Loc. cit.

91 Woodroffe (1973, p. 321). Dasgupta (1974) indicates that the Buddhist equivalents are generally known as āli and kāli (pp.153ff.) and provides a list of synonyms for these two channels.
92 Loc. cit.
93 Govinda (1975, p. 156).
94 Leadbeater (1927).
95 Woodroffe (1973, p. 115).
96 Op. cit., p. 148.
97 Brown (1921, p. 15).
98 Mallinson (2007, pp. 26–28).
99 Snellgrove (2002, p. 170).
100 Wilber (2007, p. 72).
101 Op. cit., p. 74.
102 Op. cit., p. 75.
103 Loc. cit.
104 Op. cit., p. 87.
105 I mention this here because a notable lacuna in Wilber's treatment of spirituality is an account of motivation, an answer to the question of why people should spend time and effort in working their way through state progressions ('a full course of meditative training ... may take anywhere from 5 to 20 years to master'; op. cit., p. 82). What does one get at the end of it that makes the effort worthwhile? In the Buddha's time, according to Pāli sources, the benefits of adopting a spiritual life were clear: freedom from suffering and rebirth. Moreover, the early Pāli sources never describe any of the Buddha's disciples taking 5 to 20 years to attain the deathless after gaining right view. This fact has been most eloquently articulated by Peter Masefield, formerly of the University of Sidney. Right view, according to Masefield, 'is defined as understanding (pajānāti) or possessing knowledge (ñāṇaṁ) of the four truths; it is to see with right insight (paññā) the uprising and cessation of the world as it really is, to have, without dependence on another, no doubt, no uncertainty that whatever uprises is dukkha [suffering] and that whatever ceases is dukkha ... Right view is, in short, to see the Dhamma, to see Nibbāna... Such a right view is, moreover, supermundane [lokuttara], anāsava [without karmic consequence] and ariyan [noble] and the means by which one comes to be born of the ariyan birth' (Masefield 1986A, p. 165).

In Masefield's account it is the acquisition of right view that makes one an ariyan, a noble one. Ariyans, in this sense, are those who see the four truths for themselves. Possessors of right view see the path to nibbāna but have not yet achieved it. What enables them to follow the path, which would be almost impossible if not completely impossible for ordinary people, is that the acquisition of right view destroys the bulk of one's karmic burden. A passage in the Sanyutta Nikāya describes it thus: 'Even so, for the ariyasāvaka [noble hearer] who has attained Right View, for the person possessing paññā [insight], this is quite the greater dukkha, this that has been destroyed, has been put to an end, while that which remains is infinitely small and does not amount to one hundredth, does not amount to one thousandth, does not amount to one hundredth thousandth, when set beside the former dukkha that has been destroyed, has been put to an end – that is at most a term of seven (births) – so great a good is (it to have) insight into Dhamma, so great a good is it to acquire the Dhammacakkhu [eye seeing the Dhamma]' (op. cit., p. 167.)

According to Theravāda tradition those who have acquired right view (ariya sāvakas, noble hearers) are of four types – type being determined by the number of hindrances destroyed and the number of rebirths that the person can expect to experience. The first of these is the sotāpanna (streamwinner), who has destroyed the three fetters of personality belief, sceptical doubts, and faith in good works and religious rituals. The streamwinner will be reborn no more than seven times. (This understanding of sotāpanna has been challenged by Masefield, op. cit., pp. 130–136.) Second is the once-returner, who has destroyed the same fetters as the streamwinner and weakened lust, ill will and dullness. The once-returner will return to the earthly realm for only one more birth. Third is the non-returner, who has destroyed the streamwinner's three plus ill will and sensuous craving. Any future rebirth for the non-returner will be in a heavenly realm. Fourth is the arahant (worthy one), who has destroyed all the above five as well as the āsavas of kāma (lust), bhava (desire for existence) and avijjā (ignorance). Some lists add diṭṭhi (views, i.e. wrong views/beliefs) to these three. The destruction of the āsavas is essentially synonymous with the attainment of nibbāna, and the arahant is one who is liberated in life. There will be no more rebirth once the karmic energy supporting the present life is exhausted.

If Masefield is correct, and the noble eight-fold (or ten-fold) path really does begin with right view as described above, then a person cannot simply decide to begin following the noble path to the cessation of suffering. One has to find a way to obtain right view. It might, therefore, seem strange that the Pāli Canon does not provide guidelines on how to get it. This, according to Masefield, is because the discourses recorded in the Pāli Canon are mostly directed at those who already have it. What we do have, though, is descriptions of a number of instances where individuals acquire right view. These descriptions have one thing in common: the individual is a recipient of an orally delivered proclamation of the dhamma by either the Buddha or one of his ariya sāvakas. Interestingly, the state of mind that a recipient enters during such a proclamation is described in terms that are almost identical to those employed in descriptions of the fourth jhāna: 'malleable, devoid of the hindrances, uplifted, devout', which was the state in which the Buddha acquired his own liberating insight. Moreover, the 'path' itself is sequential: beginning with right view and ending with the tenth step of right release. Even so, as Masefield points out, 'so soon did attainment of arahantship follow upon the acquisition of the Dhammacakkhu that talk of treading a path seems out of place' (op. cit., p.98); 'these two distinct stages in the process of liberation – initial sight of the goal and attainment of that goal – were equally unthinkable without the intervention of the Buddha with an oral teaching of one sort or another. When this second teaching had been received the goal was won – there was nothing more to be done ... except to undergo expiation of that kamma not already annihilated by the arising of the Dhammacakkhu ...' (Masefield 1986B, pp. 104–105).

The message is clear: if you want right view, find someone who already has it (ideally a Buddha) and request a teaching on dhamma. Whether such a person wears the robes of a monk or nun would seem to be far less important than whether he or she is an ariyan, i.e. a sāvaka who has gained right view. It is easy to understand why many Buddhists are not attracted to Masefield's analysis, because it tells them that unless they have experienced right view they cannot be following the noble eightfold path that leads to nibbāna. Masefield pulls no punches in pointing out the implications of his research:

> While this [means of acquiring right view] was of obvious benefit to the fortunate individual who became a sāvaka, it had the sinister implication for the Buddhist world that until such a conversion were received, almost as an act of grace on the part of the Buddha, there could be no possibility of anyone, whether monk or layman, following the eightfold way to Nibbāna nor of their becoming free of their past kamma. (Masefield undated)

106 Wilber (2007, p. 95).
107 Masefield (1986B, pp. 60, 81).
108 See the Appendix in Donaldson (1978).
109 Op. cit., p. 77. See White (2014) for an explanation of why Wilber's characterisation is misguided.
110 Gill Lloyd (senior trainer for T.K.V. Desikachar), personal communication.
111 In the Foreword to Iyengar (2002, p. viii).
112 Vivekananda (1912, p. ix).
113 Carrera (2006, p. ix).
114 Miller (1996, cover).
115 Wilber (2007, p. 110).
116 Fausboll (1881/1905, p. 197).
117 Woodward (1927, p. 29).
118 Snellgrove (2002, pp. 79–94).
119 Wilber (2007, p. 114).
120 Samuel (2008, p. 264).
121 See Snellgrove (2002, pp. 396–407).
122 Op. cit., p. 260 and 474–475.
123 Mallinson (2007, pp. 27–28).
124 Op. cit., p. 121.
125 Op. cit., p. 261.
126 Op. cit., p. 265.

127 e.g. Miller (1996).
128 See *Sāṁkhya Kārikā* 11, 21 and 22 in e.g. Larson (1979).
129 Wilber (2007, p. 15).
130 Loc. cit.
131 Jung (1971).
132 The traits indicative of extraversion were: warmth, gregariousness, assertiveness, activity, excitement-seeking, positive emotions; those indicative of agreeableness were: trust, straightforwardness, altruism, compliance, modesty, tender-mindedness; those of conscientiousness were: competence, order, dutifulness, achievement striving, self-discipline, deliberation; those of openness were: fantasy, aesthetics, feelings, actions, ideas, values; those of neuroticism were: anxiety, angry, hostility, depression, self-consciousness, impulsiveness, vulnerability. From Matthews and Deary (1998, p. 27).
133 Cooper (2002, p. 311).
134 Op. cit., p. 21.
135 Janda (2001).
136 Cooper (2002, p. 13).
137 Wilber (2007, p. 15).
138 Jones (2002, pp. 71–72).
139 Baron-Cohen (2003) offers a readable overview of many of these complexities.
140 Wilber (2007, p. 31).
141 Op. cit., p. 4.
142 Op. cit., p. 16.
143 Op. cit., pp. 43–44; 49.
144 First published in 1951 and revised for the English translation in 1964.
145 First published in 1954, second edition 1969.
146 Most of the material in this section is taken from my 'Ecstasy and Enstasy: two sides of the same coin?' (Connolly 2015).
147 Eliade (1964, p. 417).
148 *Chambers Concise Dictionary* definition.
149 Eliade (1964, p. 5).
150 Op. cit., p. 6.
151 Op. cit., p. 8.
152 Op. cit., p. 6. Eliade claims that a shaman differs from a possessed person because he or she *controls* the spirits that *possess* others (op. cit., pp. 6, 328), though he does acknowledge elements of "possession," (always printed in inverted commas), in the early stages of a shaman's career (op. cit., p. 82). I have argued elsewhere (Connolly 2000A), contra Eliade, that possession is a central feature of many shamanic experiences, and I was pleased to find, in the course of my research for this paper, some examples in Eliade's own work that challenged his claim. One of the most significant was the report of his experience by a Goldi shaman from the Amur region of Siberia (Eliade 1964, p. 28). He informed Leo Sternberg that 'When I am shamaning, the "ayami" [tutelary spirit] and the assistant spirits

are possessing me: whether big or small, they penetrate me, as smoke or vapour would. When the "ayami" is within me, it is she who speaks through my mouth, and she does everything herself. When I am eating the "sukdu" (the offerings) and drinking pig's blood ... it is not I who eat and drink, it is my "ayami" alone' (op. cit., pp. 72-73)'. This, we may note, comes from an experienced shaman, not a novice. A similar point is made by Edward B. Harper in his report on shamanism in South India: 'The Savara shamanic séance consists in the shaman being possessed by the spirit of the tutelary or by the god, whichever is invoked, who speaks through his voice at great length. It is the spirit that takes possession of the shaman or shamaness that reveals the cause of the illness and tells them what action is to be taken ...' (op. cit., p. 424). In commenting on this account, Eliade writes in a footnote, 'These are phenomena of possession and do not necessarily imply a shamanic structure or ideology.' I do not know why Eliade was so averse to acknowledging possession by spirits as a core component of his 'shamanic complex', though I would argue that any phenomenologist who based his or her typology on the evidence as presented would have to admit its centrality.
153 Eliade (1969, p. 361).
154 Loc. cit.
155 Op. cit., p. 4.
156 Op. cit., p. 5f.
157 Op. cit., p. 362.
158 Op. cit., p. 96.
159 I say *can* here because in the context of brāhmanical social ideology the yogin can be seen to perform an important political function: that of providing an alternative to living within the rigid constraints of caste culture and, thereby, deflecting the energies of the socially discontent away from social reform or revolution and into the politically harmless pursuit of metaphysical freedom.
160 For a brief introduction to Fischer and his work see the Wikipedia article at https://en.wikipedia.org/wiki/Roland_L._Fischer.
161 Fischer (1986, p. 16).
162 Fischer (1978).
163 Fischer (1971, pp. 897-904).
164 Fischer (1976). A useful discussion of state-dependent memory and altered states of consciousness can be found in Rossi (1986, ch. 3).
165 Tart (1972, p. 6).
166 Forman (1990, pp. 5-7).
167 Fischer (1969B, p. 265).
168 Op. cit., p. 251.
169 Op. cit., p. 264.
170 This diagram is taken from Fischer (1969B). It is essentially the same article as that reprinted in the Allman and Jaffe volume, though somewhat abbreviated. The change in the diagram is perhaps the most notable feature, though I am

uncertain about the place where this second version was first published. Its character, intermediate between the 1969 and 1971 versions, suggests a date of 1970 or thereabouts.
171 Fischer (1971, p. 898).
172 Loc. cit.
173 Loc. cit.
174 Loc. cit.
175 Fischer (1976, p. 308; 1980, p. 308).
176 Fischer (1971, p. 902).
177 Fischer (1969B, p. 264).
178 Op. cit., p. 267.
179 Fischer (1969A, p. 168).
180 Goodman (1988B, p. 8). While I think Goodman is making a valuable point here, I would argue that some of the phenomena she identifies as manifesting in the ecstatic religious trance also have their secular counterparts, e.g. spirit possession (religious) and multiple personality disorder/dissociative identity disorder (secular). Goodman also claims that sleep, the hypnotic state and the meditative state are altered states of consciousness different from the ecstatic religious trance. By contrast, it seems to me that ecstatic religious trance, the hypnotic state and the meditative state are all examples of what might be generally called trance phenomena. The case for this has been argued by me in (Connolly 2000A, 2000B).
181 Fischer (1978, p. 38).
182 Horner (1954/1976, pp. 291–305).
183 Fischer (1978, p. 42).
184 Fischer (1971, pp. 900–901).
185 Fischer (1978, p. 35).
186 Fischer (1969B, p. 255).
187 Fischer (1978, p. 26).
188 Op. cit., p. 50.
189 St Theresa, *The Interior Castle*, quoted in Wapnick (1969, pp. 49–66).
190 See, for example, Lynn and Rhue (1991). The article by Bowers and Davidson in this volume is one of the best critiques of the first approach and demonstrations of the validity of the second that I have come across.
191 Tart (1988, p. 81).
192 Shor (1959, pp. 582–602; reprinted in Tart 1972, p. 242).
193 Berger and Luckmann (1967).
194 Fromm and Kahn (1990, p. 90).
195 Op. cit., pp. 20, 59, 79.
196 Gilligan (1987, p. 42).
197 See www.youtube.com/watch?v=5Q7CoqFud5s (accessed 8 September 2016). This programme also films a woman having her two front teeth extracted and replaced with implants using only hypnotically induced analgesia. I suspect

that inviting people to role-play an analgesic jaw under such conditions would attract few volunteers.
198 For a discussion of this work see Temple (1989, pp. 95–96).
199 Op. cit., p. 80. Cf. Erickson (1980, p. 327).
200 Temple (1989, pp. 78ff.).
201 Quoted in op. cit., p. 85.
202 See op. cit., ch. 4, passim for details. See also Tart (1975, p. 81).
203 See, for example, Alman and Lambrou (1992); Simpkins and Simpkins (2000).
204 Gilligan (1987, p. 42).
205 See, for example, Sargant (1957, pp. 12–13), and Jaynes (1990), but especially pp. 347–353ff.
206 Ludwig and Lyle (1964, pp. 70–76), cited in Temple (1989, pp. 82–84). Temple describes the induction procedure thus:

> Ludwig and Lyle instructed their subjects to pace the floor, then to spin around the room and while doing so to sweep the room with their eyes, and to do as many knee-bends as possible. Then they were told to sit in a chair and grasp the arms as tightly as possible and then to begin rotating their heads until their necks became completely rigid. While the subjects were doing all these things, they were bombarded with rapid-fire commands of various kinds, were constantly told that they were uncomfortable, 'frozen with fear', etc. They were also instructed to allow their minds to become flooded with all kinds of thoughts and impressions, indeed that these would be 'erupting like lava from the volcano of [their] mind'. (Loc. cit.)

Temple comments on this procedure, saying 'Although this may all sound ridiculously confusing and non-conducive to inducing a trance, all of the subjects went into trances within 5 to 25 minutes of this "tension induction" procedure' (loc. cit.). To anyone familiar with hypnosis, however, the fact that confusion produced trance states is not surprising. Even without the tension elements confusion techniques can produce quite profound trances. See Gafner and Benson (2000, ch. 4) for descriptions of some 'Confusional inductions'. Ormond McGill's excellent *The New Encyclopedia of Stage Hypnotism* also contains instructions for a wide range of induction techniques.

207 Storr (1989, pp. 49–50); Will Macdonald (co-author with Richard Bandler of *An Insider's Guide to Submodalities*, 1988), personal communication. See also the similar technique described in McGill (1996, pp. 139–141). Derren Brown displays a 'light' form of this technique in *Derren Brown: Miracle* (Vaudeville Productions for Channel 4 Television, 2016).
208 See Sargant (1957, ch. 10).
209 Gilligan (1987, p. 42).
210 Brown (1991, p. 223).
211 Op. cit., p. 190.
212 Gilligan (1987, p. 23).
213 Shor (1959, 13: 582–602; reprinted in Tart 1972, pp. 239–256).

214 Michael Yapko (2011) has demonstrated, persuasively in my estimation, that many of the guided mindfulness meditations employed by an increasing number of clinicians are so similar to activities that are initiated in sessions of clinical hypnosis that they are probably best understood as variants of the same sets of mental processes. The entire book is largely a continuous argument to support this claim, but see especially the summary of common aspects on pp. 185-187.
215 Gilligan (1987, p. 24).
216 Hilgard (1986, p. 220).
217 Op. cit., p. 221.
218 See Ornstein (1991, pp. 144 ff.).
219 Gilligan (1987, pp. 46-59). Cf. Rossi (1986, ch. 3).
220 Blessings and curses are interesting in this connection. They have pronounced parallels with placebo and nocebo effects. Ben Goldacre (2014, p. 323) calls the nocebo 'the evil twin of the placebo effect, where negative expectations can induce unpleasant symptoms in the absence of a physical cause'. Both blessings and curses and placebo/nocebo effects are demonstrably rooted in human suggestibility. In these cases the power of authority seems to be the primary factor behind the amplification of suggestibility, as it was in the early days of hypnotism. See Ellenberger (1970, p. 150) on the method of 'imperative suggestion' that was used by hypnotists of the Nancy school: 'Such imperative suggestions were found to work best with persons who occupied subordinate positions in life and were accustomed to obeying orders (soldiers and laborers) ...'. Also Weitzenhoffer (1989) on 'Authoritarian and Permissive Approaches'. Carl Jung provides an interesting anecdote on this point in *Memories, Dreams, Reflections*. A woman with a paralysed leg presented herself for treatment and began recounting 'the whole long tale of her illness'. As Jung reports it, 'Finally I interrupted her and said "Well now, we have no more time for so much talk, I am now going to hypnotise you." I had scarcely said the words when she closed her eyes and fell into a profound trance - without any hypnosis at all.' After bringing her out of the trance, with some difficulty, Jung said 'I am the doctor, and everything is all right.' Whereupon she cried out, 'But I am cured!', threw away her crutches and was able to walk (Jung 1971, pp. 138-9).
221 Tart (1970, pp. 27-40; 1975, p. 81); Ludwig and Lyle (1964, pp. 70-76).
222 Banyai (1980, p. 267).
223 Vingoe (1973, pp. 176-177), quoted in Temple (1989, p. 101).
224 Deren (1975, p. 286).
225 Ludwig and Lyle (1964, p. 73).
226 Op. cit., pp. 74-75.
227 Banyai and Hilgard (1976, pp. 218-224); Banyai (1980); Goodman (1988B, p. 31).
228 See, for example, Banyai and Hilgard (1976, p. 222); Banyai (1980, p. 266); Goodman (1988A, p. 3; 1988B, p. 38).
229 Suryani and Jensen (1993, p. 112).
230 Deren (1975, p. 243).

231 Rouget (1985, p. 47).
232 Bandler and Grinder (1981, pp. 185–189).
233 Rouget (1985, pp. 47–48).
234 See, for example, Masefield (1986A; 1986B, p. 167). See also Michael Yapko's (2011) comments on the relationship between guided mindfulness meditations and hypnosis.
235 See, for example, Sherman (1972, pp. 87–91); Tart (1970); Horner (1954/1976), especially pp. 218–219. For a discussion of the Buddhist jhānas, see Thomas (1949, chs 6, 13); Patañjali *Yoga Sūtra* 1.41–1.51 and 3.1–3.8, translations by Feuerstein (1979) and Woods (1914). The Woods version contains translations of the commentaries by Vyāsa and Vācaspatimiśra but not the Sanskrit text.
236 Gilligan (1987, pp. 46–59).
237 This description should probably be qualified thus: 'They are more able to directly experience [what seems to them to be] "things as they are".'
238 Tart (1975, p. 81).
239 Temple (1989, p. 83).
240 Tart (1975, p. 81).
241 Fromm and Kahn (1990, p. 79).
242 Op. cit., p. 74.
243 de Rivera and Sarbin (1998).
244 Yapko (1990, pp. 42–43).
245 See Weitzenhoffer (1989, pp. 258–262) for a discussion of this phenomenon.
246 The Amicable Life advertisement showed a calamity for a team of vaulting horse gymnasts. The first gymnast vaulted the horse successfully, but the second got her timing wrong and crashed into it. The third, who had started her run-up before the second had arrived at the horse, did not stop her run but continued and crashed into the second. The remaining gymnasts, who were standing in line awaiting their turns, could all see what had happened, but they still ran towards the horse and contributed to the pile-up of bodies in front of it. Why did they do this? The answer, I think, is the effect that practice has on conscious processing. We may, in the early stages of practice, use our conscious mind to divide the activity into smaller, more manageable chunks. As we master each of these and link them together our performance becomes more automated and less amenable to conscious interference. Indeed, virtuoso performances demand the exclusion of conscious interference. Conscious processing is just too slow for the kind of flow that characterizes virtuoso performance. Because they exclude conscious interference automated behaviours have a trance-like quality. What seems to have happened with the gymnasts is that they had practised the entire sequence as a team and the trigger for the learned but now automatic behaviour was the commencement of the routine, at which point they entered a trance state that they could not influence consciously.

   I sometimes give students an example of this from my own life to illustrate the point: my wife likes to change the furnishings around in our house and had a couple of alternative locations for the kitchen waste bin. In the days following a relocation of the bin I would find myself going to where it had been and watch myself, in partial disbelief, empty the remnants of my meal onto to the floor. Once I started the action of 'clearing my plate into the bin' (an action I had done regularly over the previous few months) I could not stop. It had become automated. The 'handshake induction' exploits this automaticity to elude resistance from the conscious mind. In the western world, if someone offers a hand for a handshake we tend to respond with a behaviour that has become automated through repetition. If, however, the person offering the hand does not complete the 'shake' then our expected completion of the action does not occur and we remain in an automated mode, which a skilful individual can exploit to make suggestions that evade conscious filtering (see Gilligan 1987, pp. 251–258 for details).

247   See Harrelson (1987).
248   d'Aquili and Laughlin (1975, pp. 32–58).
249   See also Trivers (2011, pp. 279, 289).
250   The limbic–hypothalamic system also plays a central role in therapeutic hypnosis. See Rossi (1986).
251   d'Aquili and Loughlin (1975, p. 37).
252   Loc. cit.
253   Sargant (1959).
254   Hinde (1987, p. 65).
255   Robert Irwin (2004) recommends Husain Haddawy's translation of selections from the collection if one wishes 'to sample the *Nights* and get a true impression of the style and art of the stories ...' (p. 41).
256   Bandler and Grinder (1981, pp. 85–87).
257   See also McGilchrist (2009, ch. 1).

Part 3: Loose ends

1   Wesley quoted in Sargant (1957, p. 75).
2   Sargant (1957, p. 101; 1973, passim).
3   Stephen Gilligan (1987, p. 35) defines dissociation as 'a mental process in which systems of ideas are split off from the normal personality and operate independently'.
4   Schumaker (1995). See also note XXX above.
5   Op. cit., p. 35. See also pp. XXXff. above in relation to Eliade's comments on chaos and cosmos.
6   Op. cit., p. 21.
7   See V.S. Ramachandran's account of the man who had undergone split brain surgery and ended up with one hemisphere believing in god and the other being an atheist: www.youtube.com/watch?v=PFJPtVRlI64 (accessed 16 September 2016).

8   See Festinger et al. (1956) for an interesting exploration of this idea in the context of religion.
9   Jaynes (1990).
10 One of the problems everyone who writes about 'consciousness' encounters is that different writers mean different things when they employ the term. For some, it simply means being awake, the opposite of being unconscious or asleep. When one boxer 'knocks out' another, the one who is knocked out becomes 'unconscious'. When he is revived he 'regains consciousness', i.e. becomes 'awake' again. The Amicable Life gymnasts mentioned above were certainly awake but their behaviour was inaccessible to conscious control, whereas when I decide to look for a particular book on my bookshelf, Libet notwithstanding, my conscious mind is active. In Hilgard's terms, my central executive plans to search for the book, initiates action commensurate with that plan, and sustains my search against obstacles and distractions. My monitor scans the shelf and deploys critical judgment, based on feedback from initiated action as what is done is compared with intended goals and performances. These are just three ways in which the word consciousness is used. In her introduction to a collection of essays on *Consciousness* Rita Carter summarises part of the problem: 'Some writers make up their own terms for various states: "core" consciousness; "creature" consciousness; "phenomenal" consciousness; "access" consciousness; and so on. As yet, though, none of them are universally agreed, and different writers sometimes use the same term to refer to different states' (Carter 2002, p. 8). To Carter's list we could add terms such as 'feminist' consciousness, 'class' consciousness and 'false' consciousness. Some people – V.S. Ramachandran refers to them as panpsychics – 'believe everything in the world is conscious, including things like anthills, thermostats, and Formica tabletops ...' (Ramachandran and Blakeslee 1998, p. 228). Carter's own working definition is 'the "lights-on" state in which we are aware of our surroundings *and* aware that we are aware of them' (Carter 2002, p. 9; emphasis mine). How often do both conditions apply? How often are we aware that we are aware? The implication that when we are not aware that we are aware we are not conscious takes her understanding quite close to that of Jaynes, Dennett (in *Consciousness Explained*) and many hypnosis researchers.
11 Jaynes is not alone in making this observation. A number of classical scholars have made similar points, e.g. Adkins (1960, 1970), Dodds (1951) and Snell (1953/1982). In addition, if one reads works such as Cedric Whitman's analysis of the *Ajax* of Sophocles from a Jaynesian perspective the contrast set up between Odysseus and Ajax inevitably conjures up the shift from bicamerality to consciousness.
12 Jaynes (1990, p. 47).
13 Op. cit., pp. 65–66. Jaynes's account of what consciousness is and is not (ch. 2) finds echoes in the writings of philosophers such as Daniel Dennett, and makes it very similar to what hypnotists call 'the conscious mind'.
14 Jaynes, op. cit., pp. 93–94.

15 Though some of the essays in the Kuijsten volume put a fair amount of flesh on the bones of Jaynes's account. Michael Persinger provided the Foreword to this collection.
16 Cotton (1995, p. 186), a quotation from an interview with Michael Persinger.
17 Persinger (1987, p. 26).
18 Cotton, op. cit., p. 188. See also Smith (2007, ch. 3 "Noble automatons").
19 Lennox and Lennox (1960). See also LaPlante (1993), and Waxman and Geschwind (1974, 1975).
20 Sacks (1995, p. 156).
21 Ramachandran and Blakeslee (1998), especially chapter 9 and notes.
22 Newberg and Waldman (2007, p. 178).
23 Op. cit., p. 179. The kinds of meditation practised by these Buddhists and nuns are, if the arguments on trance are even partially accurate, forms of hypnotic induction that modify the normal patterns of interaction between cerebral hemispheres.
24 Loc. cit.
25 Op. cit., p. 182.
26 As I wrote this the following limerick popped into my head:

> There was a young man who said, 'Damn!
> At last I've found out that I am
> A creature that moves
> In determinate grooves:
> In fact, not a bus but a tram. (Clapham and Gray 2003, p. 290)

27 Op. cit., pp. 185 and 214.
28 Op. cit., p. 175.
29 Op. cit., p. 201.
30 Op. cit., pp. 176–177.
31 Op. cit., p. 205.
32 Op. cit., p. 175.
33 This account contrasts with those of other researchers who continue to work within the general framework of what psychologist Leda Cosmides and anthropologist John Tooby call the Standard Social Science Model (SSSM). This model assumes that most human behaviour, including the ways in which people think and feel, is best explained by reference to the influence of culture on human beings and that the contribution of inherited elements is minimal. The argument that they develop to reveal the deficiencies in this model is both lengthy and complex; so here I will just focus on what I consider to be salient points.

In the SSSM what we might call 'inherited human nature' is conceived in minimalist terms. Empiricist philosophers, following John Locke, described the human mind at birth as a *tabula rasa,* a blank slate. Through various processes of learning that slate is filled with knowledge and abilities that are provided by culture – knowledge accumulated over time by the group. Cosmides and Tooby illustrate this feature of the SSSM with a quotation from the anthropologist Clifford Geertz:

> Our ideas, our values, our acts, even our emotions, are, like our nervous system itself, cultural products – products manufactured, indeed, out of tendencies, capacities, and dispositions with which we were born, but manufactured nonetheless.

Geertz rejects the metaphor of the blank slate and replaces it with a modern equivalent: a general-purpose computer. This might have an operating system (the tendencies, capacities, and dispositions with which we were born) but everything else is supplied by culture or, in the language of other SSSM writers, is socially constructed. Those who work within the framework of the SSSM start from the assumption that the features of the inherited operating system 'must be constructed in such a way that they can absorb any kind of cultural message or environmental input equally well'. In short, the 'software' all comes from outside, from culture.

The dominance of this line of thought has been challenged by scientists from a number of disciplines, including those social scientists who have aligned themselves with what is currently known as evolutionary psychology. The most accessible overview of this debate, in my opinion, is Steven Pinker's *The Blank Slate: the modern denial of human nature* (2002). That work also summarises much of the research showing that human beings do have a nature that has evolved over vast, in comparison to individual lives, time scales.

Modern knowledge, which derives from modern research, is a contested arena. Innocent students who embark on personal quests to discover the current state of our knowledge about ourselves are in a precarious position. Even if they reject all religious claims to knowledge and read only those works and attend only those lectures offered by academics working in reputable universities they may still be misled. So even if we try to seek guidance on our knowledge of ourselves we cannot avoid having to make judgements about the relative worth of competing positions that are persuasively presented by clever people. It is easy to become confused.

Many of the scholars who study religion within an SSSM framework are anthropologists, whose research methods tend to be qualitative in nature, though they do also draw upon experimental research conducted by other scholars. Michael Winkelman, a former president of the American Anthropological Association, provides a good example of this approach (e.g. Winkelman 2016). It is not easy to determine exactly what the positive thesis in this article is, though he is clearly opposed to what he calls 'the traditional constructivist hypotheses'. Presumably he has in mind the kind of argument put forward by Steven Katz, though how the descriptor 'traditional' gets attached to it is a mystery to me since it challenges many religious and scholarly accounts of religious experience. Drawing upon the output of writers such as Forman (1990), Schuon (1975) and Wilber (1977, 1980), he claims that their findings 'falsify the traditional constructivist hypotheses and support instead a neurophenomenological view of mystical experiences as a biologically structured experiences [*sic*]' (Winkelman, op. cit., p. 50). As I hope to have demonstrated in the main text, such 'findings', if that is a legitimate description of them, do no such thing. Moreover, neither I nor many of the writers whose work I have consulted have sought to deny that there is a biological basis for mystical and indeed all religious experiences. As such, his conclusion seems to be rather bland. What he really wants to assert comes a few lines later: ordinary experiences are constructed. The constructivists are right about this. However, 'Meditative experiences reveal the constructed nature of ordinary perception and lead to a deconstruction of these habitual processes and *permit the emergence of neurognostic structures*' (op. cit., p. 50; emphasis mine). In other words, mystical experiences don't just seem to provide knowledge they really do open a door onto a veridical experience of otherwise inaccessible realities. This, as I hope to have shown, is just wishful thinking.

34   Nelson (2011, p. 25).
35   Masters and Huston (1966, p. 247).
36   Nelson (2011, p. 239). In the first chapter of *The God Impulse*, entitled 'What is a spiritual experience?', Nelson writes:

> Many of James's ideas on science and spirituality are the foundation neuroscientists continue to build on. Particularly important is *The Varieties of Religious Experience*. Michael Trimble, an expert in both neurology and psychiatry, calls it 'the most revealing investigation into the psychology of religion ever attempted'. (Op. cit.)

Perhaps. As one researcher's personal attempt to make sense of religious experiences it is certainly outstanding, though our understanding of both psychology and religion has progressed considerably since James's day.

37   James (1902/1985, pp. 405, 422).
38   Op. cit., p. 415 (emphasis mine).
39   Op. cit., pp. 513–514, 526.
40   Op. cit., p. 426.
41   Op. cit., pp. 426, 512, 516.
42   Op. cit., p. 426. This is the kind of claim that may be the source of the dictum 'By their fruits ye shall know them, not by their roots'. The wording itself may well come from R.D. Richardson's (2007) biography of James, where he summarises James's position on this issue as 'His mantra is "By their fruits ye shall know them, not by their roots"' (p. 392).
43   Op. cit., p. 508.
44   Op. cit., pp. 504–505.
45   Op. cit., p. 504.
46   Cited in Dundas (2002, pp. 41–42).
47   Op. cit., p. 158.
48   Op. cit., p. 160.
49   Taqī-ud-Dīn al-Hilālī and Khan (undated).

50   Horrie and Chippindale (2007); Husain (2003).
51   Huntington (1997); Kirsch (2004); Lewis (1995); Pinker (2011).
52   Horrie and Chippindale (2007, pp. 46 and 54; cf. p. 64).
53   Husain (2003, p. 3).
54   Loc. cit.
55   Beattie (2013).
56   Atran (2017, p. 87).
57   See de Blij (2012), especially chapters 5 and 6 and the section on the Islāmic front in Africa. There's a revealing map on p. 200, which shows a continuous line of conflict across the entire continent: Muslims to the north and east of it; Christians and others to the south and west.
58   For example, against French colonialists in Algeria. See, for example, Hussey (2014).
59   Lewis (1995, p. 233).
60   Op. cit., pp. 233–234.
61   Robert Spencer's recent history of jihad reinforces and expands upon my comments here (Spencer 2018).
62   James (1902/1985, p. 519).
63   Op. cit., pp. 508–509.
64   Op. cit., p. 523 (emphasis mine).
65   Indeed, many modern researchers do not even try to bridge the gulf, though some of their words in passing indicate that they would like to. A recent collection of research papers edited by Bettina Schmidt (2016) contained no overt attempts to construct that bridge though a number of covert ones are evident to the critical reader. For example, Gregory Shushan, who is primarily concerned with refuting claims that religious experiences are entirely fabricated by cultures and that they do not provide grounds for religious beliefs (I think he is right to do so), nevertheless employs a number of expressions that hint at a desire to cross the bridge.

While acknowledging that we 'do not necessarily need to believe that the person genuinely did leave the body' during near-death and out-of-body experiences (which he abbreviates as NDEs and OBEs, respectively), he nevertheless inserts statements into his account that hint at a tendency to treat at least some of the reports he considers as veridical. He claims, for example, that 'Staunch materialists and atheists have also had their convictions challenged by their NDEs and OBEs' (Shushan 2016, p. 81); presents Thomas Metzinger's conclusion about OBEs in a manner that suggests he would like to dismiss his own caveat; and presents Carol Zaleski's conclusions about NDE narratives in a manner that implies an error on her part.

In the case of challenges to materialist and atheist convictions, what we are offered is not references to research of various kinds that have produced acknowledgements from materialists and atheists that has challenged their convictions but merely instances where two previously materialist thinkers:

A.J. Ayer and John Wren-Lewis, changed their views because of their personal experiences. Such accounts do show that religious experiences can have a powerful effect on people's beliefs, but, as I hope to have shown in the course of preparing this book and as William James maintained at the beginning of the twentieth century, their existence does not require anyone else to accept the reports at face value (James 1902/1985, p. 422).

Metzinger, as quoted by Shushan, writes 'the truthfulness of centuries of reports about ecstatic states, soul-travel and second bodies as such can hardly be doubted'. As Metzinger himself indicates, that 'truthfulness' only applies to the actuality of the reports, i.e. people provided honest accounts of what they experienced, and not to their content, i.e. 'the conceptual and ontological interpretations' of those experiences. That Shushan would like to ignore this caveat is apparent from his comments elsewhere in the article, such as 'Disregarding emic testimonies and self-understandings of NDEs and OBEs is to privilege specific etic interpretations *de facto* over those of individuals who provide us with our data in the first place ...' and 'Implying that certain individuals – by virtue of the fact that they claim to have had an unusual experience – cannot make such distinctions, [i.e. between the experience and its interpretation] or are unable to differentiate between experience types, or lack the critical faculties to interpret rationally their experiences, is groundless' (Shushan 2016, p. 77).

What are we to make of this? The first thing that pops out at me is that favourite postmodernist term 'privilege'. This tends to be employed to imply a bias or prejudice on the part of those who are accused of 'privileging' without actually claiming that a bias or prejudice has been identified. Moreover, it is easy to flip this argument into its opposite: privileging experiencer reports over accumulated knowledge about human psychology reveals a level of credulity that is unbecoming in scholarly writing. Similarly, 'disregarding' transforms scepticism or a preference for an alternative explanation into a kind of blanket dismissal that is unusual in scholarly writing. We should, therefore, treat it as a rhetorical 'straw man'. Researchers can take reports of unusual experiences seriously and be respectful towards the people who provide those reports without accepting their explanations of them. Shushan makes a similar point but with a subtly different spin: 'We do not necessarily need to believe that the person genuinely did leave the body in order to respect and take seriously his or her narrative' (op. cit., p. 83). Here the respect is not directed towards the person as someone who is being as honest as possible about what it was like to have that experience but towards the narrative. What does it mean to respect and take a narrative seriously? Surely it involves, and I think that this is what Sushan was hoping for, an implication that the narrative accurately captures what actually happened.

Zaleski, claims Sushan, 'denies insider testimony comprehensively and deliberately by concluding that NDEs are imaginary' (op. cit., p. 82). Well, Zaleski's research may be riddled with 'logical inconsistencies' and her conclusion that NDEs are imaginary may be incorrect, but the fact that she draws this conclusion from her work does not, by itself, mean that she, or anyone else who arrives at a similar conclusion, denies insider testimony. It simply means that she (and others) denies that insiders who claimed that their experiences were veridical are correct.

Schmidt's own contribution to this volume is typical of much modern anthropological writing on religion. It draws heavily on ethnographic research, related theorising and subsequent speculation. Following Lambek, she is critical of what she calls 'the Abrahamic tradition' (presumably referring to Jewish, Christian and Islāmic theology) and also of 'secularism', which is characterized as a perspective that 'imagines it can look at religion from the outside' (Schmidt 2016, p. 93). Both, she claims, 'seem fundamentally faulty because they *privilege* one stance over others ...' (op. cit., pp. 93–94; emphasis mine). For her, these perspectives represent what she and Lambek describe as binary or either-or thinking. Avoiding such thinking and adopting both-and thinking instead gives us 'a crucial methodological advantage' (op. cit., p. 94). Does it really?

In the first place, the perspectives of 'the Abrahamic tradition' and 'secularism' are not the only ones available to students of religious experience. Religious traditions themselves offer a range of perspectives (see, for example, Rawlinson's typology of spiritual traditions). Secular traditions are different, because they not only *imagine* that they are outside religion, they actually *are* outside it. If people subscribe to any supernaturalist beliefs that affect their behaviour then they are appropriately described as religious. If, on the other hand, they do not subscribe to any beliefs of that kind then they are appropriately described as non-religious. They are *outside* religion. Insofar as secularists are non-religious they are outside religion, not merely in imagination but in reality.

Her technique for *privileging* (we non-postmodernists can use this term too, even when we are not engaged in parody) ethnographic research and presenting it as the 'only way to move forward with an understanding of spirit possession' (Schmidt 2016, p. 95) is to promote Lambek's notion of deixis, which converts a linguistic category into an ontological one. This supposedly promotes a 'polyphonic reading' (oxymoronic?) of all forms of religious experience and converts spirit possession into 'a deictic form of speech'. Such moves remind me of theological sophistry. An experience of being possessed is not 'a form of speech', one doesn't 'read' sounds, one hears them and listens to them. The deixis frame may be attractive to theologians and anthropologists because the particularisation (Schmidt and Lambek prefer 'provincialisation') of experiences prevents typologising and turns each context-dependent experience into a sui generis category. This, in turn, gives credibility to the debates engaged in by possession practitioners who display 'an impressive intellectualisation' through their publications, conferences, lectures and university degrees. In short, these practitioners merely are doing what Christian theologians have been doing for years.

Moreover, Schmidt acknowledges that the deixis frame is quite limited in that it does not enable one to explain what happens during spirit possession but merely 'relates to the relationship' (?) between human and non-human beings. It does not address the question of 'whether the spirits, *orixas*, or God exist'. This kind of caveat is, however, little more than a subterfuge that allows (or privileges) believer-speak and amounts to little more than a kind of phenomenological *epochê* that communicates insider understanding and confers a pre-critical level of credibility upon it. So we read, for example, that 'While an untrained medium might not be able to control the spirits, to work as a medium is allowed only after intensive training with approval of the spirits' (op. cit., p. 98) and 'The commonality [between Spiritism, Umbanda and Candomblé] is therefore the reference to something extraordinary, outside oneself, and often outside the human body' (op. cit., p. 101). Such passages clearly invite the reader to accept insider epistemologies and ontologies as both credible and authoritative. This invitation is reinforced by claims that such views challenge 'the dualistic understanding of body-mind in Western discourse' (op. cit., p. 101). One wonders which Western discourses she has in mind. Certainly not those found in the writings of most contemporary biologists and psychologists, who tend to think about the human organism much more systemically and organically while also recognising that there are sub-systems within the whole. One does not need the contributions of spirit tradition theologians to challenge mind-body dualism, our best science has already demolished it.

If the deixis frame cannot explain what is happening during experiences of possession does this mean, as Schmidt claims, that 'It is impossible to extract the essence of spirit possession' (op. cit., p. 101)? I would contend that such pessimism is unfounded. The research on trance and hypnosis outlined in Part 2 of this book goes a long way towards extracting that 'essence' even if much work still need to be done. If that 'believed-in imaginings' frame is reasonably robust then we can understand the beings who possess people as constructs created by the possessed themselves, with a fair bit of help from the surrounding culture. They may be real to the possessed and, perhaps, to those around them (including some of the anthropologists) but not, to reiterate what William James asserted over a century ago, necessarily real to or authoritative for anyone else.

66 They do mention James and his work in a couple of passing references in the final chapter (Masters and Huston 1966, pp. 258, 262).

67 Op. cit., p. 5.

68 LSD-25 (d-lysergic acid diethylamide) was synthesized from ergotamine by Albert Hofmann in 1938. The LSD acronym derives from the German 'Lyserg-säure-diäthya' plus the sequential number 25. Peyote 'buttons' are products of the cactus *Lophophora williamsii*. They contain nine alkaloids, the most potent of which is mescaline, though the others also generate some psychedelic effects, as peyote experiences differ in a number of ways from those obtained through the use of mescaline alone (Masters and Huston 1966, p. 40). Psilocybin is mainly derived

from mushrooms of the genus *Psilocybe* and DMT (di-methyl-triptamine) can be derived from a variety of plant sources, including *Mimosa tenniflora*, *Diplapterys cabreran* and *Psychotria viridis*. I mention these differences because although all of these drugs have psychedelic effects the molecular structures of each are different, and in the case of mescaline quite different. As Strassman explains, mescaline is a member of the phenethlyamine family, whereas LSD, DMT and psilocybin are all members of the tryptamine family (Strassman 2001, pp. 32–39). Differences between the experiences of people using these drugs may be the result of differences between the drugs themselves. Ideally, researchers would investigate the effects of each separately rather than assuming commonality. Indeed, Masters and Huston's own comments on the differences between peyote-instigated experiences and mescaline-induced ones should have alerted them to this possibility.

69 Masters and Huston (1966, pp. 148, 265).
70 Op. cit., p. 144.
71 Loc. cit.
72 Op. cit., p. 147.
73 Op. cit., p. 148. These levels are presented as a journey into profundity. There is no mention of 'bad trips' or anything corresponding to James's 'diabolical mysticism'.
74 Op. cit., p. 144.
75 Op. cit., p. 185.
76 Op. cit., p. 193.
77 Op. cit., p. 149.
78 Op. cit., pp. 213–216. One wonders whether any of these Jonny-on-the-spot 'historical' experiences ever yield any information that could convincingly add to or modify the versions of those events that have been produced by historians using standard historical methods.
79 Op. cit., p. 214.
80 And on and on ... op. cit., p. 222. It is quite clear in a number of these accounts that the participant's immersion in these unfolding experiences has been triggered by suggestions from 'the guide'. In this case the guide handed the participant a cross (presumably some kind of Christian crucifix). In another example (op. cit., p. 226), the guide says 'Perhaps instead of thinking of a desert, you will find it possible to think of a void, a black, silent void. A void beyond life, beyond existence, beyond you, beyond me, beyond everything. Now there is a light coming into this void. A light that is beginning to dimly illuminate the landscape. Tell me what you see there.' As I read this I was reminded of a training day for hypnotherapists that I attended on past-life regression. Similar formula; different content.
81 Op. cit., pp. 148–150.
82 Op. cit., p. 148.
83 Op. cit., p. 266.

84 See op. cit., ch. 9 passim, and especially pp. 261-265, 274 and 303.
85 Op. cit., p. 267.
86 James (1902/1985, p. 415).
87 Philosophers have drawn attention to some of the problems inherent in our notions of truth in connection with epistemology. Many people would say something like, 'if a statement accurately describes what happened or what is the case it is true; if not, it is false'. This way of understanding the situation is probably the most common, and it has received general support from eminent philosophers such as Aristotle, Bertrand Russell and J.L. Austin. It is often called a 'correspondence notion of truth' or a 'correspondence theory of truth'. This is the notion of truth that one finds in courts of law, for example: *Do you promise to tell the truth, the whole truth and nothing but the truth?* The assumption here is that there is a kind of direct relationship between statements (sentences that can be true or false) and the world. This common sense notion has been challenged, however.

Two of the most influential challenges have to do with what we can call levels of application.

Challenge 1. The correspondence theory of truth works quite well with everyday, specific examples and we can all think of other examples that are relatively straightforward because they are simple and easy to check. Some of mine would be:

- My fountain pen contains blue ink.
- Apples are a type of fruit.
- Bertrand Russell was the author of a book called *The Problems of Philosophy*.

When we come to more general truths, however, problems start to emerge.

Take, for example, the statement 'The ancient Greeks invented democracy'.

This statement may be true and it, or ones similar to it, are often said by many people to be true. Yet it is certainly not simple and it is not easy to check against the facts. So the kind of correspondence with the way things are or were is a lot less straightforward than it was with my earlier examples. For a start, which ancient Greeks are we talking about? Certainly not the characters in Homer's Iliad and Odyssey, and certainly not the Spartans, who supported a kind of oligarchy. The Athenians then? Well, they did have a kind of democracy, but it was nothing like Abraham Lincoln's notion of 'government of the people, by the people, for the people'. Only around 40,000 adult males had the vote. So there is a kind of truth to the statement 'The ancient Greeks invented democracy'. There are also many ways in which it is false.

Challenge 2. Another way in which general truths are problematic is that many of the things we regard as true, what might be called 'facts about the world', depend for their understanding on their relationships with other ideas that are difficult to check. Sometimes these other, usually more abstract, ideas are found to be mistaken. The 'facts' that were based on those ideas are also brought into question and what once seemed to be true is now regarded as false.

For example, the idea that the world was composed of the four elements of earth, air, fire and water was once deemed to be true and is now deemed to be false. So too are the medical cures and personality descriptions that were based on the idea. Likewise, the idea that the sun, stars and planets revolved around the earth was once regarded as true, but now it isn't. Sets of ideas that were based on that idea, such as astrology, are now no longer regarded as true by many people – though it is interesting to note in this case how some notions continue to attract support even when their theoretical foundations have been undermined.

So the question arises, 'were those errors that were previously regarded as true ever true, or were they always false despite the fact that people believed them to be true? If one thinks that errors that were once believed to be true were true then but not true now then one does *not* subscribe to the correspondence theory. Instead, the correspondence theory commits one to the position that errors that were once believed to be true were as false then as they are now, because correspondence is with the way things really are, not with how they are or were believed to be. The pressing issue for correspondence theorists is the question arises about the status of ideas that we currently think are true.

Some people take the view that all 'truths' are provisional, destined to be overturned with the next major shift in our understanding of what the universe is really like. Others argue that much of modern science provides us with truths that are as certain as we can get. We can call the first group 'provisionalists' and the second group 'non-provisionalists'. The provisionalists think that the correspondence view is far too simple. One group of provisionalists, who can be said to hold a coherence view of truth, argue that what we usually mean when we say that something is true is that it coheres with or fits with what we already believe to be true. The most eminent advocate of this view was the philosopher F.H. Bradley (an idealist). This approach treats 'truth' as an embedded idea. It is embedded in or linked with lots of other ideas that tend to stand or fall together. That which is taken to be true is accepted as such because it fits with a wider picture or set of ideas. In science this wider picture is often called a 'paradigm'.

Occasionally, information that doesn't fit with the paradigm accumulates to the point where the paradigm ceases to function as an explanatory framework. At that point, one or more alternative frameworks begin to emerge and, eventually, scientists abandon the old paradigm and adopt a new one, e.g. Copernican revolution; plate tectonics. Thomas Kuhn calls this a paradigm change or shift (Kuhn 1970). In the process, many of the 'truths' that existed within the old paradigm are also abandoned. They are no longer regarded as truths. Others are reworked, recast or remodelled in the light of the new paradigm. The older versions are then regarded as being only approximations to the truth. However, those 'truths' that do fit with the new paradigm are treated as truths, or at least the closest we can currently get to truth. From this perspective, there is no such thing as 'truth' in a correspondence sense.

Another group of provisionalists who are uncomfortable with a correspondence understanding of truth are the pragmatists. For them, and the philosopher and psychologist William James is often regarded as their most eloquent spokesperson, our main way of knowing whether something is 'true' is that it 'works' for us. It has utility value. He writes:

> The possession of truth, so far from being ... an end in itself, is only a preliminary means towards some other vital satisfactions ... the practical value of true ideas is ... primarily derived from the practical importance of their objects to us ... You can say ... then either that 'it is useful because it is true' or that 'it is true because it is useful. Both these phrases mean exactly the same thing [They do not, of course, mean the same thing], namely that here is an idea that gets fulfilled and can be verified. True is the name for whatever idea starts the verification process, useful is the name for its completed function in experience. (James 1907/1999)

But what James is getting at here is that if the application of a belief to the world yields the results we expected or hoped for then the truth of that belief has been verified – it works. For example, psychologist Shelley Taylor found that the most mentally healthy people were not those who had a realistic understanding of their situation in the world but those who had an unrealistic optimism about it. These optimists believed that they were better than average at most things, that they were, overall, in control of their lives, and that their future would be a good one (Taylor 1989).

Not only were the optimists mentally healthy, they also tended to be quite successful and their success verified their optimistic beliefs so that those beliefs became true, they worked.

The non-provisionalists accept that some of what we might tend to regard as truths will, at some future date be shown to be either false or partial. They also maintain that some of our knowledge is of a genuinely correspondence type. For example, Richard Dawkins argues that the coherentist notion might have been applicable at an earlier stage in the development of scientific understanding, but now we have arrived at a point where many general and theoretical truths can be ascribed the same status as everyday specific truths. For example, 'Water is composed of two hydrogen atoms and one oxygen atom'. This is a highly embedded claim. It depends on the accuracy of our understanding of atoms and how chemical bonds are formed. It is also quite difficult to check for oneself. But it is, in Dawkins's terms, as true as any of our more everyday truths.

With regard to the pragmatic version of truth, I think Bertrand Russell is right in his argument that 'when we say of something that it exists when it *does* exist, that statement is true; when we say of something that it exists when it *does not* exist, that statement is false. The pragmatic notion allows us to claim truth for the second statement if we find that useful to us' (Russell 1999). This, he thinks, not only distorts what we mean by truth, it also robs us of a useful distinction. For example, if I find it useful to believe that God exists, because holding that belief makes me happy, i.e. is useful to me, then that belief, according to the pragmatists, is true. Likewise, if that belief makes me unhappy, then it is false. In short, the pragmatic idea of truth allows there to be many different, mutually incompatible 'truths' (op. cit.). In recent years this position has been referred to as *relativism*. The basic idea is that each culture has its own view of the world, its own truths, and no culture has the right to claim that its own truths are superior to those of another.

What we have here, I think, are two quite different meanings of the term 'truth'. The relativist uses the term truth to mean an opinion or conviction or belief that is embedded in the worldview of a culture – an essentially coherentist position. The correspondence theorist thinks that if two 'truths' are mutually incompatible then one or both of them must be false. You can have complementary truths, perhaps at different levels of explanation, but in the final analysis the world is as it is and our descriptions of it are sometimes accurate (true) and sometimes not (false). It seems to be the case then, that none of the explanations of what is meant by 'truth' are completely accurate or tell the whole story. Nevertheless, for me, despite its limitations, the correspondence theory catches what we generally understand by the term 'truth' better than do its competitors.

Underpinning my judgement on this issue is the relationship between ideas about truth and those about knowledge (epistemology). The three most widely recognised sources of knowledge are: Perception, Inference, and Testimony. Perception covers everything that we can experience directly. Inference covers everything to do with the logic of reasoning, and testimony covers everything that we learn from others. Each of these can yield reliable knowledge, and each is susceptible to generating error. One way to think about what these sources of knowledge have to offer is to create two columns, one headed knowledge, the other headed belief. Many of the disputes in epistemology are about which ideas go in which column.

We tend to use the term 'knowledge' for beliefs that are supported by good reasons, whereas we tend to use 'belief' for beliefs that we think are true, but for which good reasons are either lacking or not fully conclusive. So we might say that knowledge is 'justified true belief'. Most people like to think that their own beliefs are actually knowledge, though they are equally ready to deny that status to the beliefs of others. To paraphrase Bertrand Russell's 'conjugation of an irregular verb':

> I have knowledge
> You have belief
> She has serious delusions.

This is a tricky issue, however. Consider the following:

Farmer Field is concerned about his prize cow, Daisy. In fact, he is so concerned that when his dairyman tells him that Daisy is in the field happily grazing, he says he needs to know for certain. He doesn't want just to have a 99 per cent idea that Daisy is safe, he wants to be able to say that he knows Daisy is okay.

Farmer Field goes out to the field and standing by the gate sees in the distance, behind some trees, a white and black shape that he recognises as his favourite cow. He goes back to the dairy and tells his friend that he knows Daisy is in the field.

At this point, does Farmer Field really know it?

The dairyman says he will check too, and goes to the field. There he finds Daisy, having nap in a hollow, behind a bush, well out of sight of the gate. He also spots a large piece of black and white paper that has got caught in a tree.

Daisy is in the field, as Farmer Field thought. But was he right to say that he *knew* she was? (Cohen 2002)

Perception

Pretty much everyone agrees that the information we get by means of our five senses: sight, hearing, touching, smelling and tasting, constitutes the basis of perception. There is, of course, what is generally referred to as extra-sensory perception. Many people hold beliefs, which they treat as truths, that are based on this kind of perception. Most religious teachings can be traced back to some person's extra sensory experience, either by way of personal revelation or meditation. And often it is claimed that such experiences tap into a dimension of reality that is deeper and more true than the reality experienced through the senses.

But even if we stay with just the five senses, there is more to perception than simple sensory input. Sensory information is decoded by our brains and used to create a simulation of the external world. What we call 'experience' is not, in fact, the experience of the world but of the virtual reality created by our brains, which we can call our internal map of the world. Most of the time, the fit between our internal 'map of the world' and the world itself is sufficiently close for us not to notice the difference between them. Our virtual reality 'works', as the Pragmatists might say. So we take our experience to be the truth. Sometimes, however, it doesn't work and we misperceive things. There are many causes of misperception, for example:

1 upbringing and learning;
2 brain damage; and
3 the influence of other people.

Upbringing

All of us have been taught that the world in which we live has certain characteristics and contains certain kinds of things. *We learn* to experience it as having those characteristics and containing those things. For example, one sunny day I looked out of my bedroom window and saw my neighbour climb out of a white car. My thoughts went something like this: Must be new, his old one was black. But it's the same model: an old model. Why change the old black one for this? I had learned previously that reflected light can sometimes change the appearance of colours – black can look white. That's what had happened here. From that moment I could not return to seeing the car as white. My stored 'knowledge' had corrected my immediate sensory impressions. I later checked my experience with a ground-level viewing of his car, and it was black. This seems to be something that could be common to all humans. Here are a couple of examples from other cultures of misperception that occurred because people's learned internal maps or models of the world didn't match the world as it was:

> An especially dramatic example reported in anthropological texts concerns the South Sea Islanders, who had never seen a white man or a ship larger than a big canoe. When Captain Cook sailed into a bay of the island for the first time, the islanders gave not the slightest sign of seeing the ship, even though it right in front of them. When a small boat set out from the ship to land, was spotted immediately and the islanders were alarmed, as it seemed have come from nowhere. The idea of a boat as big as Cook's ship was inconceivable to the islanders. Boats all fell within a certain size range, they apparently had a negative hallucination of it at first. (Tart 1988, p. 104)

> With typical pygmy philosophy [Kenge] turned his back on the mountains to look more closely at what lay all around him. He picked up a handful of grass, tasted it and smelled it. He said that it was bad grass and that the mud was bad mud. He sniffed at the air and said it was bad air. In fact, as he had stated at the outset, it was altogether a very bad country. The guide pointed out the elephants, hoping to make him feel more at home. But Kenge was not impressed – he asked what good they were if we were not allowed to go and hunt them. Henri pointed out the antelopes, which had moved closer and were staring at us as curiously as ever. Kenge clapped his hands together and said that they would give food for months and months. And then he saw the buffalo, still grazing lazily several miles away, far down below. He turned to me and said, 'What insects are those?' At first I hardly understood, then I realized that in the forest vision is so limited that there is no great need to make an automatic allowance for distance when judging size. Out here in the plains, Kenge was looking for the first time over apparently unending miles of unfamiliar grasslands, with not a tree worth the name to give him any basis for comparison. The same thing happened later on when I pointed out a boat, in the middle of the lake. It was a large fishing boat with a number of people in it. Kenge at first refused to believe it. He thought it was a floating piece of wood. When I told Kenge that the insects were buffalo, he roared with laughter and told me not to tell such stupid lies. When Henri, who was thoroughly puzzled, told him the same thing, and explained that visitors to the park had to have a guide with them at all times because there were so many dangerous animals, Kenge still didn't believe, but he strained his eyes to see more clearly and asked what kind of buffalo they were that they were so small. I told him they were sometimes nearly twice

the size of a forest buffalo, and he shrugged his shoulders and said he would not be standing out there in the open if they were. I tried telling him they were possibly as far away as from Epulu to the village of Kopu, beyond Eboyo. He began scraping the mud off his arms and legs, no longer interested in such fantasies. (Turnbull 1961, pp. 227–228)

Damage to the brain

The writings of Oliver Sacks provide numerous examples. Here's one:

I had stopped at a florist on my way to his apartment and bought myself an extravagant red rose for my buttonhole. Now I removed this and handed it to him. He took it like a botanist or morphologist given a specimen, not like a person given a flower.

'About six inches in length', he commented. 'A convoluted red form with a linear green attachment'.

'Yes', I said encouragingly, 'and what do you think it is, Dr P?'

'Not easy to say.' He seemed perplexed. 'It lacks the simple symmetry of the Platonic solids, although it may have a higher symmetry of its own ... I think this could be an inflorescence or flower.'

'Could be?' I queried.

'Could be,' he confirmed.

'Smell it,' I suggested, and he again looked somewhat puzzled, as if I had asked him to smell a higher symmetry. But he complied courteously, and took it to his nose. Now, suddenly, he came to life.

'Beautiful!' he exclaimed. 'An early rose. What a heavenly smell!' He started to hum 'Die Rose, die Lillie ...' Reality, it seemed, might be conveyed by smell, not by sight.

I tried one final test. It was still a cold day, in early spring, and I had thrown my coat and gloves on the sofa.

'What is this?' I asked, holding up a glove.

'May I examine it?' he asked, and, taking it from me, he proceeded to examine it as he had examined the geometrical shapes.

'A continuous surface,' he announced at last, 'infolded on itself. It appears to have' – he hesitated – 'five outpouchings, if this is the word.'

'Yes,' I said cautiously. 'You have given me a description. Now tell me what it is.'

'A container of some sort?'

'Yes,' I said, 'and what would it contain?'

'It would contain its contents!' said Dr P., with a laugh. 'There are many possibilities. It could be a change-purse, for example, for coins of five sizes. It could ...'

I interrupted the barmy flow. 'Does it not look familiar? Do you think it might contain, might fit, a part of your body?'

No light of recognition dawned on his face ... Later, by accident, he got it on, and exclaimed 'My God, it's a glove!' (Sacks 1985, pp. 12–13)

What people tell us

A classic example of this is what has come to be known as the self-fulfilling prophecy. In 1968 Rosenthal and Jacobsen published a book entitled *Pygmalion in the Classroom*. They had set up a school-based experiment where teachers were told that around 20 per cent of the pupils in 18 classes were 'bloomers', that is they would show extraordinary development over the coming year. The idea was to assess the effect of teacher expectation on pupil performance. The so-called 'bloomers' had actually been chosen at random and did not display any characteristics that might suggest they would 'bloom' over the coming year. At the end of the year, the 'bloomers' had raised their IQ scores by 12 points as compared to the non-bloomers' increase of 8 points. This was far from being a perfect experiment, but it and other studies do point to a powerful role for expectation in the generation of performance.

Expectation can also work backwards to affect memory. Psychologist Elizabeth Loftus has conducted a number of experiments on this theme. In one, she and a colleague showed a video clip of a car accident to 150 people:

> One third were asked 'About how fast were the cars going when they smashed into each other?' one third 'About how fast were the cars going when they hit each other?' and one third acted as a control group who were not posed a question about speed. One week later, all were asked questions about the film, including 'Did you see any broken glass?' None had actually appeared in the video clip, but the number of sightings increased with the vigour of the verbs used one week earlier. Of those asked about estimated speed using the word 'smashed', 32 per cent said they had seen broken glass. This compares with 14 per cent asked using the word 'hit' and 12 per cent for those in the control group. Thus the information implicit in the question asked after participants saw the video affected their subsequent judgements and recall of the accident. (Brace and Roth 2002, p. 134)

These examples show that not only can we misperceive on occasions but also that some kinds of misperceptions, those arising out of the ways in which our maps of the world are constructed under cultural influence in childhood, can actually pervade our whole lives without us being conscious of the fact.

Inference

Inferences are constituent parts of many of our perceptions, though we are rarely conscious of making them. I might perceive a chair on the floor. That's my sense perception. I also 'know' that the chair arrived in the room after the flooring had been laid. That knowledge is not, however, given in the sense experience. I had to infer it. Inference can also take us further than this. Good detectives use it all the time. They start with clues, 'the facts of the case', and then by a combination of different kinds of inference they eliminate many of the possibilities and concentrate on the more plausible ones. Sherlock Holmes and

Hercule Poirot are the masters of this kind of thinking, which can also be found in courts of law. The film *12 Angry Men* illustrates it well. Many crimes are solved and accusations resolved through the judicious use of inferential methods. So inference can be a major source of knowledge.

Our inferences can also go astray. Indeed, they go astray so often that a special term has been invented to indicate a faulty inference: *a fallacy*. There are many ways in which our inferences can become flawed, though logicians have identified and named 20 or so as the most common. Here are three of them:

1. The argument from ignorance (*argumentum ignorantiam*). For example: 'No one has ever managed to prove that we have not been visited by beings from another planet, so we must have been.'

2. Argument at the person (*argumentum ad hominem*). For example: 'You cannot trust what Dr Bloggs says about academic salaries because he's an academic.'

3. Begging the question or assuming the conclusion (*petitio principii*). For example: 'God exists because the Bible tells us so, and we know that what the Bible tells us must be true because it is the revealed word of God.'

Testimony

For many of us, testimony is the least robust of the sources of knowledge. All of us have lied at various times throughout our lives and we are pretty sure that everyone else has too. In fact, field research based on questionnaires suggests that 98 per cent of the population tell lies at some time or other, and that the other 2 per cent are liars (joke). Much of the time, though, people do tell the truth. If you ask for directions, people usually set you on the right route. If you ask about the football score you are usually given the right result, and if you ask whether a particular shop is open until 8pm on Thursdays, people will usually give you accurate information. Indeed, our society can only function because people tell the truth most of the time. So we are probably right to dismiss the claim by Sebastian of Cambridge that all Cambridge people are liars.

In many religious traditions testimony is often given pride of place among the sources of knowledge. The testimony of the scriptures that St X or prophet Y experienced talking with God or saw the future or found the path to enlightenment is often treated as though it were above the possibility of error, though, as we have noted, the situation is complicated by the fact that religions tend to accept sources of knowledge that non-religious people are sceptical about: revelation and meditation. It is testimony based on claims of access to these distinctive sources of knowledge that religious confidence in testimony tends to be based rather than just any old testimony. Whether these extra-sensory sources of information are as reliable as religious people take them to be is one of the big debates in the philosophy of religion.

Ordinary testimony can mislead us for two main reasons: People might sincerely believe that what they are telling us is the truth even though in actuality it is not; so the problem is an epistemological one – so what we need to examine is the basis of their belief. Alternatively, they might know that what they are telling us is false and intend to mislead us. Here the issue is an ethical one and we move out of the realm of epistemology proper and into the realm of deception. There is also a third dimension to this, which leads back to problems with the correspondence theory: the relationship between lying and creativity and forms of language use that go beyond the purely descriptive.

Lying and creativity

Creativity has much to do with going beyond the merely factual and generating new possibilities. Some of these possibilities will never see the light of day, but some will. Lies are a kind of alternative scenario, a plausible version of events. The ability to create such plausible alternatives has obvious survival value if it can get you off the hook. So we can expect natural selection to favour this kind of adaptation. It is also an ability that is often prized by cultures. Two of the greatest heroes of Greek and Indian culture are Odysseus and Kṛṣṇa, both noted for their feats of deviousness. (Odysseus for the Trojan horse and his deception of the cyclops; Kṛṣṇa for his deception of Drona about the death of his son Aśvattaman).

Autistic children find it difficult to lie, and this is often taken to indicate that they lack a theory of mind, an ability to work out what someone else is thinking. As Campbell points out, 'It is touching and tragic, to find that parents will sometimes express great relief when their autistic child, otherwise intellectually able, tells his first clumsy lie in his teens' (Campbell 2001, p. 261). Storytellers and raconteurs excel at lying in that they either invent or embellish the truth. And many people do the same for their own life stories. The film *Big Fish* and Henry James's short story 'The Liar' both explore this theme and come to the conclusion that in the kinds of circumstances they explore, lying is not so bad and can even be enriching.

Non-literal forms of language

In these forms, value lies not so much in 'telling it as it is' but rather in telling it as it might be or might have been, with telling it as it should be and with communicating truth in ways that are almost the opposite of correspondence.

Let us consider each in turn.

Telling it as it might be or might have been

Myths, the grand stories that tell us about the origin of the world, of our group, of our place in the scheme of things and of the way we have always organised our social affairs, provide a broad framework for our thinking about reality. To challenge such stories is difficult, because one seems to be questioning the way things actually are – a sure sign of insanity. Simply to say, as people have at various times, that the stories are false is usually ineffective – especially if no alternative set of stories is on offer. People seem to need some kind of meaningful story within which they can locate their lives, and this, I think, goes a long way towards explaining the persistent success of religious traditions in spite of the credibility issues that critics raise in every generation. They provide cosmic stories that give human life a significance beyond mere survival and reproduction. No other human institutions do this as well. So myths offer what might be thought of as a kind of paradigm, a framework for truth, a set of stories and values into which everyday truths can be fitted.

To challenge a myth (and political ideologies are kinds of myths) one has to offer an alternative myth, a counter ideology. One cannot effectively displace a myth without offering a replacement for it. Alternative myths or ideologies offer us alternative frameworks for deciding what is true and what is false. *Dominant ideologies* and myths provide cultures with frameworks for understanding how things are. *Counter ideologies* and myths offer alternatives that are in not only the realm of what might be but also in ...

The realm of could be or should be

The issue between ideologies and counter-ideologies is largely a matter of plausibility. Does the new framework explain my life, my problems and the world better than the old one? If it does, it might be successful. The odds are usually stacked in favour of the status quo, however. The proponents of the new ideology are, metaphorically speaking, pushing their ideas uphill whereas the custodians of the old have the gradient on their side. Education and upbringing have all been permeated with ideas from the dominant myth, so the populace tends to be predisposed to give arguments that work within it the benefit of the doubt while being suspicious of the new. Of course other factors are involved too, such as who has the most powerful army, who controls the media and who controls education. But a good counter ideology can keep an alternative vision alive through years and even generations of repression, for it challenges not only the accuracy of the dominant narrative but also the legitimacy of the values it propagates, e.g. caste system; all creatures great and small.

In some respects, novels are like myths. They offer an insider, meaning and value filled perspective on human affairs. They offer alternative ways of making sense of events that we usually only access from the outside. Like counter ideologies and myths, they work within the realm of what might be or might have been the case. They can also reverse the effects of attribution errors (I deserve my success; he was lucky. I was unlucky; he deserved what he got). So although novels (and indeed, ideologies and myths) are works of fiction, they can communicate a kind of non-literal truth. Whether the very idea of non-literal truth makes sense is a moot point at the present time.

Communicating truth in a non-correspondence manner

At this point, I simply want to mention two ways of communicating a kind of truth (exactly what kind I leave you, the reader, to determine) that does not employ notions of correspondence: *irony* and *metaphor*. One may, of course, be predisposed to reject the idea that there can be truth without some kind of correspondence, though if this is the case we have to address the issue of what exactly is being communicated through these devices. Perhaps in the end, a non-literal notion of correspondence (whatever that would look like) will resolve the matter. We'll have to see.

Irony

Irony is a form of language that, taken literally, would convey the opposite of what is actually intended. A simple example would be that Mr Smith passes Mrs Brown on a wet and windy day and says 'Lovely weather we're having'. More sophisticated forms have the bite of satire or sarcasm about them. As one seventeenth-century grammarian put it, 'An irony ... hath the honey of pleasantness in its mouth, and a sting of rebuke in its tail' (Campbell 2001, p. 148). Examples would be:

- In response to someone who says 'It's simple enough, you fine a thief and execute a killer', an ironical retort might be 'O eloquent one, if the framers of our codes and laws only had access to your penetrating intellect all our social problems would be solved in an instant.'
- To someone who behaves in a loutish manner, an ironical retort might be 'How did you come by those exemplary manners?'

So the ironist says the opposite of what he or she intends to communicate, but what she/he intends to communicate is the truth. Or we could say that *irony is the communication of truth through falsehood*. In that way, says Jeremy Campbell, 'It disrupts the correspondence between word and world' (Campbell 2001, p. 148).

Metaphor

When writing about metaphor, many modern authors tend to ignore the stricter use of the term and treat similes (this is like that) and metaphors (this is that) as essentially the same. At the heart of metaphorical communication is the explanation of one thing (usually an unfamiliar one) in terms of another, usually more familiar, one. Take the metaphor, 'A blanket of snow'. A literal version of this idea might be something like 'A thick and continuous layer of snow. The main difference between these expressions is that the second works pretty much like a sign – there is a single and ideally unambiguous message being conveyed. The first expression works more like a symbol – it carries layers of meaning, in this case all the associations that go along with our idea of a blanket. A related metaphor with similar layers of meaning is 'a carpet of leaves'. Metaphors have the capacity to convey complex ideas in a relatively concise way, and when we explore our language with metaphors in mind we find that that they are pervasive. Indeed, most people would find it difficult to string more than half a dozen sentences together without employing metaphors of some kind. Metaphors, claim authors such as George Lakoff and Mark Johnson, actually allow us to communicate the truth as we understand it. Without them, many ideas would simply be incommunicable (Lakoff and Johnson 1980). So metaphors can be accurate or inaccurate, true or false, though in a slightly different way than more literal expressions are true or false.

These examples of irony and metaphor illustrate the more general point that truth and meaning are inextricably linked through language, and language can be used to communicate our understanding of the world in ways that fall outside the scope of simple correspondence notions. The idea of correspondence, it seems to me, still has a lot going for it, though it needs to be substantially enriched if it is to do justice to the subtle and complex relationship between language and the world. Simple correspondence presents that relationship, to use a metaphor, as one that works like a sign – a one-to-one match. A more sophisticated correspondence theory would need to work much more like a symbol that can communicate many levels and dimensions of meaning. So the question, 'What is truth?' remains one that continues to fascinate and challenge thinkers from a wide variety of backgrounds.

88 Masters and Huston (1966, p. 258; emphasis mine).
89 Most also seem to be sexist – in a misogynist kind of way – and have some version of the 'collection box'.
90 Theodore Flournoy, like his friend William James, was profoundly interested in the phenomenon of mediumship (which suffered a considerable decline in popularity during the twentieth century but is currently making something of a comeback under the label of 'channelling'). Although theoretically committed to a position of neutrality with regard to the existence of spiritual entities his approach tended to be thoroughly naturalistic, i.e. if he could explain spiritual experiences by reference to psychological factors alone he would do so. In his most famous study of mediumistic and spiritistic phenomena, *From India to the Planet Mars*, Flournoy consistently explains his subject's experiences of the spirits of deceased or extraterrestrial persons and her memories of her own

previous lives in purely psychological terms (through his concepts of subliminal or subconscious mental processing, autosuggestion and cryptomnesia – the 'reappearance of memories profoundly buried beneath the normal waking state, together with an indeterminate amount of imaginative exaggeration upon the canvas of actual facts' (Flournoy 1899/1994, p. 173). In order to establish the ignorance of their participants Masters and Huston would need to show that cryptomnesia, etc. was unlikely to have been operative.

91 Greenberg (2013, pp. 68–69).
92 Op. cit., p. 40.
93 Op. cit., p. 72.
94 Grof (1975/2009, p. 25).
95 Op. cit. p. Op. cit., p. 118.
96 Op. cit., p. 27.
97 Op. cit., p. 40.
98 This is a label coined by R.A. Sandison. As Grof explains it, 'The root *lysis* suggests dissolving or releasing tensions and conflicts in the human mind' (Grof 1975/2009, p. 19n).
99 Op. cit., p. 45.
100 Op. cit., p. 44.
101 Op. cit., p. 20.
102 Op. cit., p. 216.
103 Op. cit., p. 217.
104 Masters and Huston (1966, p. 185).
105 Joseph Griffin's work on dreaming also makes useful contributions to this literature (Griffin 1997; Griffin and Tyrrell 2004).
106 Grof (1975/2009, p. 97).
107 Op. cit., p. 99.
108 Op. cit., p. 103.
109 Loc. cit.
110 For example, 'realistic complex *recollections* of the original embryonal situation …' (op. cit., p. 107); 'realistic *recollections* of their fetal existence …' (op. cit., p. 110); 'racial and evolutionary memories' (op. cit., p. 105).
111 Op. cit., pp. 97, 108, 109, 136.
112 Op. cit., p. 108.
113 Op. cit., p. 119.
114 Op. cit., p. 127.
115 Op. cit., p. 132.
116 Op. cit., p. 133.
117 Op. cit., p. 135.
118 Op. cit., p. 144.
119 Op. cit., p. 158. Note the presuppositions embedded in this definition: 'expansion' and 'extension' suggest/imply actualities when the evidence he presents will only support something like 'a perceived or inferred or experienced expansion/

extension'. Consciousness may be expanded or extended during psychedelic sessions, or it may not. Is consciousness expanded/extended during dreams? If we say 'yes' then it is probably appropriate to say 'yes' to psychedelic experiences; if we say 'no' then the same conclusion may well apply to psychedelic experience. As far as I am aware, clinching evidence that can push the conclusion one way or the other is not yet available, though my own default position is that these experiences should be treated as subjective until robust evidence supporting an objectivist judgement is forthcoming.

120 Op. cit., pp. 159–160. His lists are:

Within the framework of 'objective reality':

  (b) Temporal expansion of consciousness

- Embryonal and fetal experiences
- Ancestral experiences
- Collective and racial experiences
- Phylogenetic (evolutionary) experiences
- Past-incarnation experiences
- Precognition, clairvoyance, clairaudience, and "time travels"

  (b) Spatial expansion of consciousness

- Ego transcendence in interpersonal relations and the experience of dual unity
- Identification with other persons
- Group identification and group consciousness
- Animal identification
- Plant identification
- Oneness with life and with all creation
- Consciousness of inorganic matter
- Planetary consciousness
- Extraplanetary consciousness
- Out-of-body experiences, travelling clairvoyance and clairaudience, 'space travels', and telepathy
- Extraplanetary consciousness

  (c) Spatial constriction of consciousness

- Organ, tissue, and cellular consciousness

Beyond the framework of 'objective reality':

- Spiritistic and mediumistic experiences
- Experiences of encounters with suprahuman spiritual entities
- Experiences of other universes and encounters with their inhabitants
- Archetypal experiences and complex mythological sequences
- Experiences of encounters with various deities
- Intuitive understanding of universal symbols
- Activation of the chakras and arousal of the serpent power (Kundalini)
- Consciousness of the universal mind
- The supracosmic and metacosmic void

We may, once again, note the presuppositions embedded in the terminology, e.g. not 'a universal mind' but 'the universal mind'.

121 Op. cit., pp. 162, 181.
122 Op. cit., pp. 161, xxiii, 193.
123 Op. cit., p. xxix (and p. xxx for full reference for the works cited in this passage).
124 Op. cit., p. 163 (emphasis mine).
125 Op. cit., p. 189.
126 Op. cit., pp. 193, 197, 205.
127 Op. cit., pp. 162, 164, 171, 173.
128 Dundas (2002, p. 88).
129 Johnson (2006, p. 37).
130 Op. cit., p. 45. A simple and easy-to-prepare electrolyte drink can be made using water, sugar and salt in precise proportions: one quart of water; half a teaspoon of salt, and six teaspoons of sugar (see www.webmd.com/hw-popup/rehydration-drinks?navbar=hw86827).
131 See www.youtube.com/watch?v=kIFlWe1oYlw.
132 There is growing evidence that psychedelic experiences can often have quite profound therapeutic effects, especially on conditions such as depression. See the TEDxWarwick lecture by Robin Carhart-Harris on 'Psychedelics: Lifting the veil', available at www.youtube.com/watch?v=MZIaTaNR3gk (accessed 6 June 2017). It is unlikely that such benefits as accrue from psychedelic experience depend on them providing access to reality. Indeed, there are good reasons for rejecting accurate reality testing as a criterion for mental health and well-being. Despite the fact that many psychotherapists, particularly those of psychoanalytic persuasion, have argued that this should be a primary aim of therapy and is a significant indicator of mental health, more recent research (e.g. Taylor 1989) calls this into question. Marie Jahoda emphasised this 'reality testing component' in her survey of mental health and, more recently, so too

did Robin Skynner. This probably reflects the influence of his early training in psychodynamic psychotherapy, not least because in the same work where he states that the central idea he cannot repeat too often is that 'if we can stay in touch with reality, the truth will heal us' (Skynner and Cleese 1993, p. 334), he offers Japanese social organisation as an example of one way of promoting mental health. Yet, by his own admission, 'For the Japanese, reality is negotiable ... because they value cohesion above any other quality, the Japanese are not interested in finding an accurate view of reality; they want a formula that everyone can agree on' (op. cit., p. 208). In short, therapeutic benefits are not dependent on gaining access to objective reality. Indeed, we can now recognise that a degree of reality distortion can have beneficial effects, and the kinds of transformations encountered in psychedelic experiences such as those described by Carhart-Harris may well turn out to be, in Taylor's terms, benign positive illusions.

133   Nelson (2011, p. 254).

Bibliography

Adkins, A.W.H. *Merit and Responsibility: a study in Greek values* Oxford University Press, Oxford, 1960

Adkins, A.W.H. *From the Many to the One: a study of personality and views of human nature in the context of Ancient Greek society, values and beliefs* Constable, London, 1970

Alman, B. M. and Lambrou, P. *Self-Hypnosis: the complete manual for health and self-change* (2nd ed.) Brunner-Mazel, New York, 1992

Argyle, M. and Beit-Hallami, B. *The Psychology of Religious Behaviour, Belief and Experience* Routledge, London, 1997

Armstrong, K. *A History of God* Vintage, London, 1999

Atran, S. 'The role of the devoted actor in war' in Lewis, J.R. (ed.) *The Cambridge Companion to Religion and Terrorism* Cambridge University Press, New York, 2017

Ayala, F.J. *The Big Questions: evolution* Quercus, London, 2012

Baba Ram Dass *Doing Your Own Being* Spearman, London, 1973

Bandler R. and Grinder J. *Trance-Formations: neuro-linguistic programming and the structure of hypnosis* Real People Press, Moab, UT, 1981

Bandler, R. and Grinder, J. *Reframing: neuro-linguistic programming and the transformation of meaning* Real People Press, Moab, UT, 1982

Bandler, R. and Macdonald, W. *An Insider's Guide to Submodalities* Meta Publications, Cupertino, 1988

Banyai, E. I. 'A new way to induce a hypnotic-like altered state of consciousness: active-alert induction' in Lajos, K. and Csaba, P. (eds) *Problems of the Regulation of Activity* Akademidi Kaido, Budapest, 1980

Banyai, E. I. & Hilgard, E. F. 'A comparison of active-alert hypnotic induction with traditional relaxation induction' *Journal of Abnormal Psychology*, 85:2, 1976

Barnes-Svarney, P. (ed.) *The New York Public Library Science Desk Reference* Macmillan, New York, 1995

Baron-Cohen, S. *The Essential Difference: men, women and the extreme male brain* Allen Lane, London, 2003

Beattie, H. 'Religious violence? Jihad and martyrdom in Islam' in Beattie, H. (ed.) *Controversial Practices* (A332 Why is religion controversial?), The Open University, Milton Keynes, 2013

Beattie, H. Bowman, M. and Harvey, G. 'What is religion?' in *Controversies in Religious Studies* Block 1, (A880 MA Religious Studies), The Open University, Milton Keynes, 2009

Beck D. E. and Cowan, C. C. *Spiral Dynamics: mastering values, leadership and change* Blackwell, Malden, MA, 1996

Benedetti, F. Carlino, E. and Pollo, A. 'How placebos change a patient's brain' *Neuropsychopharmacology* 36, pp.339–354, 2011

Berger, P.L. and Luckmann, T. *The Social Construction of Reality* Penguin, Harmondsworth, 1967

Bernhardt, S. 'Are pure consciousness events unmediated?' in Forman R. (ed.) *The Problem of Pure Consciousness*, Oxford University Press, New York, 1990

Bowers, K.S. and Davidson, T.M. 'A neodissociative critique of Spanos's sociopsychological model of hypnosis' in Lynn, S.J. and Rhue, J.W. (eds) *Theories of Hypnosis: current models and perspectives* Guildford Press, New York, 1991

Brace, N. and Roth, I. 'Memory: structures, processes and skills' in Meill, D. et al. (eds) *Mapping Psychology 2* Open University, Milton Keynes, 2002

Bronkhorst, J. *Greater Magadha: studies in the culture of early India* Motilal Banarsidass, Delhi, 2013

Brown, G.W. *The Human Body in the Upanishads* Christian Mission Press, Jubbulpore, 1921

Brown P. *The Hypnotic Brain: hypnotherapy and social communication* Yale University Press, New Haven, CT, 1991

Campbell, J. *The Liar's Tale: a history of falsehood* W.W. Norton & Company, New York, 2001

Carrera, J. *Inside the Yoga Sutra: a comprehensive sourcebook for the study and practice of Patanjali's Yoga Sutras* Integral Yoga Publications, 2006

Carroll, L. *Alice's Adventures in Wonderland* Macmillan, London, 1865/1927

Carter, R. (ed.) *Consciousness* Weidenfield & Nicolson, London, 2002

Cavanagh, R. 'Religion as a field of study' in Hall, T.W. (ed.) *Introduction to the Study of Religion* Harper & Row, New York, 1978

Clapham, M. and Gray, R. (eds) *A Thousand and One Limericks* Book Blocks, London, 2003

Cohen, M. *101 Philosophy Problems* (2nd edition) Routledge, London, 2002

Connolly, P. 'Religion and mental health: an exploration of the relationship between the ineffable and the indefinable' *Journal of Beliefs & Values* vol. 19, no. 2, pp.177–187, 1998

Connolly, P. 'Psychological approaches' in Connolly, P. (ed.) *Approaches to the Study of Religion* Cassell, London, 1999

Connolly, P. *A Psychology of Possession*, Religious Experience Research Centre, 2nd series Occasional Paper 23, Oxford (available at http://uwtsd.ac.uk/library/alister-hardy-religious-experience-research-centre/occasional-papers), 2000A

Connolly, P. 'Mystical experience and trance experience' *Transpersonal Psychology Review* vol. 4, no. 1, pp.23–35, 2000B

Connolly, P. *A Student's Guide to the History and Philosophy of Yoga* (revised edition) Equinox Publishing, Sheffield, 2014

Connolly, P. 'Ecstasy and enstasy: two sides of the same coin?' *Journal for the Study of Religious Experience* vol. 1, no. 1 (available at http://rerc-journal.tsd.ac.uk/index.php/religiousexp/issue/view/3), 2015

Cooper, C. *Individual Differences* (2nd edition) Arnold, London, 2002

Cosmides, L. and Tooby, J. 'The psychological foundations of culture' in Barkow, J.H. Cosmides, L. and Tooby, J. (eds) *The Adapted Mind: evolutionary psychology and the generation of culture* Oxford University Press, New York, pp. 19–136, 1992

Cotton I. *The Hallelujah Revolution, the rise of the new Christians* Little, Brown and Company, London, 1995

Cross, F. L. and Livingstone, E. A. (eds) *The Oxford Dictionary of the Christian Church* (3rd rev. ed.) Oxford University Press, Oxford, 2005

d'Aquili, E. and Laughlin, C. Jr. 'The biopsychological determinants of religious ritual behaviour' *Zygon* vol. 10, pp. 32–58, 1975

Dasgupta, S.B. *An Introduction to Tantric Buddhism* Shambala, Berkeley, CA, 1974

Davies, N. *Europe: a history* Oxford University Press, Oxford, 1996

Dawkins, R. *The Blind Watchmaker* Penguin, London, 1991

Dawkins, R. *A Devil's Chaplain* Weidenfield & Nicolson, London, 2003

Dawkins, R. *The Greatest Show on Earth* Transworld/Bantam, London, 2009

De Blij, H. *Why Geography Matters: more than ever* Oxford University Press, New York, 2012

Dennett, D.C. *Consciousness Explained* Penguin, London, 1991

Deren, M. *The Voodoo Gods*, Paladin, St Albans, 1975

De Rivera, J. and Sarbin T. R. *Believed-In-Imaginings: the narrative construction of reality* American Psychological Association, Washington, DC, 1998

De Waal, F. *Good Natured: the origins of right and wrong in humans and other animals* Harvard University Press, Cambridge, MA, 1996

Dilts, R.B. *Sleight of Mouth: the magic of conversational belief change* Meta Publications, Capitola, CA, 1999

Dodds, E.R. *The Greeks and the Irrational* University of California Press, Berkeley, CA, 1951

Donaldson, M. *Children's Minds* Fontana, Glasgow, 1978

Doniger, W. *The Hindus: an alternative history* Oxford University Press, Oxford, 2009

Doniger, W. and Smith, B.K. (trans.) *The Laws of Manu* Penguin, London, 1991

Dundas, P. *The Jains* (2nd edition) Routledge, London, 2002

Eliade, M. *The Sacred and the Profane: the nature of religion* (translated by W.R. Trask) Harcourt Brace Jovanovich, Orlando, FL, 1959

Eliade, M. *Shamanism: archaic techniques of ecstasy* (revised edition), Bollingen, Princeton, NJ, 1964

Eliade, M. *Yoga, Immortality and Freedom* (trans. W.R. Trask) Routledge and Kegan Paul, London, 1969

Ellenberger H.F. *The Discovery of The Unconscious: the history and evolution of dynamic psychiatry* Fontana, London, 1970

Erickson M.H. *Collected Works* vol. 2 (ed. Rossi, E.L.) Irvington, New York, 1980
Fausboll, V. *The Sutta Nipāta* (2nd edition) Motilal Banarsidass, Delhi, 1881/1905
Festinger, L. Riecken, H.W. and Schachter, S. *When Prophecy Fails*, Harper & Row, New York, 1956
Feuerstein, G. *The Yoga Sūtra of Patañjali*, Dawson, Folkstone, 1979
Fischer, R. 'The perception–hallucination continuum (a re-examination)' *Diseases of the Nervous System* vol. 30, March 1969A
Fischer, R. 'On creative, psychotic and ecstatic states' in Jakob I. (ed.) *Art Interpretation and Art Therapy: Psychiatry and Art* (vol. 2) Karger, Basel, 1969B
Fischer, R. 'A cartography of the ecstatic and meditative states', *Science*, 174, 26 November, pp.897–904, 1971
Fischer, R. 'Transformations of consciousness. a cartography' *Confinia Psychiatrica* vol. 18, 1975
Fischer, R. 'State-bound knowledge: "I can't remember what i said last night, but it must have been good"' *Psychology Today*, 1976
Fischer, R. 'Cartography of conscious states: integration of east and west' in Sugarman, A.A. and Tarter, R.E. (eds) *Expanding Dimensions of Consciousness*, Springer, New York, 1978
Fischer, R. 'Towards a neuroscience of self-experience and states of self-awareness and interpreting interpretations', in Wolman, B.B. and Ullman, M. (eds) *Handbook of States of Consciousness* Van Nostrand Reinhold, New York, 1986
Flournoy T. *From India to the Planet Mars: a case of multiple personality with imaginary languages* (translated by Sonu Shamdasani) Princeton University Press, Princeton, NJ, 1899/1994
Forman, R. 'Mysticism, constructivism, and forgetting' in Forman R. (ed.) *The Problem of Pure Consciousness*, Oxford University Press, New York, 1990
Fowler, J.W. *Stages of Faith: the psychology of human development and the quest for meaning* Harper San Francisco, San Francisco, CA, 1981
Fowler, J.W. Nipkow, K.E. and Schweitzer, F. (eds) *Stages of Faith and Religious Development: implications for Church, education and society* SCM Press, London, 1991
Fromm, E. and Kahn, S. *Self-Hypnosis: the Chicago paradigm*, Guildford Press, New York, 1990
Gafner, G. and Benson, S. *Handbook of Hypnotic Inductions* W.W. Norton, New York, 2000
Gardner, S. 'Aesthetics' in Bunnin, N. and Tsui-James, E.P. (eds) *The Blackwell Companion to Philosophy* (2nd edition) Blackwell, Oxford, 2003
Gilligan, S.G. *Therapeutic Trances: the co-operation principle in Ericksonian hypnotherapy* Brunner/Mazel, New York, 1987
Goldacre, B. *I Think You'll Find It's a Bit More Complicated Than That* Fourth Estate, London, 2014
Goleman, D. *The Varieties of Meditative Experience* E.P. Dutton, New York, 1977
Gombrich, R. *Theravada Buddhism: a social history from ancient Benares to modern Colombo* Routledge, London, 1988
Goodman, F.D. *How About Demons? Possession and exorcism in the modern world*, Indiana University Press, Bloomington, IN, 1988A

Goodman F. *Ecstasy, Ritual and Alternate Reality* Indiana University Press, Bloomington, IN, 1988B
Gould, S.J. *Rocks of Ages: science and religion in the fullness of life* Ballantine, New York, 1999
Govinda, L.A. *Foundations of Tibetan Mysticism* Rider, London, 1975
Green, D. *The Periodic Table in Minutes* Quercus, London, 2016
Greenberg, G. *The Book of Woe: the DSM and the unmaking of psychiatry* Blue Rider Press, New York, 2013
Griffin, J. *The Origin of Dreams: how we evolved to dream* The Therapist, Hailsham, 1997
Griffin, J. and Tyrrell, I. *Dreaming Reality: how dreaming keeps us sane, or can drive us mad* H.G. Publishing, Chalvington, 2004
Grof, S. *LSD: doorway to the numinous* Park Street Press, Rochester, VT, 1975/2009
Hardy, F. *The Religions of Asia* Routledge, London, 1988
Harré, R. *Key Thinkers in Psychology* Sage, London, 2006
Harrelson W, 'Myth and ritual school' in Eliade M, (ed.) *The Encyclopaedia of Religion* (vol. 10) Macmillan, New York, 1987
Harrington, A. *The Cure Within: a history of mind-body medicine* W.W. Norton, New York, 2008
Hauser, M.D. *Moral Minds: how nature designed our universal sense of right and wrong* Little, Brown, London, 2007
Hilgard E.R. *Divided Consciousness: multiple controls in human thought and action* (2nd edition) John Wiley and Sons, New York, 1986
Hinde, R., *Individuals, Relationships and Cultures* Polity Press, London, 1987
Hinnells, J.R. (ed.) *The New Penguin Handbook of Living Religions* Penguin, Harmondsworth, 1998
Hitchens, C. *The Missionary Position: Mother Teresa in theory and practice* Atlantic Books, London, 1995/2012
Hood, R. W. (Jr.), Hill, P.C. and Spilka, B. *The Psychology of Religion: an empirical approach* Guildford Press, Abingdon, 2009
Horner, I.B. (trans.) *The Collection of the Middle Length Sayings (Majjhima-Nikāya)*, vol. 1, The Pāli Text Society, London, 1954/1976
Horrie, C. and Chippindale, P. *What Is Islām? A comprehensive introduction* (revised edition) Virgin, London, 2007
Hultkrantz, Å. 'Ecological and phenomenological aspects of shamanism' in Diószegi V. and Hoppál M. (eds) *Shamanism in Siberia* Akadémiai Kiadó, Budapest, 1978
Huntington, S.P. *The Clash of Civilizations and the Remaking of the World Order* Simon & Schuster, New York, 1997
Husain, M.Z. *Global Islamic Politics* (2nd edition) Longman, New York, 2003
Hussey, A. *The French Intifada: the long war between France and its Arabs* Granta, London, 2014
Huxley, A. *The Perennial Philosophy* Chatto & Windus, London, 1974
Irwin, R. *The Arabian Nights: a companion* (2nd edition) I.B. Tauris and Co, London, 2004
Iyengar, B.K.S. *Light on the Yoga Sūtras of Patañjali* (revised edition) Thorsons Publishers, 2002

James, W. *The Varieties of Religious Experience* Penguin, Harmondsworth, 1902/1985
James, W. 'Pragmatism's conception of truth' in Blackburn, S. and Simmons, K. (eds) *Truth* Oxford University Press, Oxford, 1907/1999
Janaway, C. 'Aesthetics, problems of' in Honderich, T. (ed) *The Oxford Companion to Philosophy* (2nd edition) Oxford University Press, Oxford, 2005
Janda, L. *The Psychologist's Book of Personality Tests: 24 revealing tests to identify and overcome your personal barriers to a better life* John Wiley, New York, 2001
Jaynes J. *The Origin of Consciousness in the Breakdown of the Bicameral Mind* (revised edition), Penguin, Harmondsworth, 1990
Johnson, S. *The Ghost Map: a street, an epidemic and the hidden power of urban networks* Allen Lane, London, 2006
Jones, S. *Y: The Descent of Men* Little, Brown, London, 2002
Jung, C.G. *Psychological Types* (Collected Works, vol. 6) (revised translation by R.F.C. Hull) Routledge and Kegan Paul/Bollingen Foundation, 1971
Katz, S. 'Language, epistemology and mysticism' in Katz, S. (ed.) *Mysticism and Philosophical Analysis*, Sheldon, London, 1978
Kelly, C. and Breinlinger, S. *The Social Psychology of Collective Action: identity, injustice and gender* Taylor and Francis, London, 1996
King, U. 'Spirituality' in Hinnells, J.R. (ed.) *The New Penguin Handbook of Living Religions* Penguin, Harmondsworth, 1998
Kinsley, D. *Hinduism: a cultural perspective* Prentice Hall, New Jersey, 1982
Kirsch, J. *God against the Gods: the history of the war between monotheism and polytheism* Penguin Compass, London, 2004
Klostermaier, K.K. *A Survey of Hinduism* Munshiram Manoharlal, Delhi, 1989
Koestler, A. *The Case of the Midwife Toad* Hutchinson, London 1971
Koestler, A. *The Roots of Coincidence* Hutchinson, London, 1972
Kuhn, T.S. *The Structure of Scientific Revolutions* (2nd edition) University of Chicago Press, Chicago, IL, 1970
Kuijsten, M. (ed.) *Reflections on the Dawn of Consciousness: Julian Jaynes's bicameral mind theory revisited* Julian Jaynes Society, Henderson, NV, 2006
Lakoff, G. and Johnson, M. *Metaphors We Live By* University of Chicago Press, Chicago, IL, 1980
LaPlante, E. *Seized: temporal lobe epilepsy as a medical, historical, and artistic phenomenon* HarperCollins, New York, 1993
Larson, G.J. *Classical Sāṁkhya* (2nd edition) Motilal Banarsidass, Delhi, 1979
Leadbeater, C.W. *The Chakras* Theosophical Publishing House, Wheaton, 1927
Lennox, W.G. and Lennox, M.A. *Epilepsy and Related Disorders* (2 vols.) Little, Brown & Co., Boston, MA, 1960
Lewis, B. *The Middle East: 2000 years of history from the rise of Christianity to the present day* Phoenix Press, London, 1995
Lewis I.M. *Ecstatic Religion: an anthropological study of spirit possession and shamanism* Penguin, Harmondsworth, 1971
Ludwig, A. M. and Lyle, W.H. Jr. 'Tension induction and the hyperalert trance' *Journal of Abnormal and Social Psychology* vol. 69, vol. 1, 1964

Lynn, S.J. and Rhue, J.W. (eds) *Theories of Hypnosis: current models and perspectives* Guildford Press, New York, 1991

McGilchrist, I. *The Master And His Emissary: the divided brain and the making of the western world* Yale University Press, New Haven, CT, 2009

McGill, O. *The New Encyclopedia of Stage Hypnotism* Anglo-American Book Company, Carmarthen, 1996

Mackie, J.L. *Ethics: inventing right and wrong* Penguin, Harmondsworth, 1977

Mallinson J. *The Khecarīvidyā of Ādinātha* Routledge, London, 2007

Masefield, P. 'How Noble is the Ariyan Eightfold Path?' in Connolly, P. (ed.) *Perspectives on Indian Religion: papers in honour of Karel Werner*, Sri Satguru Publications, Delhi, 1986A

Masefield, P. *Divine Revelation in Pāli Buddhism*, Sri Lanka Institute of Traditional Studies, Colombo, and George Allen and Unwin, London, 1986B

Masefield, P. 'The Sāvakasaṅgha and the Sotāpanna', unpublished paper, undated

Masters, R.E.L. and Huston, J. *The Varieties of Psychedelic Experience* Turnstone, London, 1966

Matthews, G. and Deary, I.J. *Personality Traits* Cambridge University Press, Cambridge, 1998

Mayr, E. *The Growth of Biological Thought: diversity, evolution and inheritance* Belknap/Harvard, Cambridge, MA, 1982

Mencken, H.L. *A Mencken Chrestomathy* Vintage, New York, 1949/1982

Miell, D. and Pike, J. (eds) *Exploring Psychological Research Methods* Open University, Milton Keynes, 2007

Miller, S.B. *Yoga: Discipline of Freedom: the Yoga Sūtra attributed to Patañjali* Bantam, New York, 1996/1998

Moran, G. 'Alternative developmental images' in in Fowler et al. *Stages of Faith and Religious Development: implications for Church, Education and Society* SCM Press, London, 1991

Muktananda, Swami *Play of Consciousness*, SYDA Foundation, Oakland, CA, 1978

Naranjo, C. and Ornstein, R. *On the Psychology of Meditation* George Allen and Unwin, London, 1971

Nelson, J.M. *Psychology, Religion and Spirituality* Springer, New York, 2009

Nelson, K. *The God Impulse: is religion hardwired into our brains?* Simon and Schuster, London, 2011

Newberg, A. and Waldman, M.R. *Born to believe: god, science and the origin of ordinary and extraordinary beliefs* Free Press, New York, 2007

Oesterreich T.K. *Possession and Exorcism among Primitive Races, in Antiquity, the Middle Ages, and Modern Times* Causeway Books, New York, 1921/1974

Ornstein R.E. *The Evolution of Consciousness: of Darwin, Freud, and Cranial Fire: the origins of the way we think* Prentice-Hall, New York, 1991

Otto, R. *The Idea of the Holy* (2nd edition) (translated by J.W. Harvey) Oxford University Press, 1950

Paloutzian, R. F. and Park, C.L. (eds) *Handbook of the Psychology of Religion and Spirituality* (2nd edition) Guildford Press, New York, 2013

Parks, S.D. 'The North American Critique of James Fowler's Theory of Faith Development' in Fowler et al. *Stages of Faith and Religious Development: implications for Church, education and society* SCM Press, London, 1991

Parsons, P. and Dixon, G. *The Periodic Table: a field guide to the elements* Quercus, London, 2013

Paulson, S. 'The believer', *Salon*, 7 August (available at www.salon.com/2006/08/07/collins_6), 2006

Persinger, M.A. *Neuropsychological Bases of God Beliefs*, Praeger, New York, 1987

Pinker, S. *The Blank Slate: the modern denial of human nature* Allen Lane, London, 2002

Pinker, S. *The Better Angels of Our Nature: a history of violence and humanity* Penguin, London, 2011

Pompa, L. 'Philosophy of History' in Bunnin, N. and Tsui-James, E.P. (eds) *The Blackwell Companion to Philosophy* (2nd edition) Blackwell, Oxford, 2003

Power, F.C. 'Hard versus soft stages of faith and religious development: a Piagetian critique' in Fowler et al. *Stages of Faith and Religious Development: implications for Church, education and society* SCM Press, London, 1991

Ramachandran, V.S. and Blakeslee, S. *Phantoms in the Brain: human nature and the architecture of the mind* Fourth Estate, London, 1998

Rambo, L.R. 'Conversion' in Eliade, M. (ed.) *Encyclopedia of Religion* (vol. 4) Macmillan, London, 1987

Rambo, L.R. and Farhadian, C. E. 'Converting: stages of religious change' in Lamb, C. and Bryant, M.D. (eds) *Religious Conversion: contemporary practices and controversies* Cassell, London, 1999

Rangaswami, S. *The Roots of Vedānta: selections from Śaṅkara's writings* Penguin, New Delhi, 2012

Rawlinson, A. *The Book of Enlightened Masters: Western teachers in Eastern traditions* Open Court, Chicago, IL, 1997

Richardson, R.D. *William James: in the maelstrom of American modernism: a biography* Houghton Mifflin Harcourt, Boston, MA, 2007

Robinson, W.P. (ed.) *Social Groups and Identities: developing the legacy of Henri Tajfel* Butterworth-Heinemann, Boston, MA, 1996

Rosenthal, R. and Jacobson, L. *Pygmalion in the Classroom* Holt, Rinehart and Winston, London, 1968

Rossi, E. L. *The Psychobiology of Mind-Body Healing* W.W. Norton and Co., New York, 1986

Rouget G. *Music and Trance* University of Chicago Press, Chicago, IL, 1985

Russell, B. 'William James's Conception of Truth' in Blackburn, S. and Simmons, K. (eds) *Truth* Oxford University Press, Oxford, 1999

Sacks, O. *The Man Who Mistook His Wife for a Hat* Picador, London, 1985

Sacks, O. *An Anthropologist on Mars* Picador, London, 1995

Samuel, G. *The Origins of Yoga and Tantra: Indic religions to the thirteenth century* Cambridge University Press, Cambridge, 2008

Sargant, W. *Battle for the Mind: a physiology of conversion and brainwashing* Heinemann, London, 1957

Sargant, W. *Battle for the Mind: a physiology of conversion and brainwashing* (revised edition) Headly Bros., Ashford, 1959

Sargant, W. *The Mind Possessed, a physiology of possession, mysticism and faith healing* Heinemann, London, 1973

Schmidt, B.E. 'Provincializing Religious experience: Methodological Challenges to the Study of Religious Experiences in Brazil' in Schmidt, B.E. (ed.) *The Study of Religious Experience: Approaches and Methodologies* Equinox, Sheffield, 2016

Schumaker, J.F. *Wings of Illusion: the origin, nature and future of paranormal belief* Polity Press, Cambridge, 1990

Schumaker, J.F. *The Corruption of Reality: a unified theory of religion, hypnosis and psychopathology* Prometheus, Amherst, NY, 1995

Schuon, F. *The Transcendent Unity of Religions* (translated by P. Townsend) Harper and Row, New York, 1975

Schwartzberg, J.E. *A Historical Atlas of South Asia* University of Chicago Press, Chicago, IL, 1978/1992

Searle, J.R. *The Construction of Social Reality* Allen Lane, London, 1995

Searle, J.R. *Making the Social World* Oxford University Press, Oxford, 2010

Sherman, S. 'Brief report: very deep hypnosis' *Journal of Transpersonal Psychology* vol. 4, 1972

Shor, R.E. 'Hypnosis and the concept of the Generalized Reality Orientation' *American Journal of Psychotherapy*, vol. 13, pp.582–602, 1959

Shushan, G. 'Cultural-linguistic constructivism and the challenge of near-death and out-of-body experiences' in Schmidt, B.E. (ed.) *The Study of Religious Experience: Approaches and Methodologies* Equinox, Sheffield, 2016

Simpkins, C.A. and Simpkins, A.M. *Effective Self Hypnosis: pathways to the unconscious* Radiant Dolphin Press, San Diego, CA, 2000

Sinh, P. (trans.) *The Hatha Yoga Pradipika*, Oriental Books, Delhi, 1975

Skynner, R. & Cleese, J. *Life and How to Survive It* Methuen, London, 1993

Slee, N. 'Cognitive developmental studies of religious thinking: a survey and discussion with special reference to post-Goldman research' in Fowler et al. *Stages of Faith and Religious Development: implications for Church, Education and Society* SCM Press, London, 1991

Smart, R.N. *Reasons and Faiths* Routledge and Kegan Paul, London, 1958

Smart, R.N. *The Religious Experience of Mankind* Charles Scribner's Sons, New York, 1969

Smart, R.N. 'Interpretation and mystical experience' in Woods, R. (ed.) *Understanding Mysticism*, Athlone Press, London, 1980

Smart, R.N. *Concept and Empathy: essays in the study of religion* (ed. D. Wiebe) Macmillan, London, 1986

Smith, D.B. *Muses, Madmen, and Prophets: rethinking the history, science, and meaning of auditory hallucination* Penguin, New York, 2007

Smith, J.Z. 'Religion, religions, religious' in Taylor, M.C. (ed.) *Critical Terms for Religious Studies* University of Chicago Press, Chicago, IL, 1998

Snell, B. *The Discovery of the Mind in Greek Philosophy and Literature* Dover, New York, 1953/1982

Snellgrove, D. *Indo-Tibetan Buddhism: Indian Buddhists and their Tibetan successors* Shambhala, Boston, 2002

Spanos N.P. and Gottleib, J. 'Demonic possession, mesmerism, and hysteria: a social psychological perspective on their historical interrelations' *Journal of Abnormal Psychology* vol. 88, pp. 527–546, 1979

Spencer, R. *The History of Jihad: from Muhammad to ISIS* Post Hill Press, New York, 2018

Stace, W.T. *Mysticism and Philosophy* Macmillan & Co., London, 1961

Storr A. *Solitude* HarperCollins, London, 1989

Strassman, R. *DMT: the spirit molecule – a doctor's revolutionary research into the biology of near death and mystical experiences* Park Street Press, Rochester, 2001

Suryani, L. & Jensen, G. D. *Trance and Possession in Bali*, Oxford University Press, New York, 1993

Tajfel, H. Human *Groups and Social Categories: Studies in Social Psychology* Cambridge University Press, Cambridge, 1981

Taqī-ud-Dīn al-Hilālī, M. and Khan, M.M. (trans.) *The Noble Qur'ān* (English translation of the meanings and commentary) King Fahd Complex for the Printing of the Holy Qur'ān, Madinah, K.S.A., undated

Tart, C.T. 'Transpersonal Potentialities of Deep Hypnosis' *Journal of Transpersonal Psychology* vol. 2, pp. 27–40, 1970

Tart, C.T. (ed.) *Altered States of Consciousness* (2nd edition) Anchor, New York, 1972

Tart, C.T. *States of Consciousness*, E.P. Dutton, New York, 1975

Tart, C.T. *Waking Up: overcoming the obstacles to human potential* Element, Shaftesbury, 1988

Taylor, S.E. *Positive Illusions: creative self-deception and the healthy mind* Basic Books, New York, 1989

Teilhard de Chardin, P. *The Phenomenon of Man* Harper & Row, New York, 1961

Temple, R. *Open to Suggestion: the uses and abuses of hypnosis* Aquarian Press, Wellingborough, 1989

Thomas, E.J. *The Life of Buddha as Legend and History* (3rd edition) Routledge & Kegan Paul, London, 1949

Torrey, E.F. *Witchdoctors and Psychiatrists: the common roots of psychotherapy and its future* Harper and Row, New York, 1987

Trivers, R. *Deceit and Self-Deception: fooling yourself the better to fool others* Allen Lane, London, 2011

Turnbull, C.M. *The Forest People* Jonathan Cape, London, 1961

Van Gennep, A. *The Rites of Passage* Routledge & Kegan Paul, London, 1960

Varenne, J. *Yoga and the Hindu Tradition* Chicago University Press, Chicago, IL, 1976

Vasu, S.C. (trans.) *The Gheranda Samhita*, Theosophical Publishing House, London, 1976

Vingoe, F. 'Comparison of the Harvard Group Scale of Hypnotic Susceptibility, Form A and the Group Alert Trance Scale in a university population' *International Journal of Clinical and Experimental Hypnosis* vol. 21, no. 3, pp. 176–177, 1973

Vivekananda, Swami *Rāja Yoga* Longmans, Green and Co., London, 1912

Wallace, A.F.C. *Religion: an anthropological view* Random House, New York, 1966

Wapnick, K. 'Mysticism and schizophrenia' *The Journal of Transpersonal Psychology* vol. 1, pp. 49–66, 1969

Watzlawick, P. *The Language of Change* W.W. Norton, New York, 1978

Waxman, S.G. and Geschwind, N. 'Hypergraphia in temporal lobe epilepsy' *Neurology* 26, pp. 629–36, 1974

Waxman, S.G. and Geschwind, N. 'The interictal behavior syndrome associated with temporal lobe epilepsy' *Archives of General Psychiatry* vol. 32, pp.1580–1586, 1975

Weightman, S. 'Hinduism' in Hinnells, J.R. (ed.) *The New Penguin Handbook of Living Religions* Penguin, Harmondsworth, 1998

Weitzenhoffer A.M. *The Practice of Hypnotism* (vol. 1), John Wiley and Sons, New York, 1989

Welch, A.T. 'Islām' in Hinnells, J.R. (ed.) *The New Penguin Handbook of Living Religions* Penguin, Harmondsworth, 1998

Werner, K. *Yoga: its beginnings and development*, British Wheel of Yoga, [no location], 1987

White, D.G. *The Yoga Sutra of Patanjali: a biography* Princeton University Press, Princeton, NJ, 2014

Whitman, C.H. *Sophocles: a study of heroic humanism* Harvard University Press, Cambridge, MA, 1951

Wilber, K. *The Spectrum of Consciousness* (1st. edition) Quest, Wheaton, IL, 1977

Wilber, K. *The Atman Project* Theosophical Publishing House, Wheaton, IL, 1980

Wilber, K. *The Spectrum of Consciousness* (2nd edition) Quest, Wheaton, IL, 1993

Wilber, K. *Integral Spirituality: a startling new role for religion in the modern and postmodern world* Integral Books, Boston, MA, 2007

Winkelman, M. 'Ethnological and neurophenomenological approaches to religious experiences' in Schmidt, B. E. (ed.) *The Study of Religious Experience: approaches and methodologies* Equinox, Sheffield, 2016

Wolff, D. H. *Psychology of Religion: classic and contemporary views* (2nd edition) John Wiley and Sons, New York, 1996

Woodroffe J. *The Serpent Power* Ganesh and Co., Madras, 1973

Woods, J. H. (trans.) *The Yoga System of Patañjali*, Harvard University Press, Cambridge, MA, 1914

Woodward, F.L. (trans.) *Kindred Sayings* (vol. 4), Pāli Text Society, London, 1927

Yang, C.K. *Religion in Chinese Society* University of California Press, Berkeley, CA, 1967

Yapko, M. D. *Trancework, an introduction to the practice of clinical hypnosis* Brunner Mazel, New York, 1990

Yapko, M.D. *Mindfulness and Hypnosis: the power of suggestion to transform experience* W.W. Norton and Co., New York, 2011

Zaehner, R.C. *Mysticism: sacred and profane* Clarendon Press, Oxford, 1957

Zaehner, R.C. (trans.) *The Bhagavad Gītā* Oxford University Press, Oxford, 1969

Zimmer, C. *Evolution: the triumph of an idea* William Heinemann, London, 2001

Zubieta, J.K. and Stohler, C.S. 'Neurobiological mechanisms of placebo responses' *Annals of the New York Academy of Sciences* vol. 1156, pp.198–210, 2009

Index

aesthetics 69, 178
altered states of consciousness (ASCs) 11, 57, 82, 95–99, 103, 106, 136, 179–180

Bhagavad Gītā 1, 46
bicameral/bicamerality 126–127, 185
Buddha 1, 26, 29, 36, 41–42, 50, 61, 63, 72, 82, 85, 102, 104, 128, 170, 175–177

cakra 77–81, 87, 173–174, 209
Candomblé 31–33, 44, 112–113, 192
cartography 9, 53, 62, 93–98
Cavanagh, R. 20, 155, 212
cholera 66–67, 149, 172
Christian 2, 19, 24, 28–30, 35, 47–50, 59, 63, 72, 77, 87, 92, 124, 129, 134–135, 139, 150, 160, 162, 169, 189, 191, 193
common core/common goal 3–4, 6, 33, 53, 135, 153
communal religion 15–16
conscious mind 11, 106–107, 109–110, 119, 125–27, 131, 183–185
consciousness 11, 23–24, 29, 34, 36, 39–40, 42–43, 57–58, 61–62, 67–68, 77–78, 82, 95, 105–116, 126–127, 137, 145–146, 149, 178–180, 185, 208–209
constructivism 4–6, 153

Dawkins, R. 160, 163, 178, 202
dissociation 32, 106, 110, 125–128, 131, 158, 184
dualism 17–18, 60–63, 76–77, 192

ecstasy 24, 29, 93–95, 98–99, 101, 104, 106, 178
EEG 55, 96, 98, 100–103, 170
Eliade, M. 31, 44, 45, 47–48, 50, 79, 93–95, 112, 156, 159–160, 165, 169, 174, 178–179, 184, 213
emptiness 63, 85, 102–103, 117
enstasis/enstasy 94–95, 99, 178

Fischer, R. 55, 62, 93–104, 122, 179–180
Fowler, J. 70–77, 173

generalized reality orientation 106
Gilligan, S. 107–111, 114–116, 180–184
glossolalia 102, 129
Goleman, D. 55–60, 170, 171
Gombrich, R. 15–16, 155, 214
Grof, S. 142, 148–155, 213

hallucination 97–98, 100–105, 115, 129, 199
hierophany 47, 51
Hilgard, E. 108, 110, 182
homo religiosus 25, 44, 47–48, 130, 165–166
horse and canary pie 66, 172

Hultkranz, Å. 31–32
Huston, J. 137, 142, 144–149
Huxley, A. 4, 153, 215
hypnosis 6, 10, 106–108, 111–115, 125, 129–130, 145, 181–185, 192

integral spirituality 62–70, 84, 88, 90–93
Islām 1, 16, 28, 72, 128, 133–135, 150, 166, 191

Jains 18, 20, 35, 76, 84, 104, 133, 135, 148, 150, 168
James, W. 5, 34–36, 44, 116, 131–136, 141–142, 148, 151, 154, 159, 188–190, 192–194, 196, 206, 216, 218
Jaynes, J. 126–128, 181, 185–186
Jhāna/dhyāna 36, 41–42, 61, 88, 102, 114, 176, 183

Katz, S. 39–43, 62, 130, 159, 187
Kohlberg, L. 74.

Leuba, J. 21, 132
LSD (d-lysergic acid diethylamide) 10–11, 100, 136, 143–146, 192–193, 215
Ludwig, A. and Lyle, W. 108, 112, 115, 181–182

Mallinson, J. 81, 86, 175, 177
Masefield, P. 42, 159, 175–177, 183
Masters, R. 137, 142, 144–149
Mencken, H. L. 26–28, 157, 217
Methodist 49, 123–124
mindfulness 42, 55–57, 85, 88, 109, 171, 182–183
monism 17–18, 28, 35–38, 60–61, 76, 78
monotheism 18, 175–6
Myers-Briggs type indicator 89
mystical experience 17, 19, 33–43, 87–88, 100, 104, 108, 114–117, 130–131, 136, 139–141, 144, 148, 159, 188, 212, 219–220

Naranjo, C. 55–60, 170–171
Nelson, K. 131, 150, 159, 188, 210
NLP (neuro-linguistic programming) 10, 65
numen/numinous 4, 16–17, 19–33, 43, 58, 108, 130–131, 140, 148, 166, 215

Oesterreich, T. K. 29–30, 130, 158, 217
ontology 17–18, 60–63, 76, 133, 155
Ornstein, R. 110, 170, 182
Otto, R. 16–29, 49, 58, 155–157, 217

Patañjali 40, 54, 60–61, 84, 87–88, 98, 102, 104, 141, 170–171, 183
Pentecostals 129–130
perennial philosophy 4, 153, 215
Persinger, M. 127–128, 186
phenomenology 7–9, 16, 55, 88
polytheism 18, 63, 76, 134–135
Popper, K. 13, 160
possession 19, 57, 24, 29–33, 102, 111–113, 125, 130, 158, 178–180, 191–192, 212, 214, 216–217, 219–220
postmodernism 62, 93, 190–191
psychedelic(s) 14, 16, 106, 142–145, 148–149, 152–156, 198–199, 214–216

ramification 38–39
ranking 2–4, 6, 25, 39, 53, 62, 140, 153
Rawlinson, A. 55, 58–60, 85, 133, 141, 171, 191
reductionism 7
Roman Catholicism 9, 11, 33, 38, 47, 129, 160–165

St Theresa 103–104
Samādhi 35–36, 40–42, 55–56, 61, 84, 87–88, 94–95, 97–99, 102–106, 114
Sargant, W. 119, 123–125, 128, 181, 184
schizophrenia 100–101

Shor, R. 106, 109, 180–181
Smart, N. 8–9, 17–18, 22–23, 33–36, 38–39, 54, 62, 155, 159, 219
Snellgrove, D. 81, 85–87, 175, 177
soteriology 15–16, 40, 132–133
spirituality 15–16, 46, 58, 60–63, 66–68, 70, 78, 88, 90–94, 130, 133, 136, 151, 156, 166, 172, 175, 188, 216–217, 221
Stace, W. T. 34–41, 141–142, 159, 220
stages of faith 70–74
sui generis 20, 155, 191
supernatural premise 1, 22, 45

Tantra 42, 69, 79–81, 86–87
Tart, C. 95, 106, 115, 179–183, 199
theory 4–5, 53–54, 60–62, 70–74, 83, 106, 123–125, 144, 147, 157, 170, 194–197, 203, 206
trance 8, 23, 31–32, 61, 94, 102, 105–119, 125–126, 142, 159, 180–183, 186, 192
truth 1–2, 6, 35–36, 40, 49, 59–61, 72–73, 75–76, 82, 84–85, 87, 94, 104, 119–120, 131, 135–136, 141–142, 146, 154, 170, 175, 190, 194–198, 202–206, 210
typology 8–9, 15–16, 38, 53–60, 88–90, 179, 191

Underhill, E. 83, 87–88

Vedānta 1, 35, 60, 76–78, 82–83, 92–93
Voodoo 31–32, 111–112, 158

Wallace, A. 1, 22, 45, 153, 155, 220
Wilber, K. 55, 62–93, 171–188

Yang, C. K. 15–16, 155, 221
Yapko, M. 115, 182–183
Yoga 10, 35–42, 54–57, 60–61, 81, 84, 86–88, 93–104, 141, 157, 170–171, 183
Yoga Sūtra 40, 54, 60, 84, 87–88, 98, 103, 141, 170–171, 183

Zaehner, R. C. 37–39, 46, 153, 160, 221
Zen 55–57, 60, 96, 98, 100–103, 109

www.ingramcontent.com/pod-product-compliance
Lightning Source LLC
Chambersburg PA
CBHW071840230426
43671CB00012B/2015